CARE-CENTERED POLITICS

CARE-CENTERED POLITICS

From the Home to the Planet

ROBERT GOTTLIEB

The MIT Press
Cambridge, Massachusetts
London, England

The MIT Press would like to thank the anonymous peer reviewers who provided comments on drafts of this book. The generous work of academic experts is essential for establishing the authority and quality of our publications. We acknowledge with gratitude the contributions of these otherwise uncredited readers.

This book was set in Adobe Garamond Pro by New Best-set Typesetters Ltd. Printed and bound in the United States of America.

Library of Congress Cataloging-in-Publication Data

Names: Gottlieb, Robert, 1944- author.
Title: Care-centered politics : from the home to the planet / Robert Gottlieb.
Description: Cambridge, Massachusetts : The MIT Press, [2022] | Includes
    bibliographical references and index. | Summary: "Care-Centered Politics provides a
    framework for the vision and the linkages needed to help create a more care-centered
    society and planet"—Provided by publisher.
Identifiers: LCCN 2021029470 | ISBN 9780262543750 (Paperback)
Subjects: LCSH: Social change. | Social policy. | Social justice.
Classification: LCC HM831 .G687 2022 | DDC 303.4—dc23/eng/20220228
LC record available at https://lccn.loc.gov/2021029470

10   9   8   7   6   5   4   3   2   1

To Andie and Casey, for their deep care for others in their work, and Marge, for her care, resilience, and compassion.

Contents

Acknowledgments

In fall 2014, I decided to structure a lecture I was slated to give at Occidental College that summarized my approach to action research, and the ideas and organizing activity I had participated in over the previous five decades. In pulling together the material for my talk, I discovered the notes I had made from a 1967 meeting with André Gorz in Paris. I was then a brash twenty-three-year-old who wanted to tell this modest, unassuming French Left intellectual how important he had become for New Leftists like myself in the United States searching for an approach to social change as well as the changing dynamics around work and class. I also began to gather material at the time of my talk that would examine the changes I had experienced in the nearly fifty years since my meeting with Gorz, and especially those of my friends and colleagues in the *movement*, as we identified our amorphous yet compelling organizational work. I enjoyed pulling together the lecture, yet I felt there was more I wanted to explore in identifying "my action research journey" that stretched from participation in the 1960s' New Left to my activities and writing about the issues of environmental and food justice.

A few years after the talk, I began to have discussions with Vivian Rothstein, one of those longtime friends from the 1960s, about our respective journeys. Vivian had had an amazing career as a community organizer, cofounder and first executive director of one of the first women's liberation groups of the late 1960s and early 1970s, staffer dealing with homeless issues for a city government, leader in a community service organization, and union organizer for hotel and restaurant workers, many of them immigrants and people of color. I shared with Vivian my exploration of the journeys of longtime friends and colleagues. We talked about whether there was a common thread in their stories, given their diversity of experiences. It was still about social change, she ventured, and their wanting to make a difference in how they cared for others and what they cared about. A politics of care, I thought; perhaps that was the thread.

In conversations with another friend, Emily Abel, a community health historian and now retired UCLA professor who has written extensively about care issues, I realized I wanted to pull together the research that would link more directly those issues of environmental justice, food justice, and climate change that I was still engaged with to the politics of care.

This became part of my next journey: to help identify a care-centered politics in its broadest context as a social change philosophy and practice. I had settled into the research when the events of 2020 and 2021 began to unfold—the pandemic, climate change–related events, Black Lives Matter demonstrations, and deep inequalities and huge wealth gaps that the 2020 and 2021 events had further revealed. This book is also a product of those events; much of the writing occurred during the pandemic's sheltering in place and the lessons they provided that are so central to an understanding of what a politics of care can represent in the midst of such huge dislocations.

For this journey, I want to thank Vivian, Emily, and others who have given feedback on and helped guide the direction of this project. They include Peter Wiley, Jessica Lipnack, Leon Canter, Rick Abel, Norm Fruchter, Diane Horwitz, John Meyer, Martha Katz, Marge Pearson, Ellen Friedman, Louis Blumberg, Christine Loh, Suzanne Langridge, Ruth and Bob Langridge, Cathy Langridge, Liz Langridge-Notis, Andrea Corker, Casey Pearson-Gottlieb, Bhavna Shamasunder, Tony Platt, and the four reviewers for the MIT Press who were thorough and insightful, and helped frame the book's direction for me. I am also grateful to Anthony Zannino at the MIT Press and my editor at the MIT Press, Beth Clevenger, who worked closely with me on this book. It has been a joy to make this happen!

1 CARE POLITICS: AN INTRODUCTION

THE YEAR 2020

In the year 2020, four history framing events occurred: climate change–related fires and hurricanes, a spreading pandemic, massive demonstrations that called for an end to systemic racism, and an election that generated intense fears along with a palpable desire to either elevate or remove a president from the body politick.

As the year approached, in December 2019, representatives from 197 countries under the auspices of COP 25, the annual UN Climate Change Conference, met in Madrid. Yet despite the sense of urgency, no major agreements were reached to slow the warming of the planet. The United States and Australia, even after they had experienced their own recent firestorms and severe air quality problems, were most responsible, along with Brazil, for blocking any major action.

As the COP 25 meeting began to break up, several thousand miles away a novel coronavirus outbreak was unfolding that led to its first victims in the city of Wuhan, China. The outbreak in Wuhan quickly spread. Within a few months, by March 2020, it would be declared a global pandemic by the World Health Organization. One immediate result, among its many disruptions, was that COP 26, the next climate change meeting scheduled for Glasgow in 2020, had to be postponed.

A few months later in May and after the COVID-19 cases had reached their first peak in Italy, Spain, and the United States, hundreds of thousands of people began to march under the banner of Black Lives Matter.

Over an intense next several weeks, more than two thousand street demonstrations took place in all fifty states in the United States, with additional protests around the world. Identifying a wide range of issues associated with systemic racism, demonstrators also noted how the pandemic and climate change had further underlined as well as intensified the enormous racial and economic disparities impacting those with the fewest resources to deal with the devastation that was occurring.

Among those impacted were the pandemic's "essential" workers in health care, food production and access, childcare and schools, and care for the elderly, including as many as 50 percent of those workers engaged in care work or care activities. While celebrated, the essential workers remained vulnerable, with only limited support, whether in the form of protective equipment or a livable wage. Yet the role of these workers—as well as the care they provided in the midst of a pandemic, climate change events, and protests about systemic racism—could not be ignored.

Climate change, economic and social turbulence, pandemic events, systemic racism, and deep inequalities have all underlined the importance of care in responding to disasters and daily life needs. Each of the events in 2020 that extended into 2021 have raised immediate and long-term issues about inequalities as well as economic, health, and environmental disparities; the role and purpose of governments and institutions, and unchecked power and resources of the wealthiest people and largest corporations; the plight of both urban and rural underserved and underresourced communities; and the interconnections as well as limits of a global politics and global economy. In responding to those issues, the need for mutual aid, social solidarity, trust, new social relations, reparations, reimagining work, and a new economy have pointed to the possibilities of a *care-centered politics*— a strategy for economic, social, and cultural change during a period of crisis and turmoil.

The cascading events of 2020 culminated in a November election that served as a referendum on whether to keep in office the most intensely anticare president of the past century and more. The immediate outcome of the election as well as the increased recognition of the import of the pandemic and climate change have made it clear that a care-centered politics can no longer be considered marginal in assessing what happens next, and where we go from here.

DEFINING CARE

Care is a simple yet evocative word that has multiple reference points and meanings. These include:

Care is about processes and relationships, including between those who provide care and those who receive it. Such relationships can and should be mutual, supplying a bond between caregiver and care recipient that increases the knowledge and awareness of both. Such a bond, according to University of Minnesota professor Joan Tronto, constitutes a "caring with" rather than just a "caring for" approach that reduces power differentials and leads to greater equalities. Care is also a social construct and is about social relationships. These relationships can take place at a community, institutional, and global level, and can be experienced in race, class, and/or gender terms. They can be found in multiple cultures and histories.[1]

Care is a form of labor, both paid and unpaid, and an economy. Paid care labor has become a rapidly growing labor segment, even as it remains marginal in the eyes of policy makers and economists for its contributions to the "real economy" as measured by the gross domestic product (GDP) and production of things. The US Bureau of Labor Statistics estimates that the employment of home health and personal care aides alone will increase by 36 percent between 2018 and 2028, faster than all other occupations. Moreover, those who work in job sectors such as health, education, retail, and other daily need-based industries are increasingly understood as care workers. Paid care workers, many of them low income, are heavily represented by people of color, and have become a leading example of racial and gender exploitation as well as deep inequalities in the United States and globally.[2]

A huge amount of labor, in the household and other settings, is also unpaid or outside formal market arrangements. Unpaid care work, especially in the home, represents, as economist Nancy Folbre argues, an "'invisible' domain, not counted as part of GDP and undervalued despite the important contribution it makes to well-being, social development and the (re)production of the work force." Unpaid care can take place in the home, or in response to a family or friend's need, such as caring for older adults or children, or maintaining a household. The market economy, says Folbre, "provides only a small portion of the goods and services we rely on," and she estimates that as much as half of all labor hours are associated with nonmarket work inside and outside the household. In evaluating the gender and class dimensions of care labor, particularly unpaid and household-based care undertaken by women, Oxfam asserts that it is "crucial to our societies and to the economy. . . . Without someone investing time, effort and resources in these essential [care-related] daily tasks, communities, workplaces, and whole economies would grind to a halt."[3]

Care involves institutional and sectoral relationships, and can influence multiple issue areas. These areas may range from the environment and climate change to health and pandemics. Issues like care for the climate and health care have become more prominent among environmental and health researchers as well as researchers and advocates focused on care of the household, children, and elders. One group of care-related conference attendees identified care as "work that includes care for others, future generations, animals, and the environment, so as to move beyond the domestic labor debates and questions of monetary compensation." A care perspective reframes the concept of "green" to incorporate "human well-being"—an approach essential to an environmental justice perspective.[4]

Care is an ethic. Care may involve an activity, such as how someone or some situation is cared for. A care ethic has the capacity to involve any or even all aspects of political, economic, social, and individual daily lives. Care is ubiquitous: everyone needs and receives care in some capacity, and most people provide care to others. Care relationships, as Tronto argues, "are part of what marks us as human beings." An ethic of care signifies that "people are entitled to what they need because they need it; people are entitled to care because they are part of ongoing relations of care." The Ethics of Care network has formed to promote that broader vision and create linkages with others engaged in different social movements. A care ethic in turn can help inform a food ethic, environmental ethic, health ethic, climate justice ethic, right to housing ethic, social well-being ethic, and community or societal ethic.[5]

Care is a practice. Care practices can influence and frame relationships, institutions, and workplaces, such as parenting, gardening, K–12 classrooms, community health clinics, transportation providers and users, sanitation workers, and postal employees, among many other situations and settings. Care practices reference trust, connection, fairness, mutual aid, and empathy, among other community-building attributes. "In practices of care," feminist philosopher Virginia Held contends, "relationships are cultivated, needs are responded to, and sensitivity is demonstrated."[6]

Care is a form of solidarity and interdependence. "An injury to one is an injury to all," "we are all in this together," and "care for each other" have been expressions of solidarity and interdependence between as well as among individuals and groups, highlighted during the pandemic. It can also identify solidarity and interdependence between communities as well as between states and nations in response to meeting needs, such as during disasters. Care as solidarity and interdependence can help shape and inform attitudes and policies toward immigrants and refugees, and influence behavior, such as whether to wear a mask during a pandemic. As the authors of *The Care Manifesto* put it, a caring world is one where there is understanding that "as living creatures we exist alongside and in connection with all other human and non-human beings, and also remain dependent upon the systems and networks, animate and inanimate, that sustain life across the planet."[7]

Care is a politics. Care-centered politics, the focus of this book, provides a framework for the vision, and establishes the linkages for the struggles to create a more care-centered society and planet. It informs a wide array of issues, whether a living wage, environmental hazards, military spending, incarceration, community food security, or recognition of the centuries of harm from racism along with the need for repair and reparations. It seeks to incorporate care as a component within all institutions and aspects of production and consumption, and engage the totality of environmental and social justice issues. Care politics is deeply engaged with questions of race, patriarchy, violence, ethnicity, immigration, and age relationships. It seeks to overcome inequalities and discriminatory practices, whether based on race or class, or gender or sexual preferences and identities. It focuses on the public sphere and global as well as local issues. It challenges efforts to privatize care, and advocates for social and human rights, such as the rights to health, a clean environment, a living planet, a place to live, and well-being. As a politics, care can help inform and be incorporated into the Green New Deal, Medicare for All, and many other feminist, racial, ethnic, environmental, and class justice demands. It can guide climate change advocacy and the response to a pandemic, and provide a pathway for addressing centuries of racial harm and injustice. And it can supply the basis for new visions of sociability, even as struggles are waged to contest power, save human lives, and protect our world and planet from daily life assaults and unimaginable disasters.

LES TREINTE GLORIEUSES AND THE ANTICARE NEOLIBERAL ERAS

The 2020 pandemic crisis that stretched into 2021 along with the cascading climate change events and predictions of future catastrophes can be considered bookends from two prior eras. The first included the thirty-plus years of post–World War II expansion (circa 1945–1975), also known in France and Europe as *les trentes glorieuses*, or the Glorious 30. Celebrated as a period where a capital-labor compact and the expansion of a consumer culture (higher wages and more to consume) held sway, the concept of thirty glorious years was also something of a misnomer in the United States given the country's continuing poverty, racial, and gender divides as well as imperial forays, dressed-up neocolonialism, and the rise of a military-industrial complex warned about by President Dwight Eisenhower in his farewell address in 1961. The second period involved the forty-plus years of a neoliberal ascendancy (1980–2020) where the huge concentration of wealth, expansion of market intrusions into everyday life, enormous income inequality, erosion of a social safety net, huge spikes in the incarceration of African Americans and people of color, forever wars, and promotion of individual (and acquisitive) rather than social (and caring) behavior became dominant.[8]

During the first period, the strike waves and militant actions right after World War II that pushed for new economic and social reforms gave way to labor peace and social contracts as well as modest efforts to develop the rudiments of a welfare state (far more developed in Europe than in the United States). The postwar vision of leading economists and politicians was of a new type of humanism based on increased productivity to be sheltered by agreements between labor and capital (higher wages and fewer worker disruptions), and an increase in levels of consumption made possible by those higher wages. Through the 1950s and into the early 1960s, for example, the top marginal tax rate remained high—as much as 90 percent during the Eisenhower years, and only lowered to 70 percent in 1964. Combined with higher wages, especially in unionized manufacturing sectors like auto and steel, income inequality was reduced to some of its lowest levels in the United States during the twentieth century.

The wealth, however, was not shared across the board. The 1960 presidential election identified significant parts of the country such as the Appalachia region with major pockets of hunger and poverty. Two years later, Michael Harrington's best-selling book, *The Other America*, placed poverty as a central policy issue, culminating in President Lyndon Johnson's 1964 rollout of his War on Poverty program. Although Black workers experienced modest wage gains, these increases were considerably lower than their white counterparts received, and were also undercut by a range of racist policies in housing, health care, and education. The civil rights protests of the 1950s and 1960s further revealed this deep-seated racism and extensive discriminatory practices, not just in the South, but in northern states.

Any labor gains among workers during this period was made possible and also disguised by the role of women in unpaid household labor—one aspect of *social reproduction*. This included caring for children, cleaning and cooking, taking care of elders, and otherwise making possible the ability of (mostly) men to join the labor force. Then as they entered the paid workforce, women experienced a double form of exploitation: lower wages for paid work and no wages for their unpaid work.

The presumed trade-off for a segment of workers with higher wages and engaged in labor peace as well as for women engaged in household tasks was the greater availability of things to buy. Increased opportunities to consume goods like automobiles as well as lifestyles, travel, home amenities, entertainment, and more became the raison d'être for the labor peace and focus on wages leading to greater consumption. This was not just conspicuous consumption available for the rich (albeit working-class consumption had an element of the need to demonstrate what had been purchased). Rather, as Austrian-born, French radical intellectual André Gorz put it, this was "compensatory consumption," the system of rewards for labor discipline and the unpaid household labor roles.[9]

Consumerism became a dominant ideology, furthered by marketing messages linking consumer brands to personal identities. Advertising, a relatively new method to enhance such messages, got a jump-start in the 1920s, extended its presence through the 1940s, and then mushroomed in the 1950s and 1960s with the near-ubiquitous penetration of television in US (and European and other developed country) households. Television, as one of its foremost historians, Erik Barnouw, argued, was the "perfect advertising medium," and by extension the promulgator of the consumer culture. The television show delivered the audience to the advertiser.[10]

Yet similar to the anger directed at the stubborn persistence of poverty, continuing racial divides, and double exploitation of women, consumerism had its downsides and critics. An emerging New Left politics in the early and mid-1960s challenged the compensatory consumption model, maintaining that it resulted in a diminished quality of life, and disguised an imperialism that extracted resources and the material components that made consumerism possible.

Perhaps most challenging for the social compact of the postwar years was the eruption of domestic racial conflict and the turmoil of the Vietnam War that exposed the lack of a consensus regarding the US imperial role. An expanding environmentalism further questioned the assumptions and outcomes of the growth models associated with the social compact. For a brief period during the late 1960s and early 1970s, not only the social compact, but the very foundations of a capitalist world order seemed to be challenged.

At the end of this era, especially by the late 1970s, a political malaise had set in. Stagflation, higher oil prices, and a push to deregulate and undercut the role of government led to a political and market-centered counteroffensive that brought together think tanks funded by the right wing and a more aggressive pushback by newly organized corporate bodies such as the Business Roundtable. Together these trends of the late 1970s began to eat away at the more care-friendly social welfare policies put in place during the postwar years. This counterrevolution extended to the reassertion that women's care roles were unique and the unpaid household labor needed to remain intact, even as women continued to enter the paid workforce and thus were obliged to perform their double duty. Though no longer the sole breadwinners, men were nevertheless not seen as needing to participate in this aspect of the care economy. With Margaret Thatcher and Ronald Reagan's ascendancy in 1979 and 1980 in the United Kingdom and United States, respectively these antigovernment, gender-biased, antilabor, austerity policies and market-promoting politics established the neoliberal capitalist regime—a politics fundamentally hostile to the role of care in the workplace, and as an ethic and practice.

The ravages produced by neoliberalism in developed and lesser-developed countries alike as well as within the United States began to immediately undermine the limited social compact established through the 1950s, 1960s, and early 1970s. As Marxist geographer David Harvey and others have described it, neoliberalism became a political project seeking to undermine the ideas and policies stimulated by the social movements of the 1960s and early 1970s, such as environmentalism, antiracism, anti-imperialism, and a feminist movement that started to articulate a critique of women's work with the beginnings of a new care politics. Neoliberal politics countered with its own ideas and policies, which became the foundations for the savage austerity that decimated community and indigenous networks and social safety nets; produced deep inequalities that rivaled even the most unequal periods like the Gilded Age of the 1890s; led to a financialization of the state and economy, where the circulation of money supplanted the production of things; and established an expulsion regime that led to a loss of housing, food security, and other basic daily needs, while expanding the numbers of migrants escaping wars, economic collapse, climate change, and political violence. Neoliberalism also led to privatization raids and takeovers of countless institutions and sectors that cut deep into the social as well as economic fabric. Daily life experiences came to be subsumed under market forces, enabling them to penetrate much of daily life, from birth to death. Neoliberalism, essentially a more draconian form of capitalist relations, took on and extended the mantle of anticare, from its political project to the realm of ideas and conditions of daily life.[11]

AN EMERGING POLITICS OF CARE

Despite the ascendance of the neoliberal order and its oft-mentioned slogan that there was no alternative, political challenges and contending ideas continued to surface through the neoliberal years. New Left thinkers like Gorz wrote, as early as the 1960s and 1970s, of the ambiguous role of technology and automation with its potential to liberate work, in contrast to the market-driven upending of the workforce and realities of precarity. Given those changes, Gorz argued that new types of social relations needed to be created based on the "new ways of producing, associating, working and consuming [that would be] the fundamental precondition of any political transformation." The joining of work and consumption, or rather the pitfalls of *work for the purposes of consumption*, Gorz asserted, undermined the very basis of working-class identity, long associated with the sphere of production.[12]

Traditional notions of working-class identity were also enjoined by those focused on the sphere of social reproduction, a Marxist concept turned on its head by an increasingly vocal set of civil rights and feminist activists and theorists. In spring 1972, the inaugural issue of *Ms.* magazine featured an angry polemic by Johnnie Tillmon, the head of the National Welfare Rights Organization, that linked antiracist and feminist arguments. Tillmon savaged the racist attacks against welfare moms and the presumption that they were not doing "real work" but instead gaming a system through welfare payments. Subsequently characterized as "welfare queens" and "lazy Black con artists," welfare recipients were continually subject to verbal and policy onslaughts during the 1970s, 1980s, and early 1990s. It included Reagan's 1976 and 1980 presidential campaign pronouncements and culminated in President Bill Clinton's 1996 "ending welfare as we know it" legislation that forced the transition of welfare recipients into what the neoliberals considered real labor market work. This was work all too often associated with subminimal wages and lack of childcare. Women's unpaid work in taking care of their children, elders, and households, Tillmon proclaimed, was indeed real work that required sufficient compensation in some form, above and beyond the minimal support of programs like Aid to Families with Dependent Children, which was restructured through Clinton's legislation. What we need instead, Tillmon declared, was a *guaranteed adequate income*. Such an approach called for sufficient support and true recognition, a bread-and-roses appeal against a racially inspired, antifeminist counterrevolution.[13]

These contentions resonated with a growing group of Marxist feminists, whose writings first appeared in Italy in the late 1960s and then began to be articulated by US feminists during the 1970s. It had become increasingly apparent that the advocacy of second-wave feminists to enable women to enter the paid labor market had highlighted that proverbial double bind: women were paid less than men for equivalent work, while they continued to do almost the entire workload in the household economy of childcare, eldercare, and household maintenance. Moreover, this household economy work was not compensated nor were the additional hours required to fulfill it included in any assessment of what constituted women's real-time labor.

During the 1970s and 1980s, these feminist arguments about childcare, household care, and eldercare work constituted the beginnings of a new politics as well as a developing theory of care. Care theorists reframed the Marxist concept of social reproduction, or activities that made labor participation in production possible, as not just the reproduction of labor in the Marxian sense but rather biological reproduction (giving birth, and caring for infants and children) and social practices (associated with socialization and the fulfillment of human needs). Social reproduction was thus linked to "life-making activities," asserted Purdue University professor Tithi Bhattacharya.[14]

Silvia Federici, one of the leading Marxist feminist critics, maintained that the capitalist focus on production of commodities contrasted with the social reproduction focus on everyday life, particularly at a community and neighborhood as well as individual level. In countering the neoliberal argument that there was no such thing as society, just individuals and families, to paraphrase Thatcher's widely cited remark, Marxist feminists like Federici emphasized the *social* dimension of social reproduction. By doing so, they sought to incorporate institutions like schools, the environment, health care facilities, and health workers as part of social reproduction, and thereby asserted that a care workforce and care institutions extended beyond the household/care economy into the broader arena of social reproduction. These were institutions, work, and activities basic to human life, and available for a transformative view of social relations. Such a view countered the invidious and market-dominated penetration of daily life characteristic of neoliberalism. Against a capitalism that asked, "How many things can we produce, because things make profit?" social reproduction champions held that human needs along with social, household, and daily life concerns needed to be incorporated into any care-centered politics approach toward the systems of production and consumption.[15]

The focus on care politics with its relationship to social reproduction and transformative potential led care politics advocates to champion new forms of community and social solidarity as well as an overall politics of care. This conflicted and contrasted with the austerity-imposed, debt-laden, anticare assaults on communities, nation-states, and the young and elderly through such policies as structural adjustment that became the hallmark of the neoliberal capitalist regimes. Even during the darkest periods of austerity imposed on countries like Greece and Spain by the European troika (the European Commission, European Central Bank, and International Monetary Fund) following the 2008–2009 Great Recession, grassroots cooperatives and social solidarity initiatives sprang up in those countries, linked at times to the support and care for refugees and displaced migrants.[16]

The Great Recession also made visible the stark disparities in wealth and income that had been increasing during the neoliberal period. The favoritism toward the rich during the Great Recession extended into the

also citizen/nation building

subsequent limited and tepid recovery period that failed to address the needs of those at the bottom, memorialized by the slogan of the 1 versus the 99 percent and taken up by the 2011 Occupy movements in the United States as well as their counterparts among the Indignados in Spain, Greece and other antiausterity movements.

While the Occupiers highlighted those huge wealth disparities through their slogans about the 1 percent, their actions sought to identify direct democracy practices and cooperative arrangements that turned Occupy encampments and Indignados movement protests into a revival of alternative living experiments. During the late 1960s and early 1970s, experiments in communal living and cooperative forms of organization had gradually diminished as the neoliberal celebrations of the market and individual gain took hold during the 1980s and 1990s. Then with the Great Recession and subsequent protests, cooperative and care-based initiatives reinvented themselves through new forms and stronger links to social movements. When the COVID-19 pandemic swept through countries in 2020 and 2021, including its most widespread reach in the United States, and earlier climate events such as when Superstorm Sandy in New York and Hurricane Maria in Puerto Rico decimated infrastructure and people's livelihoods, grassroots efforts to respond cooperatively and through a care-centered lens became magnified and inspirational as a response. A crisis of care was making possible an alternative care-centered politics.[17]

THE ELEMENTS OF A CARE-CENTERED POLITICS

There have been differing interpretations among care researchers and activists about how to best situate care, including its political dimension. Care for some largely falls within the domain of parenting and the family, and suggests that care is intrinsically "relational," involving primarily two people: caregiver and care recipient. Others situate care in a social and individual context, identifying care as an essential component of social justice as well as care for the environment and social well-being.

In an influential 1990 essay, Berenice Fisher and Tronto highlighted care as an activity that includes "everything that we do to maintain, continue, and repair our 'world' so that we can live in it as well as possible. That world includes our bodies, ourselves, and our environment, all of which we seek to interweave in a complex, life-sustaining web." Their argument was also directed at economists and politicians who often saw care as a marginal economic category, with its low-wage sector and "nonproductive" nature. What needs to be valued, Tronto asserted, in seeking to link care to democratic values, "is not making money or making stuff, but caring. If we prefer to use this metaphor of making, then let us speak of 'making livable lives' . . . and sustaining the world, and let us act to create a politics to move us toward such a world."[18]

That approach resonated with social justice and environmental advocates—particularly those focused on climate change—who had not previously engaged in the decades of feminist-led discussions about the importance of care in daily life. Writer Naomi Klein, a leading climate and social justice activist, became one of the first to embrace the concepts of "care and repair" as central to the climate arguments.[19]

In addition to the climate change issues, the focus on care as a social and political construct expanded significantly during the 2020–2021 COVID-19 pandemic with the recognition that care workers and an ethic of care was shared by a wide range of people engaged in providing essential daily life services. Care became a widely used reference point for discussing how these workers were responding to crucial health needs and other everyday concerns. Care politics, however, had yet to fully emerge as a more comprehensive form of political advocacy, even though targeted measures such as living wages and sick time benefits for the care workers were widely supported. The outcome of the 2020 election helped to change that dynamic, as more care issues and a language of care worked their way into pandemic and climate change political discourse as well as policy and legislation, such as the new Biden administration's March 2021 stimulus, recovery-related American Rescue Plan Act.

Even prior to the 2020 election, both climate change events and the COVID-19 pandemic had already begun to lay the groundwork for a care-centered politics. Arguments by a number of young radical researchers and activists such as Kate Aronoff, Gabriel Winant, Daniel Aldana Cohen,

Alyssa Battistoni, Sarah Jaffe, and Thea Riofrancos linked social and environmental justice as well as a care economy as a necessary response to climate change and the need for social transformation. The demand for a universal basic income, frequently cast as unrealistic and hostile to a work ethic, quickly became a possible and popular option in the form of those stimulus payments during the pandemic to address the collapse of institutions and employment. To make such changes central to policy agendas, however, still required a political leap in how social movements, progressive policy makers, and care advocates could more fully translate their agendas into a more comprehensive social and environmental justice language coupled with a politics of care.[20]

This book seeks to identify that agenda and language by identifying the elements of a care-centered politics. This includes the discussion of *care work*, whether paid or unpaid, defined in market terms, or *care activity* as an essential part of life. The care workforce is largely, though not entirely (depending on the type of work), female, people of color, and immigrant. It is for the most part highly exploited and poorly recognized for its value in everyday life.

Care work is nevertheless expanding rapidly and will likely grow even further in the wake of COVID-19, despite workplace conditions becoming even more hazardous. Eldercare is especially experiencing some of the fastest growth *and* increased hazards and stress among those who care, whether in the home as unpaid labor or at in-home care facilities. The COVID-19 and climate change events have further extended the debate about what constitutes care work, even within the health care, eldercare, and childcare sectors. As care work changes and expands, including becoming part of new labor market sectors, it has the potential to further change the nature of work itself.[21]

A care politics has also started to be incorporated into *environmental discourse.* This is particularly the case among environmental justice groups that have identified a politics of daily life (the environment is where we live, work, play, worship, or eat) as central to the environmental justice argument. Care and healing work along with care activity and politics can also be central to a low-carbon, green economy transition, as Klein and others have argued in supporting, although pointing to the limits of, the Green New Deal concept.[22]

Environmental discourse is often care centered. Care for the land, care for the planet, and care for living things are central to an environmental ethic and ethic of care. Gardening and the growing of food represent a type of care-centered work and activity along those lines. Beyond caring for the land, gardening can become health enhancing and a healing activity, such as through horticulture therapy, for those who do the gardening as well as those who reap its rewards. Growing and producing food as care centered also contrasts with fossil-fuel-based (and corporate-dominated) food-related production with its massive environmental and occupational hazards. A care-centered politics approach to food extends to an eater's ethic as well as a producer's care for how food is grown and accessed. Other food sector workers such as school food service employees (e.g., the "lunch ladies" in school cafeterias) can become care-centered healthy food advocates, if given the opportunity and healthier food fare is available. Farm-to-school programs have been especially effective when the food service staff become part of its development and implementation. The "farm-to-table" concept, moreover, has represented a form of resilience in the wake of a pandemic or climate change event, as exemplified by the reworking and expansion of the community-supported agriculture (CSA) model, or interest in gardening as a form of food provisioning as well as healing during a crisis.[23]

Similarly, the language of a care politics has helped frame the arguments for a different type of economy in the era of climate change. Harvey, for one, has contended that a climate politics especially needs to address the hypergrowth strategies embedded in capitalist economies, led by the two largest carbon emitters, the United States (the second largest by volume and largest per capita) and China (the largest by volume, based on its own version of state-driven capitalism and likely to become the largest per capita in the near term). A care-centered politics, in challenging the hypergrowth model, seeks to be grounded in the notions of a social commons and sufficiency, or what Gorz characterized as "less is better."[24]

This concept of a *care economy* includes a system of production based on the infrastructure of daily life and a form of consumption based on the idea of sufficiency. Such an approach counters the capitalist logic of hypergrowth, deep inequalities, and what ecofeminist economist Mary Mellor calls the "careless and reckless accumulation economy." A care economy seeks to sustain lives and living things. Its notion of well-being contrasts with the dominant focus on economic growth as the all-encompassing goal of all climate-impacting systems, whether neoliberal or state capitalist. Even for the Green New Deal, whether its US, European, or UK versions, economic growth, albeit *green* economic growth, remains an underlying objective. A care economy perspective reverses that objective in favor of the notion of sufficiency—to have enough for all as well as understanding "what is enough," as Buddhist wisdom would have it. The social justice dimension of sufficiency in a care economy requires an agenda of redistribution for those who lack an essential livelihood, whether at the local, national, or global level. A care-centered politics thus seeks to establish universal well-being (enough for everyone), and value and care for the environment and the earth, which demand a voice as part of a care economy. "Enough should be a human right, a floor below which no one can fall; also a ceiling above which no one can rise. Enough is a good as a feast—or better." Kim Stanley Robinson writes in *The Ministry for the Future*.[25]

The continuing capitalist pursuit of hypergrowth is further bound up with the notion of making and consuming things. Economists and the mainstream media frequently assert that consumption drives the economy—a perspective that initially led to panic as the COVID-19 pandemic in its first months shut down the consumption/hypergrowth economy. Yet the concept of consumption is a relatively recent invention. In his book *Keywords*, cultural critic Raymond Williams wrote that in early English and French preindustrial capitalism, to consume meant to "completely devour, waste, spend" and "to destroy, to use up, to waste, to exhaust." Williams also distinguished the term *customer*, which implied some degree of regular and continuing relationship to a supplier, whereas *consumer* indicated a more abstract figure in a more abstract market.[26] The consumer and the primacy of consumption as a central economic driver became preeminently US concepts, thanks in part to the rapid rise from the 1920s onward of the use of advertising and other consumption-inducing strategies that heralded as well as helped manipulate the idea of an individual's free "choice" in selecting what and how much to consume as central to capitalist ideology.

Prior to the pandemic, the idea of sufficiency and an ethic of care had already begun to challenge the assumptions of endless growth and compulsive consumption. In a climate change and pandemic era, the development of new forms of sufficiency and connections between cooperation and care have taken on more urgency as they start to be explored in urban places and multiple institutional settings. The 1960s' New Left argument for a "long march through the institutions" will need to be revised in order to identify how best to restructure patriarchal systems as well as market-dominated institutions and sectors in *immediate* as well as longer-term trajectories. Such restructuring begins with institutions available for a care-centered politics. As part of any such shift, the relentless push for inequitable economic growth along with its increasingly dire environmental and climate consequences will need to be challenged.

Care-centered places like libraries and schools, or potential care institutions such as postal operations, will need to be supported and allowed to redefine themselves as essential care-related services. Activities like walking, biking, or gardening and the growing of food will need policies along with institutional support mechanisms to make them accessible to all individuals and communities. At the same time, the financial and time pressures as well as outcomes of the neoliberal order that have led to endemic problems, such as homelessness, mental health challenges and crises, precarity, and uncertainty about daily life needs, will require a transformative approach to how our institutions, economies, and politics need to be challenged as well as remade. Internet-based services, now beholden to a market orientation and assuming an oligopolistic form, will need to be remade from a care politics approach into a type of public utility and operate in the public trust. Expulsions from homes and withdrawal from daily life services, and creating barriers against migrations and refugees fleeing from violence and climate change, will need to be reversed and replaced with the embrace of a right to place along with a celebration of difference and diversity, all of which need to become part of a care-centered politics agenda.

The importance of a care-centered politics and its related need to remake our institutions is most pronounced when it comes to climate change, pandemics, and the need for system transformations, including undoing centuries of racial and sexual harm as well as violence against African Americans and women, among others. Climate change does not respect enforced boundaries. It requires public action at a local, national, and global scale. It deeply impacts the most vulnerable, whether individuals, communities, regions, or nation-states, while increasingly affecting everyone throughout the world. It requires collective action and changes in daily life. It needs to overcome the still-potent ideology of maximizing individual economic gain and instead assert the shared value of community, and a green, care-centered commonwealth of diverse peoples, communities, regions, and nation-states.

A care-centered politics is most important and valuable in addressing the enormity and longevity of the climate crisis. Many of the climate mitigation and adaptation initiatives promoted by individuals such as business magnate Bill Gates, and policy makers, industries, and the media, including in the United States and China, have emphasized the role of technology and scale. These initiatives are often an extension of the powerful hold of the market and GDP-type, production-oriented growth strategies in fashioning such initiatives. For example, vast solar farms established by large investors working with the investor-owned utilities are favored over small-scale solar projects that serve and can be controlled by communities and neighborhoods.[27]

A care-centered politics needs to address mitigation as an opportunity to change dependence and create alternatives to the major contributors to climate change—an approach that requires a different set of institutional arrangements, a focus on their relation to inequality, and a different sufficiency and care paradigm to reverse the logic of hypergrowth. In relation to climate adaptation issues, a care-centered politics seeks to restructure existing infrastructure to meet social and environmental needs that are also designed to respond to the intensity and unpredictability of climate change. Such unpredictability will substantially increase until and unless far greater efforts toward prevention and mitigation take place. Radical restructuring then extends beyond technical solutions to daily life and institutional transformations, the centerpiece of a care-centered politics.

While climate change represents an unfolding series of challenges, COVID-19 created an immediate need for change as the global economy, reliance on compensatory consumption, and promise of unending hypergrowth all faced potential collapse during the uncertainty of the first months of the pandemic. The early wisdom during those months was that a return to normalcy meant a rapid increase in consumption levels too, and eventually greater fossil fuel use and increased carbon emissions, as happened in the years following the 2008–2009 Great Recession. The recovery from the pandemic was predicated on such a return to normalcy, which meant a return to the hypergrowth model, albeit a green hypergrowth. The events of 2020 and 2021 nevertheless created uncertainty about future trends, including the response to the huge numbers of unemployed and return of poverty levels not experienced since the Great Depression of the 1930s. The possibility of hitherto-unimaginable transformations, including an ascendant care politics, seemed incredibly difficult yet more necessary than ever.

It also became clear in 2020 and 2021 that a care-centered politics needed to be part of challenging the system-wide and historical forms of racism as well as social, economic, and environmental inequalities. By doing so, a care-centered politics approach could counter prevailing beliefs, attitudes, and language, create a call to action, and become a guide to transformative change too. And it could provide some modest yet essential hope in the midst of a world in turmoil.

"To be truly radical is to make hope possible, rather than despair convincing," Williams once argued.[28] Those thoughts have become a necessity in a climate change and pandemic era, and where racial, social, economic, and environmental injustices require immediate as well as long-term structural change. Such transformations are also integral to a care-centered politics. And as 2020 came to an end, the outcome of the US election reinforced the idea that hope was indeed a radical idea, and care could help facilitate it.

2 CARE WORK/CARE ACTIVITY

"Work must lose its centrality in the minds, thoughts, and imaginations of everyone. We must learn to see it differently: no longer as something we have—or do not have—but as *what we do*. We must be bold enough to regain control of the work we do.

—ANDRÉ GORZ, *RECLAIMING WORK*

WAGES FOR HOUSEWORK?

what does this / leave out?

In his 1976 book *Keywords*, Raymond Williams did not include the word *care* among the 131 terms he parsed and situated in historical context. He did, however, elaborate at some length regarding the word *work*, including its most common reference as "paid employment." Williams noted that this was a market or wage labor rather than a household economy concept, based on the distinction frequently made between a woman who runs a household and raises children, and a woman "who works" by taking regular paid employment.[1]

At the time *Keywords* was published, a sharp and often-contentious debate was taking place about what constituted work, and whether and how it should be compensated, including household and care work. During the 1960s and early 1970s, feminist advocates such as Betty Friedan, under the banner of a second-wave feminism, argued for women to enter the paid workforce. Their advocacy was largely confined to middle-class women who also had the capacity to reduce household labor time constraints by utilizing services such as childcare programs, or purchasing assistance for household and childcare tasks by hiring housekeepers, nannies, or other contracted home service work.

That option did not extend to low-income women or households whose employment income, if jobs were available, was minimal. Low-income women, particularly those who didn't have jobs or husbands and relied on the limited support provided by welfare payments, were stigmatized as freeloaders who didn't work. Yet low-income women often had the sole responsibility for raising their children, dealing with older family members, and fulfilling the myriad tasks of maintaining a household. Social movement advocacy organizations, such as the National Welfare Rights Organization, pushed back against the definition of work as solely waged work, especially in the context of the barriers for low-income women and women of color. Moreover, participation by men in the household economy and care for children or elders remained at the low levels that existed prior to the publication of Friedan's *The Feminine Mystique* in 1963, even as more women entered the workforce. It had become clear that the issue of care and unwaged labor had a direct gender (and racial and class) character that was prevalent in both wealthier and poorer countries.

In the late 1960s and early 1970s, a handful of feminists began to question the assumptions and structure underlying what they called "unwaged work"—an issue that had a long history, including advocacy by nineteenth-century feminists such as Susan B. Anthony and Elizabeth Cady Stanton. Initially organizing in Italy and rallying around the concept of "wages for housework," these subversive Marxist feminists, as many called themselves, identified wages for housework as less a campaign than a "provocation" and "revolutionary strategy" to undermine what they saw as the capitalist division of labor between work and the family.[2]

In December 1971, the Italian Marxist feminist Mariarosa Dalla Costa drafted a manifesto titled *The Power of Women and the Subversion of the Community*. Working with Selma James, a US expat then living in the United Kingdom, the manifesto was circulated in Italy, the United Kingdom, the United States, Canada, and eventually several other countries in Europe. It immediately triggered debates among feminists about the role of household labor that extended to housewives as well as women who worked at waged labor and then returned to the home to continue working without compensation.

The US wages for housework advocates focused especially on working-class women who had two jobs: the paid work, itself frequently at lower wages compared to men who held equivalent jobs, and the uncompensated household and caring work of cleaning, feeding, raising children, taking care of elders, and other work around the home and family. Such domestic and caring work could constitute as much as half a day declared Dalla Costa at an International Women's Day event that launched the wages for housework organization in Italy. According to Dalla Costa, this was work that "no-one has ever recognized, no-one has ever paid."[3]

The advent of capitalism brought about and then extended the separation of waged labor and nonpaid domestic work, Dalla Costa and James wrote in *The Power of Women and the Subversion of the Community*. The capitalist division of work and home also meant that domestic work was no longer shared work, and women, presumably by their nature, would be assigned their assumed role. Given such expectations, it had become clear that all women were now housewives, Dalla Costa and James asserted, and "even those who work outside the home continue to be housewives." The family and its working-class housewife thus became "the very pillar of the capitalist organization of work," and were indispensable to capitalist production due to the reduced wages of women in the paid workforce and ability to escape paying for the cost of the unpaid labor. "We must refuse housework as women's work, as work imposed upon us," Dalla Costa and James concluded their manifesto.[4]

The Dalla Costa and James publication was translated into English and published in the United States in 1973. By then the wages for housework idea within the US women's movement had become controversial, particularly regarding the role of women as change agents in their capacity as housewives. The issues were different in the United States than in Italy, some wages for housework critics contended, since few women had entered the waged labor workforce in Italy while more than 50 percent of women in the United States had paid employment at that time.[5] Socialist feminist critic Carol Lopate argued in an article in *Liberation* magazine that wages for housework was an unrealistic demand when seeking to reform capitalism. The cost for such compensation would be prohibitive, not easily calculated, and rely on taxes that would also negatively impact male workers whose own wage levels would suffer, and thereby the household income would be reduced. Lopate and other wages for housework critics also decried the entrance of the state into the affairs of the home—even making an analogy to abortion restrictions.[6]

Nicole Cox and Silvia Federici, two of the leaders of the New York Committee on Wages for Housework, the largest of such groups in the United States, issued their own rebuttal of the critics, focusing on the Lopate article. They argued that the critics refused to see work other than in the form of waged labor and were especially sharp in their criticism of the presumed time constraints for men related to their jobs. "Many of us have lived with men who work an eight- or ten-hour day while we have found ourselves preferring or finding less consuming jobs which have left us more time for house care," Lopate wrote, suggesting that any man would find it difficult to rearrange their work schedule in order to equally share in child and house care. Such an assertion, Cox and Federici countered, institutionalized exploitative relationships presumed to be "a natural, unavoidable and even fulfilling activity to make us accept our unwaged work." By reinforcing the assumption that housework is not work, it prevented women from struggling against it, "except in the privatized kitchen-bedroom quarrel that all society agrees to ridicule, thereby further reducing the protagonist of a struggle. We are seen as nagging bitches, not workers in struggle."[7]

For the wages for housework advocates, the home and the demands of housework had become the "social factory," and the concept of social reproduction had become central to their argument. While social reproduction commonly at that time referenced domestic work, procreation, and childcare as part of the reproduction of labor (making it possible for men to work for wages), the wages for housework advocates wanted to undo the capitalist division between home and work. Elevating the concept of social reproduction as central to life activities outside waged labor, they established a framework for situating social transformation as more

REPRO AS WORK

specific charges of movement

than a change in production. Social reproduction, for Federici as well as Dalla Costa and James, referenced the range of life activities, including care for the land and environment.[8]

Throughout the debates in the 1970s, the wages for housework advocates continued to assert that they weren't seeking reforms or even pursuing an organizing strategy. Instead, they wanted to redefine the terms and in what form social transformation should take place. Despite the emphasis on wages for housework as a "perspective" and "tool for demystification," there were nevertheless also implied arguments for specific changes that could be transformative. The advocates promoted the concept of a "social wage" or "guaranteed adequate income" that the National Welfare Rights Organization had raised. They also maintained that the hours required for domestic or household care work as well as waged labor needed to be reduced. "To have time," the wages for housework advocates declared, "means to work less." Reduced paid labor time could mean increased household and family work time for men too—work to be now shared with women. These ideas of a social wage and reduced working hours continued to percolate even after the wages for housework organizations faded, although the ideas never disappeared. They would eventually become central to the arguments about a care economy.[9]

Forty years after she helped coauthor the original wages for housework manifesto, James was interviewed by the *Guardian* about her writings and activism, including arguments about care and wages for housework. James had had a fascinating and politically diverse history. Born Selma Deitch in Brooklyn in 1930, she was infused with Jewish left-wing politics as a child and young adult. She gravitated especially toward the struggles of people of color, and connected with different groups and individuals on the Left, including an attraction to the charismatic Trinidadian writer, historian, and activist C. L. R. James. A confidante of Marxist revolutionary Leon Trotsky and author of the *Black Jacobins*, an influential and widely acclaimed book on Toussaint Louverture and the Haitian slave rebellion of the early nineteenth century, C. L. R. took Deitch under his wing as his assistant and go-to person. Despite their thirty-year difference in age, Deitch would marry her mentor in 1956 shortly after his detention on Ellis

Island, and then release and deportation to London. Deitch then changed her pen name to Selma James and later followed C. L. R. to Trinidad, where she edited its proindependence paper. She settled again in 1969 in London, where she began her collaboration with the Italian Marxist feminists while continuing her life of writing and activism. James remained close to C. L. R. even after they divorced in 1980.

Wages for housework was just one of many struggles that James participated in, though it remained central to her writings and advocacy. She embraced the concept of care, and saw herself as both care advocate and critic in how care had come to be defined as well as structured by capitalism. In her 2012 interview with the *Guardian*'s Becky Gardiner, James explained that care work was not like other work. "By demanding payment for housework, we attack what is terrible about caring in our capitalist society while protecting what is great about it, and what it could be," James asserted. What it was and what it could be would also become a key focus for those engaged in care work, care advocacy, and politics.[10]

CARE WORKERS —? VISIBILITY

On April 4, 2020, at the onset of the pandemic in the United States, care researcher Nancy Folbre wrote in her blog, "Who exactly are the care workers, other than the people we need most right now?" Care workers had become among of the most visible essential workers. They included the health care providers, or those who tended to the elderly or infirm in places like nursing homes, or who supplied care in people's homes or provided childcare. Essential workers also included grocery workers, garbage collectors, farmworkers, meat plant workers, janitorial workers, postal employees, home repair workers, warehouse workers, and the people delivering packages, groceries, or other items brought to people's homes while they sheltered in place.[11]

Care workers, as the pandemic revealed too, engage in industries that help "produce, develop, and maintain the nation's human resources," as three care work researchers described the range of care industry sectors. Many essential workers, including workers involved in taking care of others, receive low wages with poor and often-unsafe working conditions in their jobs. These conditions have long prevailed in childcare and elder-care, including after the 1980s, 1990s, and 2000s when these care sectors experienced a major expansion, as did health care and mental health services. The workforce they required doubled in numbers and then doubled again. Increases were due to multiple reasons, such as greater numbers of women entering the paid workforce, the need for preschool education and care, and demographic changes, including an aging population.[12]

Wage differences in the paid workforce have also been prevalent between professional or middle-class and professional-aspiring care workers who receive a modest wage such as registered nurses, and the most exploited paid care workers who frequently have the most precarious type of employment and among the lowest-paid care jobs. Some of those involved in care work, such as physicians or surgeons, are among the highest paid in a care sector like health services and have continued to obtain major increases in pay. While the median wage of care work in the health care sector has been going up thanks to those high-paying jobs, this has occurred despite the increase in numbers of low-wage health care workers whose wages have basically stayed at the same level. The pay differential associated with the different care work categories has also contributed to the increased job polarization in the US economy that increased significantly during the 1980s and 1990s, and has today become its dominant feature.[13]

Paid care work has been further shaped by the market along with the pressures for standardization, routinization, and cost containment, such as cutbacks to Medicare that determine what is allowed and not allowed in home health care. It has been subject to privatization, with corporate entities consolidating ownership of facilities like nursing homes, of which about 70 percent are for-profit entities. From 2015 to the period prior to the pandemic, 190 private equity deals totaling $5.3 billion were made to take over nursing homes. The push for profits in turn reduced transparency, created pressures to cut costs such as reduced nursing care and higher patient-to-care-worker ratios, and as one research study documented, led to increases in the short-term mortality of Medicare patients by as much as 10 percent. There were also declines in patient mobility and increased

care work is not monolith

Medicare-related taxpayer funding. These trends have led to an even greater reliance on low-wage workers, including undocumented workers. Furthermore, care workforce employers have relied on a steady flow of global immigrant labor from places like the Philippines, thereby creating its own care crisis (or "care deficit") in those countries, some of whose workers compare the conditions of their work to a form of servitude.[14]

One difficulty in assessing changes in care work has been identifying who fits the label of "care worker." The wages for housework debate pointed to the importance of including those engaged in unpaid care work as part of a broader definition of care work itself. The number of hours spent at unpaid care work have not substantially changed since the publication of *The Power of Women and the Subversion of the Community* fifty years ago, including notably for women engaged in the double shift of paid and unpaid work. The annual time-use surveys by the US Bureau of Labor Statistics and Census Bureau have continued to find that women on average report greater hours spent on unpaid household and care work than paid work hours, while comparable numbers for men are reversed. Moreover, 61 percent of the women taking care of a family member are also engaged in paid care work jobs, compounding the stress of the double-time bind they face. Based on those numbers, UK economist Diane Elson has argued that gender equality in the paid work sector requires not only wage parity for paid work but also a redistribution of unpaid work hours between men and women. Such a change, she remarks, will depend on policy changes like significant increased paid leave for men as well as women along with a cultural shift regarding who is responsible for care.[15]

The most frequent association of the roles connected with both paid and unpaid care work is relational, which generally references a face-to-face service that helps develop the care recipient's capacities in their physical and mental health. Workers who provide a face-to-face service might include teachers, nurses, childcare workers, and therapists, among other job categories. Even while assessing the work roles associated with the relational or face-to-face aspect of care work, distinctions are made between a "nurturant role" that is often higher paying (e.g., a therapist or counselor) and the low-wage "nonnurturant" work (e.g., cleaning, providing food, bathing, etc.) that is also necessary to sustain care.[16]

From 1980 through 2020, the heart of the neoliberal ascendancy, two related changes significantly impacted the nature of the care workforce. The first involved its major expansion, with key groups such as the home health care, assisted living, and childcare workers far outstripping the increase in the overall workforce. The second change involved de-skilling, increased productivity, cost containment, and privatization, or its "overcommodification" due to the increased pressures of market forces. At the same time, as care itself became more commodified, it reduced access to care by limiting it to the ability to pay. For institution-based relational or interactive care work, this market orientation of care work reduced its quality, caused low-wage care workers to seek multiple jobs at different facilities that further reduced face-to-face time, and shifted funding from the relational work to the administrative and managerial positions in a facility.[17]

These changes have been most apparent for adult care workers, including those working in homes such as home health care aides or institutional settings such as nursing aides in nursing homes. The demand for adult care workers has continued to grow as the population ages, with estimates of double-digit growth in the next decade as the baby boomer generation reaches the age of sixty-five and older. A 2018 Census Bureau report estimated that those sixty-five and older would constitute 21 percent of the overall population by 2030, and bypass the population of those eighteen and younger by 2034. Partly based on those demographic trends, a 2019 (prepandemic) Bureau of Labor Statistics report estimated that the growth of home health and personal care aides would far outstrip the increase in overall employment (36 compared to 5 percent).[18]

Yet the growth of a labor force to meet the workplace needs of the home or long-term care, intermediate care and assisted living sectors including nursing homes, and assisted living facilities for the elderly and/or those with disabilities did not represent an increase in the wages of those who worked at those jobs, or the social value seen in such care work, even including during the pandemic when the health risks multiplied. Moreover, these jobs are less impacted by automation and robotics than other job sectors such as in manufacturing. Eldercare, for one, is not only labor intensive but also does not easily lend itself to robots taking over many of the daily care work tasks. Care sector robots have been most effective in countries like Japan where they have been utilized in as many as 60 percent of the nursing home facilities, particularly for assistance in the physical demands of the job such as lifting people who have trouble getting up. Still, even where such robots have been utilized, they have required human labor to manage and assist robots in their tasks, thus increasing or maintaining rather than reducing the care labor required.[19]

The 2020–2021 pandemic highlighted the poor working conditions and risks associated with the low-wage care work sector—"a critically needed but persistently marginalized workforce," as one study characterized the sector. Nursing homes had among the highest numbers affected by the coronavirus, including those testing positive as well as the deaths of both patients and care workers. Since their low wages and job precarity led many care workers to hold two or three jobs, this increased the potential spread of the virus to multiple facilities as well as the care workers' own homes, where many of the workers had care responsibilities for others in the family. Meanwhile, facility operators eagerly accepted and even solicited new COVID-19 patients with their higher reimbursable rates, and then displaced other lesser-paying patients, including those with dementia, to make room for the new COVID-19 patients.[20]

Some of the risks and challenges of paid care work during the pandemic were especially prevalent among home care workers engaged in eldercare, childcare, housecleaning, or other domestic care roles. A survey in New York, Florida, and Massachusetts conducted in May and June 2020 by the National Domestic Workers Alliance (NDWA) in conjunction with the Institute of Policy Studies found that high percentages of workers were exposed to COVID-19 yet lacked medical insurance, personal protective equipment, and core safety net resources. In addition, many of the care workers experienced housing insecurity and job loss fears. Another pandemic-related survey of family childcare workers also identified major burdens such as lack of health insurance, fears of exposure for themselves and their families, and less financial support to address new needs due to the pandemic. The survey researchers characterized their survey group as "unsung heroes in the COVID-19 crisis," and identified the pride the family childcare workers took in their role as essential workers along with their ability to quickly adapt their routines and educational practices as a result of the pandemic.[21]

These types of conditions in the eldercare and childcare paid care work sector—low wages, job precarity, high risk, time and market pressures, and job devaluation—reduce opportunities and the capacity for relational care too, undermining the connections and reciprocity in the job. The loss of such capacities can also be found among the higher-paid medical professionals where "curing" rather than caring predominates, according to writer and geriatrician Louise Aronson. Those who incorporate care into their medical practice, like geriatricians, reside at the bottom of the medical hierarchy in terms of power, prestige, income, and respect compared to the surgeons, internal medicine specialists, treatment specialists, and others who focus on medical interventions that may not always be in the interests of the patient and society. Geriatricians engaged in eldercare, Aronson points out, are among the medical professionals with the highest job satisfaction in their care of older patients, and are happier and more fulfilled. Given their lower status, these care practitioners do their work "for the reasons that give life meaning: it interests and inspires you, you believe in it, and it gives you pleasure," she writes. At the same time, she argues for a new "care paradigm," where those providing the care can connect with as well as learn from those who receive the care.[22]

Why then is eldercare or much of care work itself seen as having low value, whether for the patient or recipient of care, or the low-wage eldercare worker, medical professional, or medical practitioner? Eldercare, for one, is devalued, according to Federici, because of the devaluing of social reproduction (care as one dimension of social reproduction) rather than making things (as a form of production) or moving money (as a form of financialization). Elders, Federici asserts, are no longer seen as productive, and thus are devalued when they need to be valued for being "the depositories of collective memory and experience."[23]

To value elders, including those who receive care, also requires a shift in how care providers receive the support necessary to undertake effective care as well as for those who receive the care. The positive dimensions of care work—reciprocity, connection, and care with dignity—have been the central organizing principle of the NDWA and its various offshoots, including We Build in Black, which seeks to build the power and visibility of Black caregivers, nannies, and professional cleaners, Caring across Generations, focusing specifically on eldercare, and Care in Action, which represents the political arm of the alliance, and whose ultimate goal, along with Caring across Generations, is to "transform the long-term care system and change the way we care in this country." The groups concentrate on three core constituencies: families that lack financial resources to afford long-term care, care workers who experience exploitative wage and working conditions, and consumers of care like elders and those with disabilities who want to live with dignity. To address their needs and create linkages between them, a series of targets and objectives for action have been identified, including challenging unequal access to care, excessive institutionalization, and the widespread ageism that devalues elders.[24]

A key strategy of the NDWA has been passage of the Domestic Workers' Bill of Rights at the national, state, and local levels. First adopted in New York State in 2010, the bill's passage impacted as many as two hundred thousand domestic workers. The New York legislation included overdue policy changes that workers in many other industries have long enjoyed. Domestic workers, along with farmworkers, for example, had been excluded from New Deal labor legislation and even more recent civil rights legislation. Resistance to the passage of the legislation in New York and elsewhere created numerous barriers, but also expanded and intensified participation in the campaigns, which gave added emphasis to the importance of their victory. The policy changes in the legislation included provisions for overtime pay, providing one day of rest per week (important for home care workers), three days of paid leave per year, and antidiscrimination language. After its adoption in 2010, the New York legislation became the model for other states and localities; over the next decade, similar bills were adopted in ten states along with the cities of Seattle and Philadelphia. A national Domestic Workers Bill of Rights program along the same lines was also introduced in 2018, and although it didn't pass during that session of Congress, it continued to be a visible goal among progressive policy makers and was incorporated into one of Joseph Biden's four planks in his Build Back Better economic recovery plan during the 2020 presidential campaign.[25]

Many of the Domestic Workers' Bill of Rights changes incorporated into legislation have been relatively modest and long overdue as essential worker protection measures. Efforts to overcome centuries of exploitation of domestic workers that date back to slavery conditions have faced enormous political and cultural barriers to change the conditions of the work as well as the rights of domestic workers. Yet even when these measures have fallen short around specific goals, such as a 2021 Virginia Bill of Rights that sought to include a workers' compensation provision, supporters, while celebrating their success in the passage of the overall legislation, still vowed to continue mobilizing to expand such rights. In this way, the NDWA's Domestic Workers' Bill of Rights efforts identified as much an organizing strategy as a set of legislative goals.[26] →similar to WFHW

One of NDWA's more visionary policy initiatives is the Universal Family Care program, focusing on three interdependent goals: comprehensive universal early childcare and education, family and medical leave policy, and a long-term support and services social insurance program. The group argues that the framework for Universal Family Care needs to be fully funded, durable, integrated, unified, and interdependent. Its platform, based on a study by the National Academy for Social Insurance, calls for it be developed as a social insurance program, which would enable it to become part of the social contract in the United States similar to what Social Security and Medicare have become. The NDWA's Universal Family Care approach also includes crucial support for the care workforce, which has often been neglected when discussing family care, even in those European countries that have greater benefits for recipients of care or family caregivers. Current public policy in the United States has the worst of both worlds, based as it is on limited resources that create a zero-sum game that ends up pitting user and worker against each other in the quest for resources and support.[27]

NDWA cofounder Ai-jen Poo has become a recognized international advocate for changes in income and working conditions for care workers, and a visionary who has identified the multiple ways to think about and practice care. Organizing around care issues since 1996, she has become a magnetic, creative, and inspirational figure who views care as an essential infrastructure issue with deep race, class, and gender dimensions. Poo sees the organizing as a way to politically build a "caring majority" in the United States, estimating that possibly more than a hundred million people need care in some form at any one time. In that context, Poo and her colleagues like to start meetings by asking participants to tell a personal story of someone who cared for them in their life. Most everyone at some point, she argues, is a caregiver or receives care, thus providing the formula for building a majoritarian movement.[28] *CARE AS MAJORITY*

Care is also, and increasingly, an intergenerational phenomenon. Poo, for example, points out that home care workers who have served as nannies in some households have begun to be asked to care for those elders living in the home who require assistance or suffer from disabilities like dementia. As part of their network, these home care workers have sought training to enable them to undertake both childcare and eldercare, even within the same household. Training and participation in reviewing and contributing to managing the conditions of work has also been a feature of the South Bronx Cooperative Home Care Associates, the largest care worker cooperative in the country. Similar to Cooperative Home Care Associates, provisions for training have become an additional goal of the NDWA and its Domestic Workers' Bill of Rights initiative. Poo further argues that a universal family care policy entails a care worker, family, and community approach to care. She calls this approach the "care squad" of "sisters, siblings, family members, neighbors, friends, professionals, all of us together, making sure that the people that we love can live with dignity, regardless of their ability or their age."[29]

Even as some modest though important policy victories have happened in the past decade, the challenges for care workers remain formidable.

Cultural biases that contribute to devaluing the work, despite the enormous need for such work, are prevalent and often associated with racial biases related to low-wage work, particularly for African American and Latinx workers, who constitute the majority of the low-wage care workforce. The average pay for home care workers, for instance, is still as little as $15,000–$16,000 a year—less than what is considered a living wage. Injuries on the job for home care workers are widespread, including chronic back, shoulder, arm, and leg pain from musculoskeletal injuries where workers continue to work out of financial necessity, despite the ongoing pain.[30]

Yet Poo projects a strong sense of optimism while recognizing the challenges and inequities that need to be addressed too. The work requires "a boundless sense of compassion and humanity," Poo told an interviewer during the pandemic, suggesting that the moment represented "a once-in-several-generations opportunity to transform and update how we care for one another in this country."[31]

CARING LABOR

Among care advocates, there is an aphorism about care that has been stated on numerous occasions. Former first lady Rosalynn Carter, for example, repeated it in an August 2019, *Des Moines Register* op-ed. "There are only four kinds of people in the world," Carter wrote, "those who have been caregivers, those who currently are caregivers, those who will be caregivers, and those who will need caregivers." Carter herself was a long-standing care advocate. She developed an institute bearing her name that focuses on the need and support for caregiving, including in family settings such as a family member experiencing dementia. For other care advocates like Poo or care researchers such as Joan Tronto, Carter's observation corresponds to their own commentary about the ubiquitous nature of care, including its social and political dimensions.[32]

"Care is everywhere, all around us," Poo wrote in her book, *The Age of Dignity*, and she has continually emphasized the interdependent nature of care relationships, and need to make changes and transform the way we value such relationships. Her argument is at once political and cultural:

change the conditions of work through political action, particularly for low-wage workers, so many of whom are engaged in care activities, and change the ways we encounter the world through our relationships with others and all living things.[33]

Similar to Poo, Tronto frames her analysis of care work and activity by extending care's political and moral boundaries. In an essay about care and democratic politics, Tronto writes that instead of just limiting accounts of care to family or other close relationships, care in its broadest sense provides "a different map that includes and reorders human activities so that care participates in, and is a large part of, virtually all human activity." Such an expansive interpretation includes the various forms of care work.[34]

Folbre and fellow economist Thomas Weisskopf also sought to broaden the discussion about care work in a 1996 presentation that became a book chapter in an edited volume on economics, values, and organization. Folbre and Weisskopf distinguished the product of the work, or provision of the care service as commonly used in referring to care work, from the attitude or motivation in doing the work. They use the term *caring labor* to describe work where caring is part of and defines the attitude and motivation for the provision of a care service. Caring labor then includes any paid work where such a service is provided and people are cared for as well as unpaid work where caring attitudes or motivations are involved. A person who cares, they state, is someone "who is concerned about the welfare of other people and will act on the basis of that concern . . . [and that] within the discourse of left political economy, caring is closely associated with solidarity."[35]

Twenty-five years after Folbre and Weisskopf presented their ideas about caring labor, the 2020–2021 pandemic highlighted how many essential workers, especially those who worked in a service capacity, would be considered caring labor, whether or not their prepandemic jobs were organized that way. Those whose prepandemic work roles necessitated a service to others, such as teachers, health workers, or social workers, had already been seen as engaged in caring labor in some capacity. Motivation was an important, if not defining, feature of the work: teachers cared for their students, health care workers such as nurses cared for their patients, and social workers cared for their clients. The economic or market calculus—pay or salary as central to the motivation about the work—was inevitably a factor, yet not the exclusive nor necessarily determining one. Jobs benefited most when care was incorporated into the work. Conversely, when market factors predominated in how the work was performed, such as by creating greater market efficiencies when classrooms have more rather than fewer students, care factors are not only undermined but the *quality of care* also suffers, as in the large teacher-to-student ratios. The pandemic, moreover, given its risks, uncertainties, immediate pressures, and the societal need for the work, highlighted even further the importance of care in sectors such as education and health that already had a visible relational and care component. CARE BEYOND TRADITIONAL FORM

What became striking too is how the pandemic revealed a less visible yet still significant caring labor dimension with other essential jobs. For grocery and pharmaceutical workers, for instance, the risks—and need for care—extended both to worker and customer. The need to care during the pandemic—wear masks, keep physical distance, address fears about limited supply and stockpiling certain goods, reduce tensions between customers, and be attentive to those most vulnerable—became critical to the job. Market factors—keeping the job amid an economic free fall—clearly motivated grocery workers to continue to work. Yet the health risks to continue to do the work and the fear of exposure for their families led workers to protest unsafe working conditions, including initial company policies that even involved a ban on wearing masks. At the same time, the issue of the welfare of shoppers and others also led to the recognition that as grocery workers, they were now first responders, and their job meant providing a broader social responsibility.[36]

A caring labor perspective applies to a number of other essential work situations. Postal letter carriers, for example, engage in an essential function—delivering the mail on a daily basis—even as risks on the job increased considerably due to the pandemic. Postal employees deliver essential goods like medicines to those who have come to depend on them. They also can look after and serve some of the most vulnerable residents—a situation magnified by the pandemic and in other crisis moments, such as climate change events like drought or flooding. "We're the ones," a postal employee told the *Nation*, "who are going to every address, often conduct welfare checks on people, knocking on the door and saying, 'Hey, are you OK?' That's our traditional role, it goes back for a while." Postal carriers have supplied daily connection, especially important during periods when people have been obliged to shelter in place. "We hit the same house, at the same time, every day," another letter carrier said of their work. "There are some customers who look forward to that. That might be their only human contact the entire day. It lets them breathe a little bit easier, like, all right, things are bad, but we still have some sense of stability going on."[37]

Caring labor can be found in places such as libraries even when they are considered nonessential and closed to public use during a pandemic. Libraries have been characterized as crucial democratic public spaces, while librarians have incorporated care as part of their work role. Libraries serve as sanctuaries for those who otherwise have no place to inhabit or be part of, whether the homeless or those seeking refuge in books. Susan Orlean, in her account of the 1986 fire at the Los Angeles Central Library along with its history and recovery, identified the library as a "government entity, a place of knowledge, that is nonjudgmental, inclusive, and fundamentally kind." Library workers also facilitate care functions like providing for children and a type of childcare as well as by creating places for the elderly to have needs met, including overcoming social isolation. Library workers seek to accommodate and provide for diverse communities, including those individuals and groups otherwise marginalized due to cultural, ethnic, class, or language differences. In pursuing these activities, librarians have largely functioned outside or despite market pressures that otherwise reshape or reduce care functions. They also offer a link to other community-based ways to turn books and knowledge into public goods, such as the "little free library" book-sharing movement.[38]

During the pandemic, even as libraries closed their doors, librarians continued to play numerous care-related roles. Librarians who were furloughed volunteered as contact tracers, utilizing their skills at human connection and tracking information. They volunteered at cooling centers and shelter sites for people experiencing long-term and recent homelessness.

They brought meals to sheltered-in-place seniors. The contact tracer work by librarians was particularly valuable as they became one of the key groups seeking to provide that critical need during the pandemic. "Library staff bring empathy, commitment and a relentless focus on community and service. They're used to stepping up, being nimble and adapting services to address real needs," Los Angeles head librarian John Szabo told the *Los Angeles Times* about the contact-tracing effort.[39]

Librarians are especially important in rural areas, where community resources are often more limited or scattered. The Nebraska-based Center for Rural Affairs has argued that the "sense of belonging and welcome provided by libraries, combined with the staff's adaptability and willingness to work to meet the needs of their community are what make these institutions so revered," particularly in places like rural Nebraska. Even after their libraries were shuttered during the pandemic, library staff in some Nebraska towns came up with multiple ways to continue to meet people's needs. These included the curbside pickup of books, establishing virtual online resources such as audio and e-books, making online databases and internet connectivity available, establishing access to learning games and language-learning apps, and creating a summer reading program for youths and adults in 2020. "Though obstacles have been thrown at them," a Center for Rural Affairs staff member said of the libraries and library staff, "libraries continue to be a refuge that people rely on." These kinds of services were likewise available at libraries in small, medium-size, and large urban areas.[40]

Essential workers and industries deemed essential may be subject to working conditions that preclude a care role for either the workers or industries they work for. The meatpacking industry as well as other meat and poultry operations utilize highly exploitative and what could be considered anticare strategies toward both workers and the environment while capitalizing on their "essential industry" status. Operating during the pandemic exacerbated those conditions. These included long shifts of ten to twelve hours with minimal breaks, assembly lines with no distance between workers, and colder environments with poor air circulation. The meat companies like Tyson also used the fear of meat and poultry shortages to justify continuing to operate their plants much as they had done prepandemic. Companies in fact increased exports during the pandemic, such as shipping pork to China. As a result, meat plants became COVID-19 hot spots, with thousands of workers contaminated and hundreds of deaths, as spikes occurred periodically throughout the pandemic. Moreover, three of the largest meatpacking companies, JBS, Smithfield, and Tyson, which already by summer 2020 accounted for more than 40 percent of the known COVID-19 worker deaths, either refused to release results of tests at their plants, stopped testing, or failed to identify future plans for testing. The push for change came from the workers, who also lived in the same communities directly impacted by the health and environment problems created by the industry practices. Yet the changes required to adopt more care-friendly practices above and beyond the pandemic have been recognized as more systemic, related to the organization and need for change in the food system itself.[41]

Scholars and writers like Juliet Schor and Arlie Hochschild have written compelling accounts of how and why the market has increasingly intruded its way into a wide range of caring activities, including for caring labor that focus on key aspects of life or social reproduction, such as childcare or eldercare. Market factors, moreover, are continually squeezing the nature of the jobs that relate to daily life, even as the need for those jobs has only increased.[42]

Many of those jobs remain so highly exploitative in relation to wages, benefits, work hours, and working conditions that recruitment is targeted to reinforce a kind of low-income or poverty chain. As one researcher on preschool labor put it, "We want them [preschool teachers] to ameliorate poverty, even as they live in it themselves." The biggest barrier to caring labor's ability to engage and extend its care role is how capitalism itself, in its neoliberal forms, reduces the support and structures the work.[43]

CARING ACTIVITY, REIMAGINING WORK

In 1994, Gorz wrote a short volume titled *Reclaiming Work* that included and extended the thoughts that he had developed for more than thirty years about the changing nature of work in capitalism, and the need to reinvent it as a type of activity rather than an area for exploitation. Gorz argued that the advanced industrial countries no longer had a "normal" worker, whether blue collar, white collar, or more broadly a "wage earner." Instead, increasingly there was the "insecure worker" with uncertain employment and shrinking pay for reduced hours who nevertheless worked longer hours at multiple jobs. Work was no longer identity creating, Gorz asserted, and the search for some fulfilling time occurred in the gaps between working hours. This included a leisure time that had itself become limiting and unfulfilling.[44]

Gorz's contention, though bleak in its assessment of the changes around work and the loss of traditional working-class identity, was none-theless positive about what changes could take place. As opposed to the exploited insecure worker, working could become "a mode of life one chooses, a mode that is desirable, one that is regulated and valued by society, a source of new culture, freedoms and sociality, establishing the right of all to choose the discontinuities in their working lives without experiencing a discontinuity in their income." To make that happen is a political project, a need for transformative action. The centerpiece of such action to change society, he maintained, is the need to "'change work,' and by changing work, to change society." Work, Gorz argued, would need to be divested of all its constraints such as hours, hierarchy, and the push for productivity—constraints that reflect the subordination of work to capital and determine what is meant by work. To undo that subordination would require reconciling work with "a culture of daily life, an art of living, which it would both extend and nourish, instead of being cut off from them." Such a political project, with action goals and a process that could enable change to happen in stages, also required for Gorz the capacity to "think differently" and imagine what is possible rather than what seems inevitable.[45]

While Gorz didn't use the idea of caring labor and care politics directly, more than a decade later, Marxist feminist Kathi Weeks picked up on Gorz's themes about reimagining work in the context of a social reproduction politics. Weeks highlighted two central goals based on ideas that had been raised by Gorz as well as the wages for housework strategists. This included the idea of an unconditional, universal, continuous, and sufficient income that allowed one to escape the constraints of waged labor. Weeks, following both wages for housework and Gorz, further argued for the shorter work-week to transform how work or waged labor also constrained time. "The demand," Weeks held, "would be for more time not only to inhabit the spaces where we now find a life outside of waged work but also to create spaces in which to constitute new subjectivities, new work and nonwork ethics, and *new practices of care and sociality*." By framing work in relation to a more open-ended and expansive set of goals, including by demanding shorter hours for "what we will—and resisting the impulse to dictate what that is or should be," Weeks envisioned a more progressive coalition and more democratic discourse. "The struggle against work is a matter of not only securing better work, but also the time and money necessary to have a life outside of work," Weeks asserted.[46]

Weeks, like Gorz, sought to construct a utopian imagination. She envisioned a "post-work society" where life activities as opposed to those of the market would define daily life. By confronting work's overvaluation, political struggles within the context of social reproduction would seek to redefine and restructure work, although interim political goals, including an unconditional basic income and shorter workweek, would still need to be developed.[47]

Yet immediate issues of vast inequalities, a severely frayed social safety net, the types of exploitation in the actually existing conditions of work, and the deep-rooted racism and sexism that have prevailed at work and in society as a whole—issues that were magnified by the pandemic—have cried out for immediate changes as well as envisioning long-term structural changes. In recognition of the need for political struggle on multiple fronts, the authors of a care-centered policy landscape have argued that a policy agenda needs to extend far beyond issues like increased pay for care work-ers or parental leave to enable shared responsibilities for unwaged labor. Care policy, they maintain, can also involve advocacy and changes regard-ing Social Security, food stamps, the Earned Income Tax Credit, school lunches, housing policy, occupational health, minimum wage, overtime policy, the criminal justice system, and education policy—all of which can be considered just the short list.[48]

The need to transform work and specifically care work is tied into what New School professor and critic Nancy Fraser has identified as the "contradictions of capital and care," where contemporary neoliberal capitalism continually undermines care work, both paid and unpaid, and more broadly, social reproduction. Fraser asserts that while the organizing, activism, and creativity around care and social reproduction issues are important markers, they currently are too dispersed and unable to rise to the level of a transformative approach, including as a political project. Yet Fraser sees possibilities in efforts to link multiple issues and movements, such as the "struggles for a shorter work week, for an unconditional basic income, for public child care, for the rights of migrant domestic workers and workers who do care work in for-profit nursing homes, hospitals, [and] child care centers." When you add "struggles over clean water, housing, and environmental degradation, especially in the global South," Fraser contends, it can lead to a demand for new ways of organizing social reproduction. Such struggles can be located everywhere even if they have not been defined that way. By linking them as part of an interconnected political project, and recognizing that capitalism's care crisis reflects the subordination of social reproduction to production, a broad movement for social transformation could be established, Fraser declared in an interview for *Dissent* magazine.[49]

Subordinating social reproduction to production and thus to the dictates of the market represents an anticare politics—one that continues to be prevalent even in the midst of a pandemic or other life- and species-threatening crises such as climate change. At best, the current productionist-oriented system and its financialization underpinnings see care as an adjunct to a continual growth economy, while starving care of resources necessary to sustain it and life itself. Care work, paid or unpaid, will always be seen as having limited value compared to making things or, more directly, money. To transform care work requires, then, a politics that constructs an "alternative paradigm that starts from, and ends with, the value of care in human life," while also extending the concept of care to all living things and the earth itself.[50]

3 EARTH CARE

CARE FOR THE LAND

During the 1870s and 1880s, a contingent of Mormons established a series of community settlements designed to sustainably manage their land and water resources. Organized as cooperative enterprises, they were part of the United Order, communities that the Mormon Church established on lands toward the southern end of the Great Basin Kingdom. Unlike other frontier settlements at the time, United Order members saw themselves as stewards, as caretakers of the land and water, with each participant supportive of their neighbors in order to establish their shared commons. This form of cooperation would eventually be disbanded as the Mormon hierarchy was obliged to turn toward a more capitalist-oriented approach and an accommodation with the reigning forces of Western expansion.[1]

After the United Order settlements began their decline, another type of debate unfolded at the turn of the twentieth century in the United States about how to protect or manage lands that were under stress in the areas west of the 100th meridian. The westward expansion by then had run its course, and undeveloped land sites were shrinking. Mining companies, timber companies, the railroads, and large land interests had ravaged the lands in search of new opportunities for development. At the same time, successful efforts to supplant Indigenous communities by means of military assaults, economic and health weapons, and policies favoring tribal extermination and juridical disenfranchisement had also made it possible to carve out a few undeveloped areas with protected status. This included, notably, Yellowstone National Park, established from lands that had been inhabited by the Shoshone, Bannock, Blackfeet, and Crow tribes, among others. The cooperative spirit and land stewardship approach of the United Order had largely disappeared and was no longer a factor in that debate.

Instead, two other distinct positions emerged: advocacy of wilderness protection, and a land and forest management approach. The most prominent figures staking out those positions were John Muir, the wilderness advocate, and Gifford Pinchot, who promoted a scientific approach toward the "wise use" of resources. Pinchot criticized the destructive forms of resource exploitation, and called for the effective management of resources as opposed to the waste and spoliation of the land and forests through the unregulated private development that had become so prominent by the turn of the century. Trained to apply resource management techniques that he had learned while working in Germany, Pinchot became the leading figure in the United States advocating the utilitarian, scientific management approach to resource development that allowed for maximum use. His connections to Theodore Roosevelt led to his appointment as the first head of the newly established US Forest Service, which Roosevelt announced in his first message to Congress as president when he emphasized that the "preservation of our forests is an imperative business necessity."[2]

The authority and power that Muir utilized was less a connection to public figures than an evocative use of language and writing to inspire others to advocate for protecting rather than exploiting undeveloped lands. Muir especially loved to hike and ski in the woods and high mountainous places where he could separate himself from the lowland inhabitants of the cities. On several occasions, Muir would cast negative aspersions on Indigenous peoples, immigrants, and the poor, whom he felt failed to appreciate the beauty and wonder of these undeveloped lands. He would speak of his own physical regeneration once in the wilderness, where he could "shake out and clear away every trace of lowland, confusion, degeneration and dust." His vision was of a nature set apart, and his plea was for protection to keep it that way. His poetic and captivating description of these places contrasted with his scorn for the people of the lowlands. That type of perspective would subsequently frame an environmental-oriented advocacy of latter-day wilderness and eugenics advocates like Henry Fairfield Osborn and Madison Grant. It was an advocacy of nature without people, protected for the few who, they assumed, could best appreciate it.[3]

A more democratic approach to wilderness appreciation was elaborated by the peripatetic hiker and explorer Bob Marshall through his writings and activism in the 1920s and 1930s. Marshall, a socialist, New Dealer, and wilderness advocate, wrote movingly of his experience in the Arctic in the 1933 best seller *Arctic Village*. The Arctic, for Marshall, was a "vast lonely expanse where men are so rare and exceptional that the most ordinary person feels that all other people are likewise significant." Marshall's love of wilderness was a love he wanted to share. He became a strong advocate of opening up opportunities, in places like the Appalachian Trail and Adirondacks, for the urban working class and African Americans who lacked access, or in the case of African Americans, were excluded.[4]

Marshall also sought to distinguish between three contending strategies: the private ownership of forest land, and the owners' role in the overproduction and destruction of a regenerating forest; the public regulation of private use and ownership, which had become the conservationist or wise use approach of the Pinchot-influenced US Forest Service; and public ownership, which was Marshall's own position. In his book *The People's Forests*, Marshall argued that with public ownership, "social welfare is substituted for private gain as the major objective for management." Marshall's concept of care for the land through both social welfare and wilderness protection represented an early version of a type of hybrid green politics where care for the land was complemented by social goals and care for people's well-being.[5]

Marshall's hybrid green politics and socialist inclinations nevertheless did not lead him to consider where and how green spaces could be found as well as established with access for all, beyond those wilderness-related green retreats he so loved. Could those green spaces in fact be found in Muir's much-scorned lowlands—urban areas or even rural communities not directly adjacent to a monumental, preserved wilderness? The idea of an urban nature, a green oasis in the complex, often-polluted, and frequently degraded urban landscape, was slow to take shape given the long-standing framing of the environmental discourse about care for nature as a place apart. The focus on making urban places livable and healthy as well as care for the land and its people in an urban setting could be found more in the ideas of public and workplace health champions like Alice Hamilton along with urban reformers like Jane Addams and Florence Kelley, whose advocacy occurred in the same period that Muir and Pinchot introduced and acted on their ideas. The notion of an explicit urban and more people-centered environmentalism became more visible with the rise of an environmental justice discourse in the 1980s and 1990s. Increasingly, the environmental justice mantra—environment is where we live, work, and play—identified nature as a part of and not separate from people's daily lives, particularly its lowland inhabitants—the immigrants, African Americans, Latinx, Asians, and Pacific Islanders, the urban and rural poor, and Indigenous people who had also been displaced from their lands.[6]

By the twenty-first century, the question of access to green spaces, especially in urban inner cities, became a prominent focus of environmental justice like-minded activists. In 2010, a resident of a neighborhood at the edge of South Los Angeles took on the charge of care for the land when he had the inspiration to do some planting in the strip of land in front of his home that ran adjacent to where cars parked and otherwise ruled the roadways. This was neglected city-owned land that contributed to the bleak cityscape. The resident, a thirtysomething (he didn't like telling his age) African American named Ron Finley was a creative, imaginative, and environmentally oriented entrepreneur type who had most recently established DropDead Collecxions, a company that used natural fabrics for tailored clothes that he sold to some higher-end retailers like Saks, Nordstrom, and Neiman Marcus. Though his business had lasted more than twenty years, the 2008 Great Recession caused him to leave it, and he hadn't yet found something new to develop.[7]

Though Finley was something of a foodie and loved to grow things, he hadn't directly connected to the budding food movement in Los Angeles that included the development of the Los Angeles Food Policy Council, one of whose working groups dealt with urban agriculture and community garden issues. There was also a passionate cadre of guerrilla gardeners in

Los Angeles: people who would pick out neglected areas on sidewalks or streetscapes, and then assemble in the middle of the night to do their planting, which often includes plants and flowers or the occasional vegetable like kale that would otherwise not require much maintenance and could enhance the community. For more than thirty years since the early 1970s, guerrilla gardeners had been undertaking such forays—"cultivating partnerships between people who care about the earth and believe in the power of community gardening to transform neighborhoods," as one guerrilla gardening organization put it. By 2010, guerrilla gardeners were planting on urban lands around the globe, including in the Global South. With the internet and expanding cell phone technology, a level of coordination was available by then that allowed the planting to happen quickly and largely without notice until the plants were in the ground.[8]

When Finley decided he'd undertake his own personal, guerrilla-gardener-like mission to do planting, he hadn't connected with others engaging in similar actions, or a food movement that had begun to change the discussions about food and the environment, food and race, and food and the urban landscape, including the desire to care for the land. Finley was aware of the lack of healthy food options in his own neighborhood, but his motivation, as he would later say, was his love of making something happen that was different. Planting food in a parkway filled with weeds met that need.[9]

That spontaneous individual act made Finley a visible figure, particularly after he was given a citation for illegally planting food on the city-owned parkway. Finley fought back, making his situation visible through a petition campaign. He was soon besieged by press interviews and contacted by various alternative food advocates such as the celebrity chef Alice Waters. With his imaginative use of language—he talked about "gangsta gardening" and "gangsta soil"—and his own growing familiarity with the language of the food movement such as calling his neighborhood a food desert, Finley was emerging as something of a minor celebrity. He was invited to give a TED Talk in 2013 that ultimately reached more than a million viewers, and with two other people, created his own advocacy group, LA Green Grounds. Drawing on his entrepreneurial skills, he transformed the land in the back of his home to showcase a large and striking food and garden oasis, and established his own master class in gardening.[10]

As an African American operating in the shadow of South Los Angeles, and through his love of gardening and by planting his seeds on an unutilized strip of land, Finley became a champion of an urban nature and for growing food in the inner city. In doing so, he became an advocate, encouraging all to become caretakers of the land. His actions and the parallel ones of the guerrilla gardeners became the twenty-first-century urban version of care for the earth more than a century after the United Order settlements had created their version of stewardship of the land.

ENVIRONMENTAL JUSTICE

Like *care*, the word *environmental justice* has multiple roots and meanings. It includes care for the land, care for the earth, and perhaps most important from an environmental justice perspective, care for the people who live on the land, including places that have become subject to environmental harm. Most contemporary accounts link the first major illustration of environmental justice advocacy to a years-long struggle involving a rural, predominantly poor, African American community's opposition to a PCB landfill in Warren County, North Carolina. Their struggle eventually gained national attention after a large 1982 demonstration about Warren County's issues highlighted the type of disproportionate environmental harm faced by low-income communities and communities of color.

The roots of environmental justice, however, date back to changes to the urban and industrial order in the United States in the late nineteenth and early twentieth centuries. Those changes in workplaces and communities generated opposition and resistance to the hazards and changing environments that workers and community residents were experiencing. While this resistance was not identified as "environmental," it nevertheless generated similar types of conflict involving opposition to unwanted land uses, toxic exposures to substances like lead, and workplace hazards.

During the late 1960s and 1970s, a self-defined national environmental movement began to take shape based on the use of expertise, litigation, and lobbying focused primarily on the passage and implementation of several new environmental laws like the Clean Air Act as well as regulatory bodies such as the Environmental Protection Agency. Parallel yet also distinct from these national, more mainstream environmental groups like the Environmental Defense Fund and Natural Resources Defense Council, local environmental organizations mobilized and led struggles in several communities throughout the United States during the same period. Several of the local groups highlighted issues of race and class in relation to environmental impacts. One underlying theme was the concern and care for places where people lived that were under threat. *Environmental racism,* the term initially applied to some of these struggles, particularly impacted communities of color subject to toxic and hazardous wastes as well as other negative and unwanted land uses, as in the Warren County conflict. The use of the term *environmental justice* would come later, but one continuing association has been the issue of disproportionate negative impacts in communities and workplaces under threat.[11]

Efforts were made to create a more expansive and unifying language around environmental justice when nearly 600 people, including 350 delegates representing local groups and organizations, gathered in Washington, DC, on October 24–27, 1991, for the First National People of Color Environmental Leadership Summit. The document that resulted from the gathering, "The Principles of Environmental Justice," served for a number of years as a broad statement of the ideas, values, and targeted issues for environmental justice, particularly in contrast to the larger, white-led, mainstream environmental organizations. Among the first principles put forth in the document, there was language about care for the earth: "the sacredness of Mother Earth," and "ethical, balanced, and responsible uses of land and renewable resources in the interest of a sustainable planet for humans and other living things." While not identifying an explicit policy agenda, the summit nevertheless resolved to establish a broad environmental justice focus around such issues as transportation, affordable housing, land and sovereignty rights, and other issues of community and daily life. In a defiant talk at the summit aimed at mainstream environmental groups, Dana Alston, one of the summit organizers, asserted that the new environmental justice groups would not be bound by narrow definitions. Alston also introduced the language that became the signature phrase of the movement: environment is where people live, work, and play; this phrasing reinforced the idea that environmental justice is focused on place-based and everyday life issues.[12]

Among the summit principles was language about compensation or reparations for damages done to communities and individuals due to environmental harms, centering again on unwanted land uses in low-income communities and communities of color. Although federal legislation had addressed the problem of contaminated sites, such as a 1980 bill that created a Superfund provision for the cleanup of waste sites, the environmental justice participants at the summit utilized a civil rights lens with respect to their struggles to end the range of negative hazards and land uses that communities of color experience. The desire to more broadly define environmental justice also opened up opportunities for the groups to move beyond their oppositional stance, and affirm what was needed through social and environmental change as well as establish alliances with other social justice groups and causes. These included issues of transportation equity, affordable housing, and health care, among others. Issues related to food emerged as one of the more prominent examples of one of those opportunities for linkage, and they have also become illustrative of an ethic of care and care-centered politics.

CARE AND RESILIENCE IN THE HEART OF THE COTTON KINGDOM

The civil rights–type language and political focus associated with the People of Color Environmental Leadership Summit drew on the intense struggles that an earlier generation of activists had experienced in places like Mississippi and Georgia. Transformative civil rights struggles became life-changing odysseys, particularly for their participants and the people they reached. They also left legacies about the struggles for basic human and social rights, including the right to care for the land—struggles that still resonate today for environmental justice as well as a care politics agenda.

The sixty-year efforts to change the politics, culture, and people's personal lives in southwest Georgia represented one such odyssey.

That journey began in summer 1961, when Charles Sherrod, a twenty-two-year-old divinity student, dropped out of school to become a field organizer with the Student Nonviolent Coordinating Committee (SNCC). SNCC was already emerging as the leading edge of civil rights activism among a younger generation of organizers who were ready to put their lives on the line to help reclaim dignity and rights for the residents they sought to mobilize and came to deeply care about. The committee had assigned Sherrod to oversee voter registration and other civil rights–related issues in the state of Georgia. Sherrod and two other SNCC staff decided to focus on southwest Georgia, including the city of Albany and a rural belt that had once been a former slave-trading center in the heart of the cotton kingdom. Their SNCC colleague John Lewis, who would later join them in Georgia, called the Southwest region "probably the most oppressive section" of the state.[13]

For the next several years, Sherrod, through his strategy of intense, face-to-face organizing, encountered innumerable dangers, including life-threatening assaults and beatings. Albany and southwest Georgia became one of the first great civil rights battlegrounds. While some, including Martin Luther King Jr., would abandon the area in the face of effective and implacable opposition, Sherrod continued his organizing work, asserting that "nothing but death could separate me from my mission of empowering young people." Sherrod eventually settled in the region, marrying one of those young recruits, Shirley Miller, whose father, Hosie Miller, a well-known and respected Black farmer, was killed by a white neighbor, who was never convicted of the crime.[14]

In 1968, Charles and Shirley joined with others to develop plans for a model community land trust development, the first of its kind in the United States. A community land trust, which resembles in part the Mormon United Order as well as other land-based cooperative arrangements, had direct bearing on the community-based, care-centered approach that Charles, Shirley, and their partners saw as central to their project's mission. It both empowered participants whose relationship to the land had been based on the scars of slavery and sharecropping, and created a community of interests and a principle of stewardship in managing the lands. "Owning the land [in Georgia], established you as somebody," Charles told an interviewer about the land development his group called "New Communities." After a difficult financing process that included Georgia governor Lester Maddox preventing the securing of a federal grant, the group finally was able to purchase nearly six thousand acres to establish its new land-based program. New Communities provided for local Black farmers to work individual landholdings as part of a collective enterprise that shared marketing and production arrangements. It was at the time the largest African American land and agriculture enterprise of its kind, and a model for a care-based strategy for land stewardship as well as the people who lived on and worked the land.[15]

For nearly twenty years, New Communities supplied land plots for multiple participants, who farmed strawberries, grapes, collard greens, corn, soybeans, and much more. It created housing for those who lived on the land along with a number of other enterprises that sustained the hundreds of people who became part of the community. During its lifetime, New Communities provided crucial opportunities for many of the residents in the communities where the Sherrods had done their organizing work, and served as an alternative community-building and food and environmental justice development.[16]

After an extended drought in the early 1980s created major operational challenges for New Communities and many of the other farmers in the region, efforts were made to secure new federal loans from the Georgia office of the Farm Home Administration to help tide over New Communities. "You'll get a loan over my dead body," the white loan officer with the administration told the Sherrods. Without new financing, New Communities was no longer able to sustain itself, and in 1985, its creditors bulldozed the homes and uprooted the farm plots. The Sherrods continued to advocate for the land trust concept along with the community-building and care-focused approach it represented. It was for them a land-based extension of what the civil rights movement had been about.[17]

In 1997, the Sherrods joined a class action suit of African American farmers against the US Department of Agriculture (USDA) for bias in its programs, including what New Communities had experienced. Known as the Pigford lawsuit for its lead plaintiff, a Black farmer named Timothy Pigford, it culminated in a victory after an initial setback more than a decade later that provided a major award to the Black farmers, including the New Communities group. With the funds from the Pigford settlement, Shirley and Charles were able to secure a new site: 1,685 acres of a former plantation, complete with a large antebellum house that had once been owned by the largest slave owner and landowner in Georgia. Through their purchase, the Sherrods converted the land into a new land trust and developed a community center. "How just it was," Shirley said of the purchase, "that the land of the slave owner would be made into a community for the descendants of slaves." At the groundbreaking ceremonies, she proclaimed that it would be a place for "resilience, resourcefulness, and empowerment." The land also represented a form of reparations, paying back for harms over decades and more generally centuries that applied to the outcome of the Pigford lawsuit.[18]

In the nearly six decades since Charles had arrived in Albany, opportunities for change continued to develop in southwest Georgia. The Sherrods' work in the region along with the institutions they created and various positions they held since the first years of the struggle in Albany demonstrated the value of a connection to place in understanding possible political outcomes. It identified their movement-building process as a care for the land and people.[19]

Fast-forward to 2018 when Stacey Abrams launched her campaign in Albany for the governor of Georgia. Abrams told the local Albany newspaper that she felt it critical that her team anchor its campaign in southwest Georgia, given its civil rights history. "This is one of the areas of the state with greatest promise," Abrams said. "It's also an area of tremendous challenge." The key to Abrams campaign was the ability to register new voters, including the residents of Albany and southwest Georgia who continued to face numerous barriers to prevent them from voting. The same was true two years later when the presidential election shifted Georgia from red to blue. Nearly six decades after Charles began to organize in southwest Georgia, and fifty years after the Sherrods had joined with others to create New Communities, the inspirational campaign of an African American woman to become governor of Georgia and subsequent shift of Georgia from red to blue identified how movements for change as well as community empowerment could lead the way for a social and environmental justice and care-centered politics.[20]

RESILIENT FARMS

The issue of resilience that Shirley Sherrod had referenced in their long political journey became a significant factor during the 2020–2021 pandemic. This was particularly true with respect to food: its growing, processing, production, distribution, and availability. By 2020, many aspects of the food system had become globalized, concentrated, and less diversified. The large, industrial-like, and global operations in turn have had difficulties responding with resilience when a crisis like the COVID-19 pandemic or climate change events occur. Once they are broken, supply chains are not immediately reestablished. The large, industrially organized facilities like the highly concentrated meat industry and its assembly-line packing plants find it difficult to adjust, and frequently resist the need for altering existing working conditions. Large big-box stores and food retail behemoths don't always respond effectively to panic demands and supply chain disruptions, despite their ability to hire new workers and cash in on their status as crisis-defined essential businesses.

What has been remarkable in these crisis moments has been the resilience of some of the local or regional food operations, including small farmers with their ability to shift cropping patterns and revise local food distribution strategies. New food growing and distribution choices have been made to accommodate changing supply and demand dynamics, including changing customer needs. Feedback loops become suppler to help facilitate better and quicker local or regional food growing, production, and distribution choices. This flexibility has happened despite the often-precarious situation of small and local farms and food operations due to a lack of funding during crisis disruptions. This stands in contrast to larger national and even multinational food businesses, including those that successfully tap into federal government support, such as the $14.5 billion earmarked in the first months of the COVID-19 pandemic for primarily larger-scale farmers and farming operations linked to global markets, and impacted by the US-China trade war fostered by the Trump administration. Even small business loans and grants went to larger entities, notwithstanding the size of some of those that received the funding.[21]

CSAs and other farm-to-table or direct marketing programs illustrate the capacity for resilience. Some of the earliest models of farm direct programs equivalent to CSAs were first developed in the United States in the 1960s and 1970s, including New Communities and its community land trust approach. An initial example included the pick-your-own farms and clientele membership clubs established in Alabama in 1974 by Tuskegee University agricultural professor Booker T. Whatley. An advocate of regenerative agriculture and direct farm sales to consumers, Whatley argued that African American farmers with small farms could succeed if they established themselves near paved roads and within forty miles of an urban center to facilitate the direct farm-to-consumer model. Through a modest annual membership fee, people could come to the farm and pick their produce, and/or sign up for the membership clubs newsletter for information about what was available and how to participate. Only a few farms in Alabama utilized Whatley's methods, though, due in part to a lack of interest among younger African American family members who had witnessed the struggles of their parents and grandparents' generation as well as the multiple racist-motivated problems they had encountered. In 1987, Whatley published a book about the farm direct approach, and while he was not able to sustain his own operation in Alabama, he helped spark interest in it. By the 1990s, a new generation of farmers markets, farm stands, and farms utilizing a CSA concept based on Japanese and European models began to catch on in the United States.[22]

CSAs have been designed to help small farmers deal with weather and market fluctuations by subscribers providing an annual or semiannual fee while at the same time creating a subscriber-farm connection. CSAs at first grew slowly, ignored by federal and state agricultural policies that favored larger growers and global exports. The number of CSA farms reached an initial peak prior to the 2008–2009 Great Recession. But the economic downturn negatively impacted small farms, including CSAs, which only began to recover from lost subscriptions when new opportunities opened up through direct sales to restaurants and schools. Subsequent to the recession, CSA numbers started to increase again, reaching a new peak of thirteen thousand CSA farms in the period just prior to the pandemic.[23]

The 2020–2021 pandemic, even more than the 2008–2009 economic downturn, started to change the dynamic for the food industry overall as well as for CSAs. In the first weeks of COVID-19 in the United States, it appeared that CSAs might well disappear as their strategy to move toward institutional sales like restaurants appeared ready to collapse once those businesses were shuttered. Surprisingly, however, a number of CSA farms quickly altered their approach and began to report an explosion of new subscribers. Many new CSA subscribers were people sheltered in place, looking to make their own meals, and wanting fresh and local items to make that happen successfully. CSA farms adapted with new plantings, utilized more creative technology and distribution strategies, and found ways to provide information, seedlings, and various tips for how to use some of the different items now supplied in their CSA baskets. Many CSAs also reworked their financial model to allow for monthly, weekly, or even onetime payments, rather than the typical six months or annual payments in advance. New distribution outlets during the pandemic such as food banks were also pursued.[24]

The CSA farms further benefited from the flexibility and resilience of farmers markets, including those that quickly and successfully restructured their operations—sometimes quicker than the large supermarket chains. In doing so, the markets revised how they operated to meet the new public health criteria, and during the pandemic, became "laboratories for new communal safety habits," as one *New York Times* article put it wryly. As more people increased their home-cooked meals and with restaurant options more limited, CSAs and farmers markets became important access points for local fresh food. At the same time, a food ethic of care among those purchasing farm direct food ("know your farmer, know your food" represented one popular slogan and bumper sticker) helped frame the decision of not only what food to obtain but where to obtain it too.[25]

GARDEN CARE

Just as the resilient local farm operations adapted, there was increased interest in new or expanded gardening during the pandemic, similar to what had happened after climate change events like Hurricane Katrina. Marguerite Green, executive director of Sprout NOLA, a New Orleans nonprofit related to community gardens, spoke of the importance of growing food during a crisis, including sustaining the sense and purpose of community. After Katrina and then again during the pandemic, Sprout NOLA developed a number of activities designed to meet crisis or postcrisis needs. These included maintaining garden plots, delivering food to those most vulnerable, and having experienced gardeners raise seedlings at home to be distributed through a spreadsheet to those who requested them to set up their own home garden. "This is actually why we build community, it's to take care of each other in a time of need," Green told the *New York Times*.[26]

Gardens have long been a source for care, comfort, creativity, and connection to others and the land during times of crisis as well as noncrisis periods. Similar to CSAs and farmers markets, they are a source of fresh food immediately available once harvested. The Victory Gardens during World War II and an earlier version (the War Garden or Patriotic Garden) during World War I emphasized the importance of increased food availability. As many as twenty million people participated in the World War II Victory Gardens, and they were estimated to have provided as much as 40 percent of the country's food supply at one point to help offset the food shortages and rationing due to the war. The 40 percent number has since been widely cited by garden advocates to identify the potential of gardens to supply a major quality food source during a crisis, particularly in low-income communities that lack access to fresh food, including fruits and vegetables.[27]

Various types of gardens have served multiple functions besides their food security role. Community gardens, for example, were first developed more than a century ago with the potato patch farms in Michigan in the midst of the recession of 1894 to provide a source of income for the unemployed as well as a source of food. One hundred years later, in the midst of the industrial decline in Michigan and most notably Detroit, African American activists began to look to urban gardens as a source of renewal. That situation became especially pressing with the 2008–2009 Great Recession that led to large numbers of mortgage foreclosures, abandoned houses, and empty lots, most dramatically in low-income, African American neighborhoods.[28]

As efforts were made to revive the auto industry and jump-start an industrial renewal in Detroit, the venerable organizer Grace Lee Boggs juxtaposed what she called illusions about industrial revival with a renewal of the city through urban gardens and related greening strategies. "You can bemoan your fate, or, as the African-American elders taught, you can plant gardens," Boggs wrote in the *Michigan Citizen*. Boggs, who had been mentored by C. L. R. James and also interacted with civil rights activist Ella Baker, spoke of the need to reimagine the concept of work as opposed to jobs. We need to "take more responsibility for each other and for our community," she wrote to promote Detroit Summer, the organization she and her husband, James Boggs, helped create in 1992. Her organization sought to have her celebrated African American elders (the "Gardening Angels") interact with youths to undertake planting community gardens, painting public murals, creating bike programs, and hosting poetry workshops "to express their new thoughts." These activities, she hoped, could serve as a "reconnection with earth and community"—a need magnified by Detroit's search for renewal.[29]

Aside from their environmental and community roles that Boggs referenced, gardens have served as a type of reconnection in other settings, such as schools and prisons. School gardens, similar to community gardens, have a history that dates back to the early twentieth century. Part of the early impetus for developing school gardens was the desire for children, including from immigrant families, or families whose parents or grandparents had moved from the farm into the cities, to regain the language and skills of growing food. School gardens also became a source of fresh food for children during the two world wars, and a central feature of the farm-to-school program initiated during the late 1990s that soon extended to thousands of schools and in all fifty states in a little more than a decade.

One of the first farm-to-school programs in the United States at the Santa Monica–Malibu Unified School District (SMMUSD) was facilitated by the role of a school garden. Rodney Taylor, SMMUSD food service director, was a savvy food service buyer who had food service industry experience through a job at the Marriott hotel chain before joining the school district. Taylor, an African American from Compton, California, with a working-class background, initially expressed skepticism about a farm-to-school program, but reluctantly agreed to try it out as a pilot that he was convinced would fail.[30]

The SMMUSD program called for farm direct produce to be offered as an alternative lunch option through what Taylor subsequently called a "farmers market salad bar." Fifty percent of the children in the pilot school selected for the program qualified for free or reduced lunch—meaning their family's income had to be below or slightly above the poverty line. Taylor decided to do an initial one-week test run, and gave the students on the first day the option of either pizza or the salad bar. To his astonishment, nearly three-quarters of the students chose the salad bar. Unbeknownst to him, the students had been provided a taste sampler in the weeks prior to the test pilot run of items that would be part of the salad bar. Many of the children compared the look and taste of the samples to the food they had grown, harvested, and tasted from the school garden, which had been established the previous year and was beloved by the students. "It's from the garden," they proclaimed, and that proved to be a tipping point for their willingness to try the new lunchtime salad bar. It also was a tipping point for Taylor, who would become one of the foremost advocates among school food service directors of farm-to-school programs and school gardens. He would later say that the experience helped him redefine his own position as a health champion who cared and was deeply engaged in providing fresh and healthy food to students who often lacked access to such food choices.[31]

Both school and community gardens became enormously popular prior to the pandemic, even as they faced numerous barriers. Despite their ability to provide food, green and beautify the urban (and rural) landscapes, allow for much-needed physical activity, and create quiet and peaceful places, many community gardens have faced precarious futures, depending on the ownership and uses of the land. In a neoliberal age, private property trumps community benefits. Once private owners and sometimes public entities decide the land value has improved (often due to the community gardens), and that development can then proceed, gardens are plowed under, even when developments are then postponed, with the former garden sometimes reverting to vacant land.

Similarly, school gardens, despite their value as teaching tools, a source of physical activity, and ability to green school grounds, have been constrained by uncertain upkeep and limited resources, particularly during periods when schools are not in session such as summer months. Teachers who help supervise garden work and do it as volunteers see it as an additional time burden in an already-overburdened schedule. Parents who help with school gardens, when allowed to do so (liability factors can sometimes prevent parent participation), are also limited by their own time constraints, including any long-term commitments. Even when policies by local and state governments, or school districts and school superintendents, identify certain goals, such as a 1995 proclamation by California superintendent of schools Delaine Eastin for "a garden in every school," they often are unable to provide the resources or establish actual policies to implement such goals.[32]

Nevertheless, community and school gardens have continued to flourish, and the benefits of gardens and gardening have extended to other institutions and places, such as prisons, domestic violence and abuse shelters, hospitals, and veterans' facilities. During the past two decades, prison gardens, for example, evolved from innovative pilot projects at a handful of locations to a widespread initiative in a number of states, sometimes in conjunction with corrections departments that have come to recognize its benefits, sometimes belatedly—not least the reduction of recidivism rates. Aside from prisons, the concept of healing through gardening, a type of care-based horticultural therapy, has been widely applied in multiple other settings where the need for changed behavior is crucial, such as for batterers and substance abusers. Unfortunately, the 2020–2021 pandemic impacted many of these programs, although adjustments were made to allow for continuing participation and even to expand their reach. This included programs enabling prison gardens to become a source of fresh food for pandemic-impacted and overextended food banks.[33]

Backyard gardening and in the home is where gardens and gardening expanded most quickly during the pandemic, as they have after climate change–related events too. "People have always gardened in hard times, but food is only one part of that story," argues Jennifer Atkinson, author of *Gardenland*, a 2018 book that highlighted the importance and value of gardening in seeking a connection with nature as well as desire for a sense of community. "There's immense gratification that comes from work that gives you tangible results," Atkinson told reporter Petra Mayer in a May 2020 interview with National Public Radio. Mayer then wrote about her own newfound pandemic-related obsession with gardening and how she wanted to share her passion with others, including colleagues at NPR.[34]

The pandemic's explosion of gardening itself emerged as a quintessential care activity in stressful times. Garden stores, seed stores, and mail-order businesses sold out many of their items, noting that among the buyers were numerous first-time home gardeners. First-timers often had little idea of how to proceed, but soon discovered the joys, comfort, and stabilizing aspects of gardening activities. Gardening "isn't some power trip," argues Rutgers University professor and ag extension agent Joel Flagler. "It's that positive control, a feeling of 'Hey I did something good here.'" A self-care response to an event like the pandemic, gardening has the capacity to become part of a broader cultural shift about the need to care for the earth as well as a form of social care when thousands of seeds are planted and bloom on multiple plots of earth.[35]

CLIMATE JUSTICE

For environmental and food justice activists in the United States, the need to care for the land along with the struggle against negative land uses and disproportionate environmental impacts at the community level has extended to global concerns about climate change. The development of a climate justice movement emerged most directly when connections began to be made between local environmental problems and the recognition of the link between the local and global as a justice concern.

One example of that recognition emerged out of the local struggles around the community and environmental impacts from freight traffic, including the movement of goods related to global trade. In the United States, low-income communities of color adjacent to ports, rail corridors, freeways filled with trucks, and warehouses where goods are repackaged and shipped to retail outlets and homes are subject to severe air quality problems, huge noise impacts, soil and land contamination, and congested roadways from the ships, diesel trains, and trucks that enter as well as leave the ports to then pass through their neighborhoods on the way to warehouses, stores, and homes. The initial environmental justice organizing around such "goods movement" issues was on neighborhood and regional impacts, which eventually expanded into a global focus given the prominent role of global trade and its links to climate change. It only took one more step for some of these groups to make those connections and remake themselves into climate justice organizations.[36]

Similar to the evolution of the freight traffic and goods movement organizing, other environmental and food justice groups have expanded their international focus, especially around climate change. In the United States, floods like Hurricane Katrina in New Orleans or Hurricane Harvey in the Houston area; drought conditions in the Southwest and California affecting water supplies and immigrant farm labor; firestorms sweeping through vast areas, putting many low-income communities and individuals in their path at risk; extreme heat events such as the unprecedented triple digit heat episodes in the Pacific Northwest in 2021, and a bitter cold front in Texas, Mississippi, and several other states that led to lengthy power outages and contaminated water supplies, especially impacting low-income communities—all these and other severe climate events came to be seen as harbingers of even more destructive climate change impacts directly experienced at the local level, especially by communities that are most vulnerable to those impacts. The language about climate impacts and care for the earth reinforced the language about protection and care for communities, and vice versa. The issue of disproportionate impacts, so central to the US environmental and food justice discourse, also led groups to consider how large parts of the Global South, often the poorest communities, regions, and nations, are most vulnerable to massive climate change disruptions.

Climate advocacy had already become most pronounced by the 1990s and 2000s among groups and nations in the Global South. Groups that embraced food sovereignty such as Vía Campesino, for example, contrasted large-scale and globally oriented industrial agriculture as a consumer rather than producer of energy, while the practices of small-scale sustainable peasant agriculture "cools down the earth." At a 2007 international food sovereignty conference in Mali, participants emphasized, in their statement of the "Six Pillars of Food Sovereignty," the importance of agroecology and other alternative agricultural practices for resilience as well as adaptation around climate change. Food sovereignty approaches, the statement asserted, seek "to heal the planet so that the planet may heal us." Food sovereignty groups have also been at the forefront of helping to mobilize climate demands at the United Nations and other climate-related international conferences, while still organizing at the local level against food and agricultural policies that undermine rural areas and communities as well as increase carbon emissions.[37]

Food sovereignty groups, along with antimining and anti–fossil fuel development groups, antitoxics and hazardous waste organizations, and sustainable livelihood advocates, have thus been at the forefront of an "environmentalism of the poor" that has taken root in the Global South. This organizing include environmental justice groups working with Indigenous communities to challenge and block efforts by transnational mining companies to extract minerals from the ground while destroying habitats and livelihoods. As global environmental justice groups became major players in climate discussions, they have been able to influence some of the language and deliberations of various international gatherings, including the Paris Agreements at the 2015 COP meeting on climate change.[38]

Once US environmental and food justice groups started to embrace their counterparts in the Global South, this helped establish an environmental and food justice discourse that became "increasingly and interactively global," as one group of researchers put it. The environmentalism of the poor climate justice demand to leave fossil fuels in the ground, for instance, preceded and eventually influenced parallel campaigns in the United States and other developed countries as well, such as the 2016–2017 struggle at Standing Rock in North Dakota led by Indigenous groups, and including a wide array of social and environmental justice participants.[39]

Climate change has now emerged as a preeminent environmental and food justice issue that is pivotal for a care-centered politics. As Welsh professor and food justice advocate Kevin Morgan put it, "How and why we care for others are some of the most important questions that societies can ask themselves in the era of climate change, which is a social justice issue as well as an ecological issue because the countries least responsible for the problem are the most vulnerable to its effects." "We care for others," Morgan argued, "because this is what being sustainable means in an ecologically interdependent world."[40]

Climate change has become a critical issue for a younger generation too. For those in the millennial generation and younger, the climate threat is perceived, more than by any other constituency, as immediate, life-threatening, and ready to inflict unprecedented and permanent damage on a global scale. The necessity of a politics of care for the earth articulated by youth organizers in groups like the Sunrise Movement complements their dark language that the failure to address climate change will rob their generation's future. Immediate action and a radical restructuring of global as well as domestic economies is required, the youth groups insist. Climate change youth ambassadors like Greta Thunberg have amplified that message and placed it in a global context, as the youth demonstrations at the COP 25 meeting did when they provided an insistent alternative voice to the sluggish pace of official governmental action. Climate and social justice, Thunberg told the *Guardian*, "are so interlinked, you can't have one without the other."[41]

Just a couple of months after COP 25 ended in indecision and inaction, and *Time* magazine made Thunberg its "Person of the Year," the climate change message came to be superseded, though also reinforced at times, by the global spread of COVID-19. The Black Lives Matter demonstrations in the United States erupted soon after and spread globally as well, at first in European countries like the United Kingdom and France, and then across continents as the issues of systemic racism and deep inequalities were perceived as rooted in regional, national, and global relationships. At the same time, the impacts from climate change and the pandemic further revealed how they reinforced, and in many instances, dramatically extended, the racism and inequalities in the United States and globally.

All these issues—climate change, the pandemic, systemic racism, and deep inequalities—have revealed that catastrophic outcomes could well happen in the near future. They have demonstrated the immediate and pressing need for transformative change too. Care for the earth and people, including the most vulnerable, an underlying message of the environmental, food, and climate justice activists, require a new and different global order as well as a different way to talk about and reconstruct social life. It also requires, in contrast to the anticare outcomes of the neoliberal capitalist worldview and its practices, an economy based on justice, solidarity, well-being, fairness, and care.

4   A CARE ECONOMY

BUILD BETTER?

In summer 2020, articles and speeches referencing the concept of a care economy began to circulate in the media and among politicians. The notion received more visibility when then candidate Biden, in unveiling his Build Back Better platform, identified a national caregiving plan (the "21st century caregiving and education workforce" plan) as one of his four major economic planks. Two of the other planks—strengthen domestic manufacturing with a focus on clean energy, and build or rebuild infrastructure—were not significantly different from the Obama administration's approach on those issues in the early days of the 2008–2009 Great Recession. A third plank in the 2020 Biden plan, "advance racial equity in America," was more unusual for an economic program, and could be considered testament to the massive Black Lives Matters demonstrations around the United States and globally taking place when the plan was released.

The fourth plank on caregiver issues was also not a traditional economic policy priority. It included early education for three- and four-year-old children through a universal preschool program; increased support for eldercare and care for people with disabilities, via both community-based and in-home care; and more support for caregivers, including higher pay and benefits. By focusing on the role of caregivers, the plank substantially revolved around enabling people, especially women, to get back to work or work longer hours—a goal highlighted by the pandemic's shuttering of businesses, schools, and childcare centers. Similar to the racial equity plank, it was testament to the organizing and policy advocacy of groups like the NDWA, and the influence of care and inequality-focused economists and progressive elected officials like Elizabeth Warren.[1]

Elevating care and racial equity to the same level as manufacturing and infrastructure suggested a change, or at least an addition, to economic development priorities. The subsequent roll out of the plan after Biden took office further indicated momentum toward incorporating this approach by including provisions related to a care economy as part of the infrastructure package proposed by the Biden administration.

Care advocates were pleased: "Not one President before Joe Biden ever used the word 'caregiving' in a public speech. Not one!" two care researchers wrote in April 2021. They also referenced a letter that more than two hundred care scholars and other experts had sent to the Biden administration outlining a more robust care policy plan. Situate care at the center of any recovery, they urged, with its capacity to quickly create more jobs than any infrastructure plan would be able to generate. The letter elaborated a number of proposals important for pursuing the role of care in the economy and daily life. It included provisions that overlapped with the Biden plan such as family leave, but included a number of policies that stretched the notion of care economy support too. These included awarding Social Security credits for family caregivers, building safe, energy-efficient, developmentally appropriate childcare facilities, and expanding a free and low-cost healthy school lunch program, among others.[2]

Care advocates have also continued to emphasize the significance of unpaid care labor, which is itself greater than many other aspects of the economy, whether in hours spent or any economic calculation about the costs of labor. They have long argued, dating back to the wages for housework debates, that the failure to provide an economic value to unpaid care labor reinforces the exploitative nature of care work as a whole. At the same time, instituting paid care work sector changes such as higher pay, more sick pay, and additional vacation time as well as facilitating the right to join a union are advocated not as an end point but rather as baseline demands for a reduction in income gaps and greater empowerment of those working in this fast-growing, heavily exploited job sector in the United States along with much of the developed world.

Beyond the paid care work sector and issues of unpaid care work, a care economy needs to be understood and supported not just in market terms but as part of a social commons too—the unpriced, nonmarket relations between people, the environment, communities, and social knowledge. In discussing the care of children, for example, Nancy Folbre has contended that care "should not be reduced to dollars: parenting is more than just another corporation." The same can be applied to other dimensions of social reproduction.[3]   *impossibility of representation*

Silvia Federici further proposes that social reproduction, including care, should reside in its own sphere between what she calls the wage and commons. Struggles around the two can be complementary rather than in conflict, Federici maintains, by advocating for a politics that supports wage equality while at the same time strengthening and expanding the role of the commons globally and in daily life. Similarly, University of East London professor of political economy Massimo de Angelis has advocated a politics of social reproduction that removes the social and natural wealth as well as labor time that are or should be part of a commons from the control of capital and the market.[4]

The question of whether to price and thereby exert market control over care extends to debates regarding whether care for the environment should be considered a market good. This is a particularly contested notion when it comes to climate politics, where policy initiatives to set up a carbon market through an emissions trading or cap-and-trade program have been developed through three major regional networks, with participation in some form from twenty-three states as well as similar programs in other countries and regions. Climate justice groups have been critical of carbon market schemes, contending that they can disadvantage vulnerable communities by polluters and carbon emitters purchasing credits that would allow them to continue to operate their facilities in those vulnerable places, albeit at possibly lower levels if emissions are capped. Moreover, by treating the environment as a market good, it assumes some level of production and consumption of goods in market terms, and precludes a more transformative approach to care for the environment that situates environment as central to the idea of a shared social commons. Even some of the cleaner and greener technologies like electric cars or eco-friendly consumption strategies like recycled content targets still assume a production and consumption cycle that reduces the environmental or climate impacts, yet does not necessarily restructure the relationship to the environment as a commons-embedded care relationship.[5]

The pandemic has also revealed the failures and devastating inequities of a market-based health system, as opposed to one that prioritizes health for its care and prevention roles. The huge pandemic-related racial and income disparities regarding those who became ill, and how they were treated, were magnified by the market-defined cost of the health care, wholly inadequate insurance systems, and such social determinants of health as work risks, food availability, and housing conditions, including a lack of affordable housing. In relation to policy, the argument that health care is a right rather than a market good underlines the Medicare for All approach that places health as a central part of the commons idea, and shifts the focus of how and where health care should be provided, and how those social determinants of health need to be addressed as central to health care and prevention.[6]

The most ambitious of the politically progressive policy proposals that emerged during the 2019–2020 presidential campaign period—the Green New Deal and Medicare for All—are important markers of a shift to a care economy. They represent transitional strategies bound up with, or at least defended or justified by, some of the dominant assumptions about the economy, such as defining economic performance through the country's GDP, the primary set of indicators of success for a country's economy that was first developed during the 1930s' Great Depression and applied especially during World War II to measure production outputs important for military capacities.

GDP privileges the production of goods, but ignores or minimizes—and in certain cases, subtracts—major components of a care economy. For example, GDP measures ignore unpaid care labor. GDP incorporates the products of polluting industries or fossil fuel–related carbon emitters without assessing and calculating some of their impacts. While it may include certain pollution control measures as products or processes that meet GDP criteria, it does not include prevention strategies that reduce the outputs. Nor does GDP address well-being and quality of life or life satisfaction measures such as happiness, connectedness, and creativity, which are also important measures associated with a care economy approach. Instead, as economist Kate Raworth has argued, the fixation on GDP has been used to justify "extreme inequalities of income and wealth coupled with unprecedented destruction of the living world."[7]

GDP's gaps and overall bias about measuring the quantity of products or goods and services as a measurement of the state of the economy at any given period of time have generated numerous attempts to develop and utilize alternative measures, including environmental, happiness, and well-being indexes, among others. Ecological economist Rutger Hoekstra's "Beyond the GDP" research has identified as many as a thousand indicators—a cottage industry of different alternatives to GDP. Three of those alternatives—the Wellbeing Economy Governments partnership (WEGo), foundational economy, and solidarity economy—all have major care components that inform their approach.[8]

WEGo was established in 2018 by the three SIN countries (Scotland, Iceland, and New Zealand), all led by women. The WEGo group challenged prevailing GDP measures of what constituted economic success, with the premise that development in the twenty-first century should entail "delivering human and ecological wellbeing." In a TED Talk in 2019, Scotland's first minister Nicola Sturgeon elaborated WEGo's critique of GDP for only measuring outputs but not the nature of them, nor other crucial indicators of quality of life. Instead, well-being measures, she argued, should include happiness, inclusivity, mental health, childcare, and parental leave, among others. In January 2020, anticipating the upcoming COP 26 Climate Change Conference in Glasgow, the WEGo group of SIN nations, along with Wales and Finland, planned to host well-being policy forums to promote their new indicator measures and seek new participation. Wales did decide to join WEGo in May 2020, partly due to the impact of the

COVID-19 pandemic, which had also caused the postponement of the COP 26 gathering for another year.[9]

The WEGo group provided a partial shift away from the dominant GDP-influenced discourse about economic performance by contending that well-being was as important as economic growth. Its assertion, however, did not entirely challenge the assumptions about what constituted economic growth and the value of perpetual increases in growth. The need to reconceptualize economic growth as well as well-being was central to the mission of the foundational economy approach, which the Welsh government embraced in 2019, partly in response to Brexit and partly in anticipation of its collaboration with WEGo the next year.[10]

The foundational economy idea, developed by a network of researchers, academics, and activists, and led by a group based at the University of Manchester, was unveiled in 2013 when the group released its initial manifesto. According to the group, the foundational economy consisted of those parts of the economy that produced goods and services that were critical to welfare and well-being. These goods and services included housing, education, childcare, health care, utility supply, and more broadly, care. Three criteria framed the approach regarding what the manifesto authors called "the sphere of the foundational." These were goods and services necessary to everyday life, consumed daily by all people regardless of income, and distributed according to population by branches and networks. This "infrastructure of everyday life," a favorite phrase of the foundationalists, was "partly non-market, generally sheltered, and one way or another politically franchised."[11]

In 2020, the foundational economy group released an updated manifesto in response to the urgent needs due to COVID-19, including the role and impacts of the coronavirus on essential workers. Many of the original issues were highlighted: housing, utility supply, health, education, and care. The branches and networks that distribute those goods and services serve essential household needs, the group argued, constituting "part of the economy that cannot be shut down."[12]

The foundational economy approach provides an alternative framework for a different type of economy, based in part yet extending beyond the existing, albeit insufficient, provision of foundational economy goods and services. Nevertheless, the group has intentionally avoided elaborating a policy blueprint or organizing strategy for how to expand those goods and services, including those that are care related. Instead, its goal is to lay out an argument about how to judge what is useful and needed in people's daily lives. The group's approach places care within a "providential" economy that includes health, education, and housing, as distinct from the material economy of water, gas, electricity, and food, also necessary for the quality of daily life.[13]

In establishing this framework, the foundational economy becomes suggestive, though not explicit about, what political and policy changes might be needed. At the same time, it provides a useful complement to the WEGo narrative, as the SIN countries plus Wales focus on what policy initiatives and programs should be supported. In this way, a different policy approach is indicated without proposing a comprehensive alternative to the dominant neoliberal economies that have continued to favor austerity, privatization, inequalities, and financialization.

The solidarity economy approach, on the other hand, emphasizes more the practices of solidarity, cooperation, and mutual aid in multiple settings than policy per se. Rather than a politics of national or global policy blueprints and programs, it provides "a politics of becoming in place" through its proliferation of local projects, as two feminist authors writing under the name J. K. Gibson-Graham described it.[14]

The solidarity economy has multiple roots and contemporary forms, from nineteenth-century cooperative societies, the anarchist initiatives in Barcelona and Basque Country during the Spanish Civil War, and the efforts to establish various networks at a regional scale. The European and Latin America versions of a social and solidarity economy have a longer, richer history than those in the United States, where the Solidarity Economy Working Group initially came together in 2007 at the first US Social Forum, an offshoot of the World Social Forum where alternative social and solidarity economy groups had been gathering since 2001. The 2007 US Social Forum meeting subsequently established a network of solidarity economy groups, including through the New Economy Coalition, which sought to provide research and studies along with its networking functions. Groups highlighted by the New Economy Coalition ranged from worker cooperatives to local and regional community-based organizing around democratic community control, such as in areas like housing, energy, food, money and finance, and the internet. They also include solidarity purchasing groups, such as the network that formed in the Emilia-Romagna region of Italy, where food and other goods are purchased collectively from suppliers on the basis of solidarity and "critical consumption"—that is, consumption based on fair prices for producers, a preference for local products, and the sustainability of production and transportation of goods, with social cooperatives as suppliers of those services. By emphasizing these kinds of local initiatives and practices, the solidarity economy suggests that a new type of politics can emerge based on ideas like the "decentralisation of power, localisation and regionalisation, self-rule (autonomy) of local communities, democratic pluralism and direct democracy, local and regional control of resources, protection of the environment, and protection of the livelihood and the basic conditions of existence of the people," as Gibson-Graham put it.[15]

As a care-centered politics becomes more prominent, including through WEGo, foundational economy, and social and solidarity economy narratives, it raises these kinds of questions: What would a care economy look like? What does it share with these and other approaches? How can it be scaled up and more widely implemented? How would it challenge the dominant anticare, neoliberal, and state capitalist economies? And what would make it distinctive and transformative?[16]

A CARE-CENTERED GREEN NEW DEAL

The issues of the environment and especially climate change loom large in pursuing the answers to those questions. They include whether the ideas and proposals associated with the Green New Deal meet the criteria for developing a care economy approach, including their ability to challenge the dominant anticare paradigms of the neoliberal period.

The Green New Deal's origins date back to the years immediately preceding, during, and following the Great Recession of 2008–2009. In

2008, the UN Environment Programme issued a call for a Green Economy Initiative to help restore economies and the job market buffeted by the economic downturn. The next year, in preparation for the G20 summit meeting to be held in Pittsburgh, the UN Environment Programme prepared a document based on a report it had solicited and later published as a book about rethinking the economic recovery through the implementation of a Global Green New Deal.[17]

The Pittsburgh Summit document called for redirecting a significant percentage of the global economic stimulus funds to green and sustainable development goals, and after the recession, dedicate 1 percent of the global GDP toward Green New Deal–type projects. These included energy efficiency and renewable energy technologies; sustainable transport technologies such as hybrid vehicles, high-speed rail, and bus rapid transit; sustainable agriculture; and ecological infrastructure such as freshwaters, soils, and forests. The use of the term *Green New Deal* was tied to the argument that green development would be an effective source of new, quality jobs—an update of the Depression era New Deal approaches toward jobs creation.[18]

Other green economic initiatives were already underway by the time the G20 conference took place. Most prominent, the Chinese government, without using the UN Environment Programme's language or blueprint, had already embarked on a massive program of infrastructure development for job creation and GDP recovery during the recession, with some, but not all, dedicated to Global Green New Deal–type goals such as high-speed rail, new subway construction, and renewable energy technologies. At the same time, however, China's infrastructure developments favored a number of polluting industries like coal.[19]

The Obama administration similarly provided support for green development goals as part of its own smaller stimulus program that constituted a relatively modest, though still important component of the US economic recovery funds. Like China, the Obama administration did not utilize Green New Deal language, nor was it able to expand the size of the economic recovery funds, as the administration soon became defensive politically over right-wing efforts to paint the stimulus as contributing to large deficits, even though it had already been whittled down due to Republican and conservative Democratic objections.

Global Green New Deal ideas had already been promoted in Europe, even prior to the 2008 economic crisis, and soon became part of the European debates about whether and how to respond to the economic crisis, given the propensity of key European political and financial players to evoke austerity rather than stimulus to guide policy. A German group, through the Heinrich Böll Foundation, the think tank of the German Greens, had pushed the Green New Deal concept, as did a UK Green New Deal group that had been active since 2007. These European Green New Deal advocates called for changes in the financial and tax systems, and through energy shifts via conservation, renewable energy and demand management. They also supported plans to create what were considered good, high-quality jobs in environmentally based sunrise industries, including through a "just transition" program for retraining workers in fossil fuel and other carbon-generating industries.[20]

The focus on jobs and sustainable or green development that emerged as part of the Green New Deal concept in 2007–2008 could also be traced to the financial and economic crises that shaped its focus on economic growth. In all the early Green New Deal initiatives, including in the United States, United Kingdom, and Europe, the language of sustainable development was integral to any goals or policy agendas. This fed off a history of international environmental and UN-sponsored gatherings such as those in Stockholm in 1972 and Rio in 1992. The language tying a green economy to sustainable development and economic growth had roots in the 1987 publication of *Our Common Future*, also known as the Brundtland Report, led by Norwegian prime minister Gro Harlem Brundtland, who chaired the United Nations' World Commission on Environment and Development.[21]

In the United States, the language of sustainable development was embraced by mainstream environmental organizations as well as a number of pundits like Thomas Friedman and policy makers like Barack Obama and Hillary Clinton. Environmental justice groups, however, remained wary of various development-centered arguments and became fierce opponents of even some presumed sustainable development businesses such as the protracted struggle against Exide, a battery-recycling plant in Southern California. These businesses, such as the Exide plant, were seen not for their environmental benefits but rather as contributing to the environmental harm in the low-income communities where they were located, due to their emissions, soil and water contamination, and negative quality-of-life impacts. The Exide issues were compounded when the company subsequently declared bankruptcy and successfully maneuvered to avoid paying for the substantial cleanup costs now borne by the public.[22]

By 2018, the question of how to address climate change became even more pressing when the United Nations' Intergovernmental Panel on Climate Change released its report warning of catastrophic consequences unless carbon emissions were curtailed dramatically—as much as 50 percent by 2030, and zero net emissions by 2050. The panel's report intensified calls for immediate and massive action by the growing climate movement, led by its youth contingent in groups like the Sunrise Movement in the United States and Extinction Rebellion in the United Kingdom. Picking up on the work of progressive US economists and think tanks that had embraced the language of a Green New Deal and helped develop some statewide Green New Deal initiatives, the climate action groups welcomed the Green New Deal concept as a potential route for action. After the 2018 US midterm elections, the climate activists found a receptive audience among the progressive social and environmental justice champions recently elected to Congress such as Alexandria Ocasio-Cortez who saw the Green New Deal as a priority for their own policy agenda.[23]

On February 7, 2019, Ocasio-Cortez and Massachusetts senator Edward Markey, with more than seventy cosponsors in the House and fourteen cosponsors in the Senate, introduced House Resolution 109 and Senate Resolution 59, which called for the federal government to recognize its duty to create a Green New Deal. The fourteen-page resolution was intended to be more of a template for future action and guide the climate debate rather than a policy document. Like some of the earlier versions of a Green New Deal, House Resolution 109 laid out a technology and jobs-related argument, but also included social and environmental goals (e.g., health care, housing, and education for all), and emphasized the importance of participation and program implementation at the local level of frontline, Indigenous, and vulnerable communities. In addition, the jobs language extended beyond the good jobs argument to call for a guaranteed job with "a family sustaining wage" and the range of benefits for "all people of the United States."[24]

Ocasio-Cortez's role also became a magnet for both supporters and opponents of the Green New Deal resolution. Her decision to join protesters from the Sunrise Movement and the progressive group Justice Democrats who decided to sit-in in Congressperson Nancy Pelosi's office on November 13, 2018, to demand action on the upcoming Green New Deal resolution seemed to backfire when Pelosi, once elected House speaker, refused to establish a special committee to review the Green New Deal. Moreover, the broader language about social as well as climate and environmental goals was criticized as detracting from the narrower language about climate action among some climate and Green New Deal advocates such as economist Robert Pollin, who focused primarily on infrastructure and had helped author several of the state-level Green New Deal proposals.[25]

While the Green New Deal resolution languished in Congress, the impact it had on the debates about climate was substantial. The Green New Deal figured prominently in the Democratic Party presidential debates and served as a proxy for the need for a massive response to the climate crisis. Its lack of a policy direction and various cost estimates, considered core legislative weaknesses, nevertheless allowed it to serve as a broad call for mobilization, and way to link issues and constituencies. Moreover, by incorporating social and economic goals along with environmental justice language, it provided a more accessible and popular way to talk about as well as organize around climate change, distinct from the more technical and obscure climate discussions about technology choices and policy debates, such as a carbon tax or the use of market instruments. Even without the ability to secure immediate legislative action, the Green New Deal became a type of baseline to judge how ambitious and, for many climate researchers and activists, absolutely necessary its implementation was to achieve needed climate action goals.[26]

From a care politics perspective, the Green New Deal, while valuable in elevating the need for large-scale climate action, would benefit by incorporating more of a care perspective in how it identified the social and economic change needed that could influence necessary climate changes too. Naomi Klein's 2015 book, *This Changes Everything: Capitalism vs the Climate*, highlighted the urgency of climate change along with the need for social and environmental justice activists to engage in the climate movement. She was supportive of the Green New Deal approach, but also sought to emphasize that the ethic of care and repair she had been promoting could strengthen as well as extend the Green New Deal argument. "Care jobs are green jobs," Klein wrote in a chapter in a book promoting the Green New Deal that was adapted for an article in *Dissent*. In her own book on the Green New Deal, Klein asserted that activists needed to tell a different story about "care for the land, water, air—and to care for one another," in contrast and opposition to an extractivist and endless growth discourse. A care economy, she wrote, should seek "to repair what had been damaged, including the land, the stuff [that is consumed], and the relationships within our countries and between them."[27]

Various feminist economists also weighed in on the Green New Deal, pointing out that the stress on job training and developing green jobs, language all found in the UK, US, and European Green New Deal versions, tended to be a male-centric one. The focus on a "green industrial policy," common to several of the Green New Deal versions and incorporated in part (without the label Green New Deal) by the initial Biden infrastructure proposal in April 2021, was criticized as "androcentric market logic," too often sidelining "the social dimension of sustainability, social rights, care and gender justice," as sociologist Christa Wichterich put it in her analysis of the European Green New Deal. The Green New Deal should not only be green, some feminists argued, but also assume a purplish tint (feminist colors) by putting forth the sustainability of caring labor as part of its green economy approach. Such an approach could be accomplished by expanding care job opportunities as well as substantially increasing care work wages and benefits (part of the good green jobs platform), and through a redistributive internalization of the costs of care into the workings of the system, parallel to and complementing the green economy approach of internalizing environmental costs. University of California at Santa Barbara professor Eileen Boris has further pointed out that care workers "draw important links between environmental and economic justice. They bring sustainability into the home—both figuratively by maintaining daily life and aiding elders, and materially by doing so healthfully." "In caring for planet earth," Boris asserted, "we can create the conditions for sustaining a more caring society."[28]

Environmental-oriented feminist economists have, in addition, argued that advocacy and changes around the care dimensions of social reproduction need to be linked to changes to the environment and climate. Such changes could be accomplished through "sufficiency provisioning," or providing enough for everyone. Sufficiency provisioning encompasses a dual objective: "the provision of the goods and services necessary for social reproduction—housing, food, drinking water, childcare, health needs—governed by the twin principles of environmental sustainability and social justice," including defining "the limits of what the biosphere can sustain, and to treat all equally within that constraint," according to feminist economist Mary Mellor. Approaches associated with sufficiency provisioning, moreover, resonate with the more care-centered language and programs in the 2019 Green New Deal resolution, such as agroecology, more local and cooperative businesses, and overall forms of production that help promote the "regeneration of the environment."[29]

In contrast to the idea of sufficiency resides the dominant language of continuing the growth and hypergrowth that guides how contemporary economies are organized. One criticism of the Green New Deal has been its avoidance of a more substantive critique of this economic growth model. Instead, Green New Dealers argue for sustainable growth, albeit more equitable growth. That critique of economic growth, activist and author Ashley Dawson writes, would require a transformation in values that could "build social resilience through the expansion of non-consumption-based sectors of the economy. Such an ecological and social reconstruction cannot take place within the framework of a capitalist economy."[30]

The contemporary hypergrowth model is intricately related to the notion of abundance through consumption, particularly the type of compulsive consumption identified as making possible a middle-class lifestyle to go along with the good middle-class jobs that the Green New Dealers advocate. Klein gently criticizes the Green New Deal's failure to discuss these issues, especially for not taking on what she calls "the outsize role that consumption plays in what used to be called 'the American way of life,'" or the way that a culture of overwork fuels cycles of disposable consumption. "Stressed and overworked people need fast and easy everything," Klein characterizes the cycle in contemporary neoliberal societies. Purple-tinted economists and sociologists, including notably Juliet Schor in several of her books and articles, have also effectively elaborated how such "work and spend" and "culture of overwork" cycles have shaped today's economies. For Klein and Schor as well as a number of other care economy advocates, how to politically address the issues of consumption along with the cultures and economics of overwork and precarity is critical to the care economy approach and agenda.[31]

COMPULSIVE CONSUMPTION

In *Keywords*, Williams noted how the evolution of the words *consumer* and *to consume* had shifted from negative associations in a preindustrial era to a neutral connotation with the development of the bourgeois political economy. By the 1950s and 1960s, the expansion of a consumer-centered economy to consume signified an individual's activity, with consumer purchases occupying a central role in the United States and other developed countries' economies. Similarly, the word *advertising*, Williams noted, when applied to earlier customer-supplier relationships about what was available, became a form of "persuasion or penetration of a market" given modern commercial advertising—a method to create "needs and wants and of particular ways of satisfying them." Following up on Williams's analysis, anarchist anthropologist David Graeber argued that with neoliberal capitalism, instead of situating consumerism as an analytic term, it had become more accurate to characterize it as an ideology.[32]

In July 1959, that ideological promotion of consumerism and the consumer economy became the backstory with the famous kitchen debate between US vice president Richard Nixon and Soviet premier Nikita Khrushchev. The exchange took place at the US Embassy in Moscow in an exhibition room featuring a model US kitchen. At the time of the kitchen debate, personal consumption expenditures per capita in the United States had been increasing steadily during the 1950s, surpassing $12,000 (in 2021 dollars). Nixon proudly pointed to the kitchen, filled with new appliances and other convenience features. These illustrated, he told Khrushchev, how "the American system is designed to take advantage of new inventions and new techniques." "What we want to do," Nixon asserted, "is make life more easy [sic] for our housewives." Purchasing those consumer goods not only helped underwrite the economy but also reinforced the gendered division between home and work.[33]

During the 1960s, as personal consumption expenditures continued their rise, consumerism critics argued that the search for convenience and continuing development of new products facilitated those manufactured needs that Williams referenced. This assertion was elaborated by German Marxist refugee and philosopher Herbert Marcuse in his 1964 book *One-Dimensional Man*, which sold more than three hundred thousand copies in its first edition and became a celebrated text among young New Leftists at the time. Marcuse maintained that advanced industrial society and its consumer economy were capable of containing the forces for social change."[34]

Yet Marcuse's pessimism appeared to be challenged by the political and cultural shifts of the mid- to late 1960s, including skepticism about an unbounded consumerism. One 1968 New Left tract titled *Consumption: Domestic Imperialism* linked US government resource extraction policies in the Third World during the post–World War II period to the rise of consumerism and its role in the US domestic economy. New Left and radical feminist critiques of consumerism paralleled and gave substance to the anticonsumerist counterculture of the late 1960s.[35]

The cultural shifts, however, failed to stem the increase in personal consumption expenditures, as they continued to rise during the 1960s and would do so for the next three decades until the 2008–2009 Great Recession. It was then, for the first time in the postwar period, that expenditures experienced a modest dip. The change was short-lived, as increases in consumer spending resumed by 2010 and reached a peak of more than $40,500 per capita in the final quarter of 2019. By then, estimates of consumer spending, dependent in part on its peak periods such as the Christmas holidays, accounted for as much as 70 percent of the economy.[36]

For some economists and various defenders of the consumer economy, the continuing growth and fading of the cultural critique of consumerism in the neoliberal period provided an ideological underpinning of capitalism. "Consumption now affects the ways in which people build up, and maintain, a sense of who they are, of who they wish to be . . . [and that] the ideology of consumerism has served to legitimate capitalism in the eyes of millions of ordinary people, if not the heart and minds of those former protestors of the 1960s," wrote English sociologist Robert Bocock in 1993.[37]

Writing around the same time as Bocock, Schor situated the link between consumption and identity, or what Schor called the "psychocultural role" of consumption, as part of the increasing commercialization of society and culture. "Advertising and marketing encourage consumers to be dissatisfied with what they have and to covet more," wrote Schor. Similar to Bocock's analysis, Schor identified how advertisers marketed identities rather than product quality. Validated by the most successful campaigns such as soft drinks representing the "new generation" or sneakers associated with desirable lifestyles, consumerism, according to Schor, became "the linchpin of modern economic, political, social and personal life." The role of advertising was further reinforced by a tax code that allowed a 100 percent deduction by businesses for their advertising costs.[38]

At the same time, *consumer choice* (itself a curious phrase, according to Williams) was touted by market economists as autonomous and near sacrosanct. In political economy terms, the doctrine of de gustibus non est disputandum —no questioning consumer choices—was elevated. Challenging the wave of political initiatives regarding consumer products during the 1960 and early 1970s, and hostile to groups like activist Ralph Nader's "Nader's Raiders" and their withering critiques of corporate practices, market economists and neoliberal champions asserted that no policies should be introduced or supported that "regulated packaging, advertising, or the sale of harmful products and services, even if those products might be harmful or embraced only after intense and manipulative advertising," wrote Gary Cross in his study of the history of consumerism about the dominant approach that prevailed by the 1980s and 1990s. "The market is always right because it 'revealed preference' in the consumer's purchases," Cross critically characterized the neoliberal economist approach. Fostered by a politics and media that elevated the consumer to be that abstract figure in an abstract market, by the end of the twentieth century the critique of consumer culture was no longer taken seriously. Yet, despaired political science professor Robert Lane, "that culture may never have needed criticism more."[39]

As the role of consumption in forging identities as well as influencing economic decision-making became pervasive in the United States, it extended to other parts of the world too and became particularly influential in China's rise as the world's leading exporter of consumer goods. The expansion globally of the consumer economy in the late twentieth and early twenty-first centuries had been fueled in part by the availability of cheap consumer goods. This was made possible by a global supply chain with low labor costs, weak or nonexistent environmental regulations, and the outsize role of China as the "world's factory." "Made in China" through much of the neoliberal era became a ubiquitous tag. The component parts of numerous consumer products were sourced from different locations throughout the world as part of the global supply chain. Goods manufactured in places like Guangdong Province, across from Hong Kong, would then be sent to Asian ports like Hong Kong, Shenzhen, Shanghai, and Singapore, to be shipped to US and European ports in places like Los Angeles and Long Beach. The end point destinations of this global supply chain traffic were the digital marketers and retail outlets, such as Amazon warehouses or big-box stores like Walmart across the United States. Through this global supply chain, 80 percent of all the world's toys, for example, were produced by China, while more than 86 percent of the toys sold in the United States came from China. The consumer economy was made in China as well as in Vietnam, Indonesia, Mexican maquiladora plants, and other places with even lower labor costs, and then bought and consumed, with corresponding identities created in greater and greater quantities in the United States and other developed countries. As a December 2020 research article in *Nature* noted, the massive proliferation of *things*, part of the overall anthropogenic or human-made mass, had come to weigh more than all the other living biomass on the planet. We had become an earth dominated by things.[40]

In 2020, the pandemic interrupted the global supply chains that dominated this production of things or stuff as well as the continuous cycle of work and spend. Consumer spending changed dramatically in the first months of the pandemic in the United States and through much of the developed countries, far greater than with the Great Recession. It also impacted global trade numbers as well as supply chain capacities, and sharply reduced spending in such areas as travel and transport, restaurants, personal care services, and cultural and sports events, among others. Yet consumer spending already began to increase by the late spring and summer of 2020 after the first stimulus funding was provided—the $1,200 payment per person in the United States, and the European Union's own economic stimulus program designed in part to save jobs. The appeal of consumer spending as an economic savior for battered economies remained as strong as ever, even though the uncertainty of the COVID-19 crisis still threatened to upend earlier patterns, at least until the pandemic was fully contained, as one McKinsey & Company report noted in October 2020.[41]

The role of China in helping to restimulate global consumer demand during the global pandemic was impacted by that country's decision to establish a "dual circulation" economic approach that identified China's own domestic consumer market as a priority—a trend that had already been developing prior to 2020–2021. While the pandemic brought uncertainty to the US and global economies, including their reliance on consumer spending stimulated by cheap exports and a now-weakened global supply chain, China remained an outlier thanks to its quicker ability to reduce pandemic impacts and aggressively pursue its domestic consumer spending reorientation. The increase in domestic consumer spending was marked dramatically when China's huge online retailers, Alibaba and JD.com, set records for online purchases in November 2020 during Singles' Day. Singles' Day is the world's largest shopping event, originally invented by the Alibaba company in 2009, and far surpasses US equivalents such as Black Friday or Cyber Monday.[42]

Along with the pandemic, an increasing number of climate change–related events, such as the Australian and California wildfires, further raised the question of whether the ideology of consumerism along with the continuing growth economies it had helped stimulate would contribute to more and even greater climate disasters. To answer that challenge, arguments were raised, including among green development advocates, that with climate change, it was technology rather than an economic and cultural paradigm shift related to the consumer economy that could slow the increase in carbon emissions. The defenders of consumerism continued to find ways to protect consumerism's favored economic status.

Yet counterarguments were raised that continual, uninhibited growth and its enabler, work-and-spend consumerism, might finally be reaching its limits. The advocates of a care economy perspective asserted that the current economic cycle of consumer-stimulated growth leading to more growth needed to come to an end for reasons of well-being and life satisfaction, and another type of model to help bring about such a change was needed. The three crises had merged: the pandemic and the economic turbulence it had created; climate change and its heat waves, fierce fires, droughts, sea rise, and even far-greater possible impacts to come; and the demands to end systemic racism along with the various forms of deep inequalities in the United States, developed countries, and Global South. With these crises, what seemed politically impossible during the neoliberal period had turned into a necessity for change.

What forms would such change take? Could a care economy approach and other radical departures from the continual growth consumer economy help shape the changes that were needed? And would such changes even be politically feasible given the entrenched and dominant discourse of a hypergrowth capitalism and market-centered manufactured consumer choice? All of these became critical questions for a care-centered politics in the immediate aftermath of the pandemic, intensifying impacts from climate change, insistent cry that Black Lives Matter meant systemic change, and continuing and dramatic increases in inequality, job loss, housing expulsions, homelessness, food insecurity, and hunger.

SUFFICIENCY AND EQUALITY

When I was a boy growing up in working-class Borough Park in Brooklyn, New York, in the 1950s, a favorite neighborhood game was stickball. Utilizing a stick (often a broom handle unscrewed), a rubber ball, some large stones to serve as bases, and an empty lot (we frequently used the after-hours schoolyard of PS 64, our local neighborhood school), anywhere from four to a dozen of us would assemble to engage in a stickball game. It was hard to be too competitive (the skill involved was highly variable), and the enjoyment flowed more from the interaction and connection rather than the outcome of the game.

This type of play, in contrast to the commoditized forms of play today in the United States, prefigures an "economy of care and connection"—a concept elaborated by environmental studies professor Jack Manno. Such a concept is associated with far lower uses of materials, energy, and carbon emissions than the globally sourced, intensively marketed, and individual versus collaborative forms of play, including with the toys that originate in China and circulate through various global supply chains.[43]

One response to the question "What would a care economy look like?" suggests an economy connected to the ideas of *sufficiency* and *equality*. In an economy guided by sufficiency, goods needed to sustain daily life, such as housing, food, individual and community health, childcare, eldercare, and clean drinking water, would be produced and provided to everyone, as the foundational and solidarity economy advocates propose. Community services such as parks, libraries, mail, cell phone, internet and other information services, utilities, the arts, and education would be considered essential public goods. To be viable, a care economy based on sufficiency requires a democratic politics that can tackle the need for equality—an economy of "to each according to their need" and for everyone to be able to live well. Such a politics needs to be at once local, national, and international, as the pandemic and climate change have made clear. "Only collective, democratic, universal provisioning can guarantee social justice," Mellor points out.[44]

Sufficiency also suggests a sharing as well as caring practice, and a care for nature and the environment. "Not producing at the expense of others and of nature-loss is the decisive criteria of sufficiency," argues Wichterich, who references the "Buddhist wisdom of knowing what is enough." A care economy and care-centered politics approach helps facilitate that awareness through its recognition that personal change is influenced by social change, and social change is made possible by a cultural shift that promotes personal, community, and global well-being. What is enough, from the care economy and care politics perspective, is only viable if it is ultimately applied on that personal, community, and global scale.[45]

Amid the dominant language of acquisitiveness and greed, celebration of wealth and policies that extend inequalities, and financialization of resources and commodification of daily life, spaces have been created that assert the practice of solidarity and the economy of care and connection too. Characterized during the late 1960s and early 1970s as alternative institutions, these spaces today, highlighted by solidarity economy advocates, include food production and provisioning initiatives such as community gardens, guerrilla gardening and CSAs, new types of energy production and distribution including decentralized microgrid and off-the-grid systems, and new arrangements for housing such as cohousing, tenant unions, or the squatter occupation of abandoned or foreclosed homes. Collectively, they suggest the mix of possibilities that move in the direction of an alternative to the dominant economy.

The challenges for a care-centered politics are obvious. How can those spaces grow and the idea of sufficiency take hold, whether based on livelihood and well-being, while addressing differences in wealth and class position, or cultural, ethnic, racial, regional, or nation-state differences? How can a care economy become viable when the pandemic, climate change, and systemic racism have made inequalities so much greater? How can one best challenge the neoliberal logic that the market governs all and there is no such thing as society? And how can social movements and a new politics overcome the type of cynicism that assumes that no change is possible. "Everybody knows that the dice are loaded [and] the poor stay poor and the rich get rich," Leonard Cohen sings.[46]

To meet such challenges and overcome the cynicism, even if at first just through partial yet still crucial approaches, will require a political project in the next decades that is the reverse image of the neoliberal political project that emerged during the 1970s and 1980s. The response to the pandemic, climate change, and the issues of systemic racism and deep inequalities, both short and long term, has the potential to begin to construct and implement the political changes required. These changes are needed at every level, whether personal, community, local and regional, national, nation-state to nation-state, or global. They can occur through individual and community initiatives, with political action and the development of intersecting social movements, by cultural shifts that unfold over time through civil society and via the government. To implement sufficiency and equality also requires a renewed and democratic public sector along with a care-based form of governance, and those robust social movements to ensure goods and resources are made available to all.

A care economy based on sufficiency and equality needs to also challenge the dominant discourse on hypergrowth and compulsive consumerism that assumes only a market-based, consumer-driven, and continually growing economy can provide for those at the bottom even as those at the top reap nearly all of its benefits. In the dominant discourse on markets and growth, a good life is defined by acquiring *more* rather than knowing what is enough as well as increasing the care and connection so central to well-being. It needs to be associated with a care-centered politics of redistribution embedded in the demands for equality, and facilitating changes in how issues of race, gender, ethnicity, and class are addressed.

One alternative perspective on sufficiency and equality that has gained followers, primarily in Europe, is based on the idea of *degrowth*, an awkward phrase in English translated from the French term *décroissance*. Since the turn of the twenty-first century, a movement for décroissance or degrowth, primarily based in France, has organized around the concept, including through a journal and publications. A French political party (Le Parti pour la Décroissance) was created to make visible its ideas. A 2018 petition that incorporated several degrowth themes gathered more than a hundred thousand signatures and was sent to European institutions, including the European Parliament.[47]

The European origins of décroissance trace back to the writings in the early 1970s of such figures as Gorz as well as Romanian mathematician Nicholas Georgescu-Roegen. In 1972, Gorz (under his pen name, Michel Bosquet) wrote that a necessary condition to achieve the earth's balance would be a form of reduced growth or degrowth of material conditions (his "less is better" argument). Similarly, Georgescu-Roegen, in his 1971 book, *The Entropy Law and the Economic Process*, applied the law of entropy in thermodynamics to argue against a wasteful and environmentally damaging economy of endless growth.[48]

In the United States, degrowth forerunners included a wide range of critics of the growth economy such as British statistician E. F. Schumacher, author of *Small Is Beautiful*, and onetime World Bank economist Herman Daly. Daly's 1973 book, *Toward a Steady-State Economy*, challenged the notion that continued economic growth would be "a panacea for problems originating in underdevelopment and maldistribution of wealth." With the growth economy, Daly argued, "there is no such thing as sufficiency because more is always better," while a steady-state economy "must be ecologically sustainable for a long future for a population living at a standard or per capita resource use that is sufficient for a good life."[49]

Degrowth advocates such as Greek ecological economist Giorgos Kallis and economics emeritus professor Joan Martínez Alier have elaborated the sufficiency and equality argument, partly by challenging the mainstream environmental assertion that green growth is a realistic political approach to pursue a more sustainable form of development. Green growth perpetuates a cycle of growth, degrowthers contend, and doesn't directly address how such growth may also contribute to inequalities and regional (North-South) disparities. Furthermore, green growth fails to challenge a market-centric notion of what constitutes well-being, reinforcing the mantra that more is better. Instead, degrowthers maintain, we need to "escape from the [market] economy."[50]

There are differences among degrowthers regarding if and when a political project is needed, and whether and how to translate degrowth into an action agenda. Most degrowthers argue, in a way similar to the wages for housework advocates, that theirs is an ideological or discourse battle, a tool "for initiating a more radical break with dominant economic thinking," including its celebration of the growth and consumer economy. A political agenda that provides only partial change, they assume, undercuts the transformative message in the degrowth reasoning. Other degrowthers, particularly those allied with ecofeminists and social justice, solidarity, and racial and environmental justice movements in the North as well as the environmentalism of the poor movements in the Global South, seek to ally with those causes and movements. Language, in this context, is critical. A degrowth concept for the wealthier countries of the North could be seen as austerity for the poorer countries of the South. Instead of degrowth, it would be more effective for a political project to talk of redistribution along with a more appropriate use of resources to live better.[51]

In order to extend beyond a type of exclusive or sectarian approach that can be found in some of the degrowth discourse, political alliances and a type of intersectionality approach is needed where the sum or integration of social movements is considered greater than the parts. Care-centered politics fits well with the intersectionality approach, including its focus on what a care economy entails, notably by underlining the centrality of social reproduction and area of life-making activities, including but not limited to the issues of gender and racial equality in the household economy. Care-centered politics broadens any discussion of political agenda and policy change to include the ideas of redistribution, unconditional and sufficient guaranteed income, community wealth creation, and a reconsideration of how to define work and activity, beginning with the presumably limited yet quite-radical reform of reduced work hours without reduced wages and by addressing unpaid household labor as part of any political project.[52]

In relation to issues of systemic racism and deep inequalities as well as pandemic and climate impacts, a care-centered politics of "care and repair" seeks to associate with the demands for *reparations*. Reparations, in the context of the care-centered politics to be discussed in the next chapter, references the issue of slavery reparations (the post–Civil War forty acres and a mule as a form of livelihood and well-being) and other systemic racial injustices up through the present day. In a North-South context, it also references the range of deep inequalities, exploitative relations, and historical and contemporary abuses, such as colonialism and austerity-induced structural adjustments.

The pandemic and climate change have further heightened the need for a care economy and care-centered politics along with the role they could play in addressing the enormity of the impacts they have had on people's livelihoods and well-being. Those impacts call into question whether capitalism as a system, already molded during the neoliberal era for perpetuating deep inequalities, can effectively adjust in an era where pandemics and climate change can no longer be ignored. In the United States, the election of Donald Trump in 2016, parallel to the rise of an authoritarian response in other countries, already suggested that new political choices needed to be made. Trump's defeat in 2020, albeit providing only the beginnings of an alternative agenda, nevertheless opened up spaces to begin to construct that new political project. Whether a quite-different political outcome will result in the longer term, including one that could draw on the ideas and hopes for a livable future embedded in a care-centered politics, remains the challenge for such a political project as well as the cultural and economic shift required to help make that happen.

5 CARE, REPAIR, AND TRANSFORM: THE CRISES OF 2020–2021

THE TRUMP INTERREGNUM

At the Republican National Convention in August 2020, when gushing speeches and self-congratulations capped Trump's nomination for reelection as president, it had already become something of a truism that the Republican Party had become Trump's party. Yet barely mentioned at the convention was that other presumed icon of the Republicans, Ronald Reagan. Missing as well was the rhetoric and platform (there was no platform) of an antigovernment, pro-market, free trade neoliberalism. Trump in fact sometimes disparaged ideological constructs like neoliberalism, substituting his own preference for a type of l'état, c'est moi self-idolatry.

Yet as economist Branco Milanovic pointed out shortly before the 2020 Republican National Convention, Trump could have been considered an unabashed neoliberal by his application of the most extreme of market ideologies and the dominance of money to the political sphere. The 2017 tax cut Trump helped shepherd through Congress, with its enormous tax breaks for the wealthy, was subsequently touted as Trump's primary legislative achievement. Trump's attacks against environmental regulations, trade unions, and social safety net programs coupled with his efforts to downsize or eliminate any form of government-mandated health care fit a neoliberal score card too, as a commentary in the *Washington Post* noted just two months into his presidency in 2017. And while providing lip service to a pro-jobs and pro-white working-class faux populist agenda, Trump fully assumed his anticare mantle by further gutting the infrastructure of everyday life, whether through his food, health, housing, childcare, immigration, and public education policies, embrace of military spending, or taxation and domestic spending decisions and regulatory cutbacks.[1]

The singular focus as well as celebration of money and wealth remained constant throughout the Trump presidency. Steve Mnuchin, Trump's treasury secretary and one of the only cabinet members to last through Trump's four years, memorably posed in November 2017 with his wife, Louise Linton, touching and reveling about a sheet of dollar bills issued by his department—the first set of bills bearing the treasury secretary's signature. While Trump and his acolytes could be considered crony capitalists, it was the overt love of money that underlined his and their political belief system.[2]

Through Trump's four years, the Trumpian hostility to anything resembling a care-centered politics agenda represented what *New York Times* columnist Linda Greenhouse called his administration's *meanness*—a direct form of anticare politics. This included its race-baiting, hostility to democratic norms, attacks against public agencies and institutions like the post office, anti-immigrant and antirefugee policies and broadsides including separating families and terrorizing children, antagonism to any public health and prevention approach to health care, and dismissal of climate change and the pandemic's impact on people's lives and livelihoods. As those attacks expanded in scope and intensified, they identified the Trump years as a period fully committed to an anticare and meanness agenda.[3]

Trump's approach to the three extraordinary set of events and crises that erupted during spring, summer, and fall 2020 prior to his electoral defeat in November 2020—the pandemic, climate events, and Black Lives Matter demonstrations—further highlighted the anticare politics of the Trump years. It was also embedded in a politics of denial: climate science denial, pandemic science denial, and dismissal of the need to address the legacies of slavery and racism. The approach raised the question, Was the Trump period an interregnum, anomaly, in-between period, high point, or continuing manifestation of the forty years of neoliberal ascendance? Would Trump and Trumpism continue to make reappearances during the coming decade? Or after a period when any semblance of a normal government was suspended, did Trump's demise also suggest that a more care-centered politics would flourish and ultimately prevail?

PUBLIC HEALTH AND PREVENTION: REVELATIONS OF COVID-19

Historically, pandemics have forced humans to break with the past and imagine their world anew. This one is no different. It is a portal, a gateway between one world and the next. We can choose to walk through it, dragging the carcasses of our prejudice and hatred, our avarice, our data banks and dead ideas, our dead rivers and smoky skies behind us. Or we can walk through lightly, with little luggage, ready to imagine another world. And ready to fight for it.

—ARUNDHATI ROY, "THE PANDEMIC IS A PORTAL"

When the Biden administration assumed office after the turbulent post-election period of electoral denial and transparent efforts to undo the results, it seemed obvious there would be changes. Science was back in favor. Climate change was not just recognized, but policies to address it were going to be actively pursued, beginning with the readherence to the Paris Agreement on Biden's first day in office. Efforts to address the pandemic, including through a massive campaign to get as many people vaccinated and a push for mask mandates, situated the pandemic at the top of the Biden agenda. Antiracism became more central to the language of the new administration. For Trump supporters, it was the deluge. For progressive advocates, including those who focused on care, it meant an opportunity to launch and extend the new political project.

Yet barriers to "bend the system," as Louis Menand characterized those opportunities, remained as formidable as ever. Legislative gridlock, due in part to the threatened, constant use of the filibuster; a Supreme Court stacked against any number of new initiatives, including any threats to property and corporate power; vast concentrations of wealth that could bend the system toward inequality and anticare policies; the deeply ingrained culture and practices of racism, misogyny, and biases against the poor as well as those newly poor due to the pandemic—all of these and more contributed to the challenges for any new political project.[4]

These were not new barriers. The events of 2020–2021 heightened the perception that capitalism's neoliberal ascendancy might have reached its limits, at the very moment when its consequences had been magnified. Still, opportunities for transformation vied with an anticare defiance and denial as well as a desire to revert not only to the past but one steeped in racial, class, and antiwomen actions and messaging too. Each of the events—the pandemic, climate change disruptions, and calls for a racial and inequality reckoning—heightened the tensions between those competing agendas and visions of a postpandemic future.

The pandemic itself provided a vivid and immediate illustration of those tensions. When people at the outset of the pandemic, in Italy, Spain, the United States, and elsewhere, came to their windows to bang their pots, sing songs, create memes, and clap hands to support frontline health care workers as well as food workers, transport workers, and all those working in numerous other services and institutions deemed essential for daily life needs in the midst of a pandemic, they did so because they felt it important to demonstrate solidarity and "clap because we care." In cities around the world, these spontaneous actions in support of care workers became a daily event. Yet while people wanted to demonstrate that they cared, systems and structures were still undermining or negating a care agenda. Care workers appreciated the demonstrations of support, but said what they wanted was workplace support, government support and direction, institutional support such as by hospitals and nursing homes, and business support to address their high-risk and, for many, low-pay work.[5]

The first year of the pandemic, particularly in the United States during the Trump period, highlighted this lack of support and blame shifting. The Trump administration's response to the pandemic represented in many ways an extension of its anticare agenda, even including its continuous desire to either ignore or simply wish that the coronavirus would disappear and no longer occupy the public discourse. It revealed a willingness to tell lies in public about the severity of the pandemic by minimizing its life-threatening impacts. Even when Trump contracted COVID-19 in

October 2020, and had to be rushed to the hospital and given an experimental cocktail of drugs and treatments not yet approved for public use, his message remained that COVID-19 was nothing to be alarmed about. For Trump, COVID-19 politics was one more extension of care for himself and not for others.

Yet the pandemic, rather than going away, exposed not just the failures of the Trump administration but also the impact of forty-plus years of neoliberalism (and indeed centuries of capitalist and colonial development) on the capacities of both the public and private sectors to address the pandemic's challenges as well as the long-term health, social, and economic issues that the pandemic had exacerbated. Once in power, the Biden administration sought to provide a different message, highlighting the dangers of the pandemic, increasing resources to address it, and vowing to have everyone vaccinated before assuming there could be a new normal. The pandemic, however, did not just go away; it suggested a reckoning with what it had revealed, and that a return to a prepandemic state of affairs was neither simple nor desirable without addressing what it had exposed.

From a care perspective, such a reckoning and challenge included:

The need to transform a health care system more focused on technologies, medical interventions, and profit centers that worked best for the wealthiest rather than one with a public health, prevention, and health care for all approach.

In 2002, under the headline "Nurses Devalued and Abandoned," the journal *Health Affairs* published a letter by Jean Chaisson of the Community Health Network in Holliston, Massachusetts criticizing how health care institutions were increasingly approaching sick people "as though they were running a factory." "Consultants," Chaisson wrote, "now refer to our most complex and vulnerable patients as 'product lines,' focusing on 'throughput' instead of *healing*. Sadly, most healthcare institutions have followed this industrial model."[6]

Such an industrial model of health care long dominated the health system, reinforced by continuing problems of health access, especially for those with limited or no health insurance. Between 1965 and 2010, from the passage of Medicare to the signing into law of the Affordable Care Act, the numbers of uninsured people climbed dramatically even while health-based private institutions and associations like big pharma and hospital chains further consolidated their political role along with their power and influence in the health system. Opposition by these private players and their political champions to universal health care remained constant, and even the Affordable Care Act, while enabling more than twenty million people to obtain health insurance, largely failed to challenge the industrial, privatized health system.

The Affordable Care Act did, however, provide some modest though important support for both prevention and public health—a major priority for a care-centered politics. The legislation did this in part by creating the Prevention and Public Health Fund, with mandatory funding to support public health. Much of the money was earmarked for state-based programs, while some funding was provided to the Centers for Disease Control and Prevention, including more than 12 percent of the center's total program funding in fiscal year 2016.[7]

Yet the Prevention and Public Health Fund failed to shift priorities away from the industrial health care model toward a public health and prevention framework. The amount of funding available was continually whittled down through funding transfers to address other financial gaps such as reduced Medicare physician payments. Republican hostility to the Affordable Care Act remained a constant, and hindered both funding and implementation. Monies earmarked for the states, moreover, failed to prevent reductions and gaps in state public health programs, including, for example, more than a 10 percent reduction in public health funding in Texas just the year before the COVID-19 outbreak. Between 2008 and 2017, fifty-six thousand local public health positions in the United States were eliminated, and forty-five states were unable to provide comprehensive public health system support for more than 50 percent of their population. Emergency funding for disasters, initially established after 9/11, also witnessed a funding decline by more than 50 percent (60 percent when accounting for inflation) in the period prior to COVID-19, resulting in health departments with out-of-date surveillance and hospital systems in COVID-19 hot spots quickly becoming overwhelmed. This combination of an industrial health care model and inability to move toward a more robust prevention and public health system along with a focus on the social determinants of health became a prime illustration of the industrial and largely private-based health system's failure to meet the challenges posed by the pandemic.[8]

The Biden administration sought to move quickly to change the response to the health challenges related to the pandemic, including through the American Rescue Plan, which was signed into law in March 2021. This included upgrading the Affordable Care Act to increase participation and lower the cost of coverage for some; providing resources for additional contact tracing and the increased production of vaccines, personal protective equipment, and other medical supplies; extending the capacity of the Occupational Safety and Health Administration to better protect health care and other essential workers subject to various risks and abuses in their pandemic-related work; providing more public health and prevention resources; and including equity criteria in responding to the pandemic, such as utilizing community-based programs and clinics for vaccine outreach.

As ambitious as it was and in contrast to the Trump administration's approaches, though, Biden's American Rescue Plan did not seek to challenge core features of the industrial and privatized health system model. For care-centered politics advocates as well as other progressive champions of alternative public and community health approaches, including a Medicare for All approach or even an interim Public Option for the Affordable Care Act, the challenge they faced was how to sustain social movement pressure for moving toward such alternatives, even while supporting the changes that had taken place.[9]

The reliance on a critical essential workforce yet the failure to support and protect essential workers, including care workers, in fundamental ways, and thus those workers become victims of a dysfunctional system that has utilized and exploited them.

On March 16, 2020, the Cybersecurity and Infrastructure Security Agency housed within the US Department of Homeland Security issued a guidance about who should be considered part of an essential critical infrastructure workforce during the pandemic. According to the agency, these included workers in medical and health care industries, telecommunications, information technology systems, defense, food and agriculture, transportation and logistics, energy, water and wastewater, and law enforcement.[10]

Missing from the guidance were some of the workers critical to the infrastructure of daily life. These included those engaged in childcare, eldercare, and disabled care separate from institutional settings. Also missing were postal workers, sanitation workers, retail workers (in hardware stores, for instance), electricians, plumbers, and social service workers, among others. Although most states adopted the Cybersecurity and Infrastructure Security Agency federal guidance during the pandemic, a couple dozen states added categories to their list.[11]

While deemed essential, many of these workers, particularly low-wage ones in care sectors, were overworked during the pandemic, received minimal or no added compensation, and were not provided with protective support, nor were working conditions changed to address exposure issues. Examples of companies failing to recognize worker safety fears were widespread, and led to pressures on policy makers at the local, state, and federal levels to put in place some minimal protections regarding safety and illness-related absences. At the same time, some of the largest companies, including, for instance, big-box stores like Walmart and Target, major distributors such as Amazon, or meat and poultry companies like Smithfield, proclaimed in ads or public service announcements (Target beamed, "[Our] employees have been MVPs," and Amazon boasted, "Our people rise to life's big challenges") that their workers were valued for their essential services, even as some of their workers protested the lack of safety and in some cases pursued spontaneous protest actions, including ministrikes.[12]

The category of essential worker ultimately revealed the pandemic's reinforcement, and further extension of a class and racial divide reflected by income and working conditions (as well as the millions of workers who lost their jobs). When efforts were made to provide a type of hazard or "hero pay" increase for essential workers exposed to COVID-19 in their work, as several California municipalities did for grocery workers employed by the larger chains, the chains struck back. They did this through lawsuits, and by threatening to close and in some cases actually closing stores, including in areas that otherwise lacked full-service markets.[13]

Such corporate responses revealed a type of hypocrisy in the meaning of the term *essential*. "Stockbrokers or Investment Bankers have not made *any* government's 'essential services' list," Tithi Bhattacharya noted wryly, arguing that "for now and forever the elite's income should reflect their utility." From a care perspective, support for essential workers, including but not limited to increased wages (at an income level that indeed reflected their utility), needed to be associated with their well-being as well as their contributions to care rather than the increased stress and fears of exposure that they experienced during the pandemic on a daily basis, and have continued to experience due to the nature and conditions of their work.[14]

The need to address the intensification of the deep inequalities and racial disparities at every level impacted by the pandemic, including the percentages of deaths and hospitalizations as well as working conditions, unemployment, job precarity, education, housing, and childcare, among others.

Through its deep reach and immediate impacts, the pandemic made visible as well as heightened the massive social, economic, and environmental divides in the United States, including among African Americans, Latinx, and immigrants. A report by the Economic Policy Institute in the early months of the pandemic situated those divides as part of the "persistent racial disparities in health status, access to health care, wealth, employment, wages, housing, income, and poverty all [of which] contribute to greater susceptibility to the virus—both economically and physically." The report observed that the divide in the COVID-19 impacted economy could already be seen in relation to work issues even in just the pandemic's first few months. It contrasted those who faced economic insecurity because of job loss or health insecurity, including essential workers, by the nature of their jobs with those able to work from home who experienced challenges but less disruption around health and economic status. This divide was only exacerbated through the course of the pandemic in 2020 and 2021.[15]

This widening divide was reflected in multiple institutional and daily life situations. School districts, for example, consisting of large numbers of low-income students were pressed to meet the needs of students who lacked the necessary resources (computers, internet coverage, and adequate areas to participate and study) when schools turned to off-site learning and virtual classrooms. When schools sought to reopen, they were faced with high-risk health dilemmas, including for children and their families living in small quarters, families displaced from their homes by the inability to pay their rent due to job loss, or one or more of their family members in high-exposure jobs such as care work at nursing homes. School employees, including notably support staff like janitorial workers, many of whom were people of color, were also among those most vulnerable to exposure due to various health and working conditions.[16]

COVID-19 hot spots further identified the places and situations where as well as how the widening divide was experienced. Prisons, with their large African American and Latinx populations; agricultural fields and meatpacking plants, with their large numbers of low-income immigrant workers; the health care sector, where inadequate protections and the potential for high exposure were prevalent; communities with large minority and low-income populations; or overcrowded refugee detention centers where spikes were identified but never adequately addressed—all contributed to the pandemic exacerbating the higher risks facing minority populations, particularly as reflected in deaths and hospitalizations.

The information available to more fully identify such risks by race and ethnicity and other population-based criteria so as to establish effective interventions such as contact-tracing strategies remained inadequate, however, through much of the pandemic. Even aggregating such information at the county or state level was spotty at first, with more than half the hot spot counties identified by the Centers for Disease Control in the pandemic's first several months failing to report racial data, while many others had data gaps. When such information became available, whether through studies, anecdotal evidence, or updated data points, it confirmed the divides, as racial and income disparities became one of the truisms of the pandemic.[17]

Among COVID-19 hot spots, the conditions at immigrant and refugee detention centers, many operated by private contractors, were among the most disturbing, representing a clear illustration of the anticare politics exhibited during the pandemic in the United States. Facilities were crowded, and protective equipment was near nonexistent. Inhumane practices had already been instituted, such as separating children "no matter how young" from their parents, as top officials in the Department of Justice had instructed border and detention employees to enforce. This was part of the Trump administration's 2018 "zero tolerance" family separation policy that was finally withdrawn after a huge public outcry. During the pandemic, even when those hot spots were reported and facilities claimed they would make changes, repeated incidences still occurred.[18]

One of the more noteworthy and reported cases of such abuses involved a facility in Georgia run by the private contractor LaSalle Corrections. This facility was particularly egregious in its anticare practices, as first identified by a 2020 whistleblower complaint by an employee to the Department of Homeland Security's Office of Inspector General. In her complaint, the whistleblower, a nurse with ten years of experience at the facility, spoke of repeated abuses at LaSalle, and this was corroborated in additional interviews conducted by journalists with the *Intercept* publication as well as reports by the *Guardian* and Associated Press. This abuse included operations performed without informed consent. One detainee, cited in the whistleblower complaint, said of the operations that he thought the detention center had become like "an experimental concentration camp. It was like they're experimenting with our bodies." The Trump administration's response was to seek to deport the whistleblowers.[19]

The Biden administration highlighted the abuses associated with the child separation policy and vowed to eliminate all such practices, including shutting down the LaSalle facility. Yet immigrant detention center problems continued after the new administration took office, including the role of private contractors, the militarization of the border, rapid deportations, and the heightened talk of a border crisis just weeks after Biden assumed the presidency. To make fundamental changes during a pandemic and into a postpandemic period required changes in the immigration system itself. This included challenging a "border-industrial complex," undertaking a cultural shift around immigrant values and rights, and making the kinds of policy and political changes that involve care as central to the debates about such changes rather than the anticare dynamics that have characterized immigration policy at the border, or how long-term immigrants living in the United States without papers or even with temporary protected status can still experience fear and uncertainties about possible deportation and expulsion from their homes and lives.[20]

The need to address food system failures, including a major increase in food insecurity and a dependence on the emergency food system.

The pandemic revealed a range of food system problems and disparities, including but not limited to increased food insecurity and hunger, which had become magnified during the neoliberal era that favored charity versus policy. These are certainly not new issues in the United States, nor globally. Goal setting to address food insecurity and hunger has been a continuous exercise. In September 2015, for example, at a UN summit meeting in New York City, the 193 members of the United Nations adopted the 2030 Agenda for Sustainable Development, which included the goal of ending hunger "in all its forms" and achieving food security by 2030. The goal was premised on increased access to "good quality food to enable people to lead healthy lives" and called for the widespread adoption of sustainable agriculture. To achieve a hunger-free world, the UN summit noted, would require greater improvements in the next fifteen years, and a more dedicated strategy to help support small farmers and sustainable agriculture goals. Yet a follow-up report in 2020 on the sustainable development goals by the Food and Agriculture Organization of the United Nations noted that the number of people experiencing hunger had gone up each year prior to the pandemic, reaching 690 million people in 2019, while parallel increases in severe and moderate food insecurity affected as many as 2 billion people, or greater than 25 percent of the world's population.

The pandemic intensified the problems of hunger and food insecurity, as the 2020 report, issued at the beginning of the pandemic, observed that 132 million more people were likely to suffer from undernourishment because of COVID-19.[21] For example, in just the first six months of the pandemic, the number of those experiencing food insecurity more than doubled. According to the Census Bureau's Household Pulse Survey, millions of people struggled to pay for food as well as housing and other basic needs. The survey's August 2020 snapshot identified that as many as 10 percent of all adults reported that they sometimes or often didn't have enough to eat in the previous seven days, or more than double the numbers compared to prepandemic times. Just four months later, in December 2020 at the height of yet another spike in positive COVID-19 tests and deaths, the weekly average had jumped to nearly 15 percent of all adults, with a slightly smaller percentage indicating their reliance on some form of "free" food, whether from a food bank or pantry, school program, or other free food providers. Those numbers in each survey were significantly higher for Black and Latinx adults and children. Such disproportionate impacts, the Center for Budget and Policy Priorities and others have argued, have reflected "harsh, longstanding inequities, often stemming from structural racism."[22]

The pandemic-related impacts on hunger and food insecurity at the global level were far more severe. The United Nations' World Food Programme, for instance, estimated that as of April 2021, 296 million people in the thirty-five countries where the organization had a presence were without sufficient food, or an increase of 110 million people from a similar survey the previous year in April 2020, at the beginning of the pandemic. Similarly, according to the World Bank's own survey in forty-eight countries in April 2021, as large numbers of people ran out of food or reduced their calorie intake and compromised nutrition, "gains in poverty reduction and health" were threatened, and that "could have lasting impacts on the cognitive development of young children."[23]

In the United States, some of the more dramatic visuals during the COVID-19 pandemic were cars lining up, sometimes a half mile or more, to access free food, often in the form of an emergency food basket. For example, the Los Angeles Regional Food Bank witnessed an increase of 125 percent of food distributed in just the first five months of the pandemic. This included 1.1 million food boxes provided for more than 3.3 million stressed families and individuals through direct distribution or the food bank's partner agencies. In the United States, food bank use during that period was up 70 percent, including 40 percent for those who had never previously obtained food from a food bank. In addition, food banks began to expand deliveries to vulnerable populations such as low-income seniors, although that service was interrupted during summer 2020 when the USDA failed to continue a waiver regarding the requirement to include commodity cheese in the food boxes in refrigerated trucks—a commodity-purchasing program designed to support dairy farmers that only made food insecurity worse.[24]

Schools also became a crucial source of food for schoolchildren and their families during the pandemic—a food provider role that schools have continually played, especially since the creation of the National School Lunch Program in 1946. A School Nutrition Association survey conducted during the first wave of school closures in May 2020, for instance, indicated that 95 percent of the schools surveyed, including those in rural, suburban, and small and large cities, had undertaken their own emergency food program. They did this primarily by providing boxed food for people either through drive-in (often again in long lines) or walk-up systems to obtain the food.[25]

Emergency food provisioning, whether through food banks or school districts, or via some of the volunteer-based initiatives that sprang up during the pandemic, was critical in responding, albeit in a limited way and through an emergency food provider system, to a hunger and food insecurity crisis. It also pointed to the gaps in the existing industrial and global food system structures to effectively respond to a crisis like the pandemic or large climate change–related events. These food system gaps paralleled those in the industrial medical and health system model in its response to the pandemic. Moreover, the events of 2020–2021 revealed the need for a postpandemic school food—and food system—reinvention. Due to the pandemic, "school lunch as we know it is over," one trade publication argued. It indicated that a food system reinvention was required not just for food insecurity and hunger but also ways to increase access to fresh and healthy food, develop alternative strategies to grow and produce such food, ensure adequate pay and working conditions for food workers, and establish new systems to increase the public control and ownership of the food system itself.[26]

Like so much else impacted by the pandemic—housing, jobs, income inequalities, racial disparities, childcare, eldercare, and all the issues associated with the infrastructure of daily life—a status quo ante return to normality seemed increasingly elusive and near impossible for those most heavily impacted. Anthony Fauci, head of the National Institute of Allergy and Infectious Diseases, argued in October 2020 that COVID-19 had shed "a very bright light on the social determinants of health"—a process that was "in essence, killing minorities." The pandemic illuminated the inadequacies and failures of the industrial, market-centered health system that had existed prepandemic, and demonstrated the need for transformative changes if those inadequacies and failures were going to be effectively addressed postpandemic.[27]

What then was normality? Throughout 2020 and into 2021, the desire to return to a prepandemic state was palpable. There were some, however, who sought to imagine and reinvent a postpandemic future. Those two contrasting desires—live again as in the past or construct something new ("The America We Need," as one *New York Times* series put it)—demonstrated not just a divided response to the pandemic but a heightened divide in relation to its consequences as well. Even for those who wished for normalcy—a return to the past once the crisis was over—recognized the difficulty of envisioning what that might be, unless they assumed that the pandemic was overblown or nonexistent. The reliance on "alternative facts"—Trump adviser Kellyanne Conway's memorable phrase at the outset of the Trump presidency—reinforced the insistence that everything seemed or at least should be normal. But it wasn't.[28]

From a care perspective, most everything was not all right, and many things were even worse. This included pandemic inequalities, racist reactions, assertions of individual rather than collective rights, overt expressions of a lack of solidarity, and a toxic individualism expressed, for example, in the hostile pushback against vaccination mandates and mask wearing. Yet spontaneous expressions of creativity, solidarity, and hope amid despair were available too, and potentially sustaining. Where communities fared better, a care perspective was significant, such as a belief in the importance of "the collective welfare," as one physician commented, regarding a survey of a Vietnamese immigrant community in Orange County, California, about responses to the pandemic. There was also a recognition of the paramount importance of a political response—finding and nurturing structural changes that had been ignored or dismissed. Postpandemic change seemed possible, even as the pandemic's biopolitics disrupted all aspects of life in communities and globally, and if the air at times seemed mephitic from the social and physical fires raging.[29]

CLIMATE DISRUPTIONS: THE FIRES THIS TIME

In the summer of 1995, the city of Chicago experienced an unprecedented heat wave that caused more than 700 deaths. The highest proportion of those deaths occurred in African American neighborhoods, particularly among seniors. Lack of air conditioning, limited green space and tree scape that heightened urban heat island impacts, and poor planning for prevention and emergency services intensified the disproportionate impacts. City officials, led by Mayor Richard Daley, denied that social or political factors had caused the disparities, and climate change was not mentioned.

Eight years later, in the summer of 2003, Western Europe experienced a series of extreme heat events. In August, nearly 15,000 people died in France. Europe's blistering summer was considered hotter than any period since the 1500s. This time, researchers began to directly point to human factors as responsible, although climate deniers sought to refute any link to global warming.

Ten years later in 2013, Shanghai experienced a red alert when the city recorded a temperature of 105°F, its hottest day in a century. That record would then be broken four years later in July 2017. According to the *Shanghai Daily* newspaper, the 2017 extreme heat episode caused a spike in physical fights and traffic accidents, as people became "more easily irritated in the extreme heat and [were] failing to exercise proper judgement." In addition, dog bites increased since dogs were also seen as on edge due to the heat. Climate change was once again not a focus for the authorities and the media.[30]

By 2020 and 2021, however, it had become nearly impossible to ignore the role of climate change in creating extreme heat events as well as a veritable cauldron of extreme weather episodes and rapidly gathering climate disasters. The Pacific Northwest sizzled with temperatures as high as 116°F. The British Columbia town of Lytton reached a temperature of 121°F and the heat and dryness sparked a fire that came so fast that it eliminated all village structures. "Lytton is gone," one resident wrote on Facebook, a scene reminiscent of the fire that had destroyed the Northern California town of Paradise a few years earlier. The fires in turn caused the skies to turn black, filled with particulate matter that also caused an increase in air pollution that required wearing N95 masks, a trademark of a response to COVID, and even a necessity in places hundreds and thousands of miles from the fires.[31]

These extreme heat events, along with the fires, air pollution, droughts, flooding, one-in-a-hundred-years hurricanes, or totally unanticipated cold fronts that wrecked infrastructure systems have been some of the continuing, tangible outcomes of climate change–related events in the United States and globally. Yet recognition of climate impacts, including the response by policymakers, as those earlier episodes revealed, has been far too slow in coming.

During the Obama years, after years of denial and intentional subterfuge by the fossil fuel and transport sector industries, and an unwillingness by policy makers to challenge the political and economic dominance of these industries when it came to climate change politics, climate change initiatives finally started to be rolled out a bit of a time, such as the promotion of green alternatives like greater fuel efficiencies as well as support for solar and wind energy. Yet even as late as the 2012 presidential election, the Obama administration was still stuck in an "all of the above energy [including oil and gas] politics" and had only begun to move more forcefully around climate change in the last two years of the Obama presidency. Those efforts included a new Environmental Protection Agency air quality regulation with respect to carbon emissions—a regulation the Trump administration immediately sought to dismantle along with numerous other climate change and air quality initiatives.[32]

Trump's climate change politics, similar to his pandemic politics, not only sought to undercut climate change policies but also climate science itself. His first Environmental Protection Agency administrator, Scott Pruitt, a longtime foe of climate change science, spoke of creating a renewed "red team/blue team" debate about the existence of climate change, while William Happer, an early key Trump adviser around climate science who was picked to head a climate science review panel, was a longtime defender of carbon dioxide and its releases into the environment. A 2014 Happer interview on CNBC became a source of embarrassment when Happer, in his insistence about the benefits of carbon dioxide, proclaimed that the "demonization of carbon dioxide is just like the demonization of the poor Jews under Hitler."[33]

While previous events such as Hurricane Katrina (2005) and Superstorm Sandy (2012) had been indirectly linked to climate change, it was during the Trump years that climate impacts became more frequent and noticeable, even as climate deniers, now in power and led by the president, worked to undermine any climate response. Yet the explosive fires, heat waves, massive flooding, and black skies made climate a more direct, visceral issue for many more people.

Despite the traumas of those events, there still remained a continuing residue of climate change denial and skepticism through 2020 led by Trump along with his enablers and supporters. Like the pandemic, there was a deep desire to assume that after a wildfire, heat wave, or hurricane, a return to normalcy would occur. This included returning to the homes, places, and daily life situations and practices as they had been. The slogan "Make America Great Again" fit directly into a climate denial discourse.

Moreover, policies or nonpolicies addressing climate change during the Trump years reinforced or at least failed to discourage a return to previous high-risk practices vulnerable to climate change impacts, even as large majorities of the United States and world's populations were now concerned about climate change. These types of anticare approaches included allowing housing to be built at urban-wildland interfaces or along coastal floodplains, or policies and subsidies that continued to support fossil fuel–based transport and industrial agriculture. Yet similar to the pandemic, the cascading climate events of 2020–2021 had also led to a shift in the recognition, at least in the abstract, that a return to a status quo ante when it came to climate change was not a likely or a viable response.

Both a climate justice and care-centered politics perspective have prioritized responses highlighting the need for change and far more transformative policies. The importance of a climate response has been particularly strong among people of color, as surveys and polls have revealed. The care politics perspective, building on the climate justice focus on climate impacts where people live, work, and play, has further addressed the need for solidarity and community as well as global responses regarding climate impacts on people's lives and environments. Such responses have required prevention, mitigation, and adaptation approaches needed for deep change, given climate change's expanding and increasingly devastating reach, and the limited time horizon available to construct and implement such approaches.[34]

From the care-centered politics perspective, there are both immediate and long-term strategies available for prevention. Each of the sectors associated with continuing increases in carbon emissions and other climate change sources, such as food and agriculture, buildings and construction, or energy and transportation, require changes from a climate justice and care politics approach that reduce their carbon footprints and contribute to well-being. With food and agriculture, for example, such changes have been linked to the call for an alternative food system through agroecological practices, short supply chains, farm-to-institution and other farm direct programs, crop diversity and soil health strategies, urban agriculture programs, direct access strategies for healthy and fresh foods, and many more strategies that characterize the food sovereignty and justice approach that also have climate change benefits. The need for an alternative food system has in turn been central to the climate justice argument—alternatives that also embrace the concepts of care for the earth, care for people, and care for all living things.[35]

Similar to the debates about the Green New Deal, a critical perspective about the role of technology and scale for climate prevention and mitigation, in contrast to the advocacy for more community-based strategies that emphasize well-being, has been central to the climate justice and care politics approach. This comes into play, for instance, with respect to the transportation and energy sectors. With transportation, substantial resources in China and more recently California have been earmarked for high-speed rail, with its climate benefits based on rail substituting for short-distance air travel, such as the Shanghai to Beijing, Guangzhou to Hong Kong, or San Francisco to Los Angeles routes. In China, which has taken the global lead in the construction of a high-speed rail system, concerns have been raised that high-speed rail reinforces the trend toward urban expansion and megaregional centers, which in turn reduce the capacities to sustain rural village life and lead to displacements during the construction of the high-speed rail network. An attachment to place is further undermined, as the urban edge extends deep into less densely populated areas—a process facilitated by the high-speed rail network reconfiguring distances and connections to place. With the California high-speed rail project, touted by former California governor Jerry Brown, who was enamored of China's rapid and aggressive rollout of its high-speed rail system as well as its potential climate benefits, the development of the system has nevertheless been plagued by huge cost overruns, expensive consultants, a shifting focus on where and how the system could achieve its goals, a failure to adequately account for impacts on the communities where the tracks are laid, support motivated as much by megaconstruction project contractors as the climate change focus, and uncertain estimates about climate benefits, especially in relation to the resources required.[36]

The megaproject focus on how best to achieve climate benefits has also come into play around non–fossil fuel alternative energy projects and proposals. Megaproject advocates continue to support nuclear power as a major climate alternative, despite its problematic nature in relation to cost, environmental impacts, spent fuel storage, and lingering safety concerns.

Similarly, concerns have been raised about those massive solar and wind project constellations that also entail huge land footprints and uneven community impacts, such as an initial Humboldt County, California, wind turbine proposal that would have impacted Indigenous communities and desecrated a sacred ancestral prayer site. Advances in solar and wind development, including their continuing decline in cost, has been an enormous benefit in helping reorient an energy future away from fossil fuels. Instead of a primary focus on the megaprojects, however, incorporating solar for a community and home-based strategy can increase community resilience too. Small-scale neighborhood solar, when widely applied, can have direct and immediate climate benefits that facilitate a more resilient mitigation and adaptation approach. It can also match the megaprojects based on the amount of climate change benefits achieved, while far exceeding the megaprojects when calculated on the basis of the resources required to achieve such benefits. Yet the push for this type of community resilience as a critical and comprehensive climate approach has tended to lag behind the emphasis and support mechanisms for the megaprojects and large-scale technology approaches.[37]

Community resilience along with the need for a collective and solidarity-based response is particularly important from a care perspective in addressing adaptation to the continuing and expanding impacts from climate change. Richard Sennett, a senior adviser to the UN on climate change and cities, has argued for a variable rather than fixed response to climate impacts on places, buildings, and/or a landmass. Fixed responses often seek to build back what had been there before, while variability efforts seek to reconfigure and reconstruct versus replicate to be better able to account for the unpredictability of climate-associated events, whether from fires, storms, floods, heat waves, or other changes to place. The lessons of how immigrants adapt and become resilient, including their ability to reconstruct and re-create a renewed sense of place, suggests the kinds of strategies needed for climate change adaptation.[38]

Yet despite the unpredictability of climate change, climate response strategies, particularly those that involve community resilient adaptation to major climate-related events, may present more immediate opportunities for social and political change, including the ability to question values that "drive inequalities in development and our unsustainability with the environment," as University of Liverpool professor Mark Pelling notes. Pelling, who has written extensively about climate adaptation, and served as a lead adviser to the UN Intergovernmental Panel on Climate Change's *Fifth* as well as *Sixth Assessment Report*, also warned that adaptation approaches have all too often been framed by identifying "what is to be preserved and what is expendable rather than what can be reformed or gained."[39]

The notion of preserving as opposed to reforming or transforming, in climate adaptation as well as with climate mitigation strategies, reinforces the bias for nonpolitical, technology-based solutions. Yet climate change is a deeply political question, both historically in relation to its progression and impacts, and with respect to its immediate and future consequences. From a climate justice and care-centered politics perspective, the history of climate change is fraught with decisions that have deeply affected the most vulnerable communities, regions, and nation-states. Contemporary problems regarding both the carbon load in the environment and climate change's disproportionate impacts can be traced historically to the advent of industrial capitalism. That includes the colonial relationships that date back to the eighteenth and nineteenth centuries that have contributed to the climate justice concern about the level of climate inequities.

In 1994, 197 countries signed the United Nations Framework Convention on Climate Change, which sought to assign primary responsibility to industrialized nations for mitigating climate change and also provide support for less developed countries, including those most vulnerable to climate impacts. Eleven years later, the Paris Agreement updated the convention's assessment, including the growing contribution of China to the increase in carbon emissions. While China had surpassed the United States as early as 2009 in the volume (though not per capita) of carbon emissions, the United States remained historically the largest carbon emitter. The United States accounted for as much as 26 percent of emissions between 1850 and 2015, while the European Union countries were the second-largest contributor at 23 percent. Those numbers represent the total carbon load or "stocks of CO_2 in the atmosphere," which matter more than annual flows in assigning responsibility for climate change. As China industrialized and globalized in the twenty-first century and continued to heavily rely on carbon sources such as coal, it began to catch up (along with a quickly developing and industrializing India) with the United States and Europe for its carbon load contributions.[40]

Colonialism and its cousin system of imperialism had already left a legacy of massive environmental destruction scattered throughout the lands it scarred, and countries and regions that were exploited—damage that contributed to climate change outcomes too. "The full impact of colonialism is revealed in its long-time impacts," journalist Daniel Macmillen Voskoboynik argues, including how it destroyed "ecosystems and human interactions necessary for preventing climate change." Part of those impacts have to do with resource exploitation. Other impacts have stemmed from colonialism and imperialism's political reconfigurations, which have exacerbated resource conflicts as well as led to the displacement and expulsions of people from their ancestral homes, including but not limited to slavery and imposed borders that have sometimes split tribal and cultural connections.[41]

From a care politics perspective, the issue of displacement and expulsion requires major attention, and a political response related to historical factors as well as contemporary and future causes, including climate change. The Office of the United Nations High Commissioner for Refugees has identified the two most prevalent forms of displacement and expulsion as violent conflict and disasters. By 2020, nearly eighty million people had been forced to leave their homes, including as many as thirty to thirty-four million children. Those numbers had doubled from the previous decade. The ability of displaced people to return to their homes also declined in recent years—a situation exacerbated in 2020–2021 by the pandemic (when borders closed and applications for asylum decreased) and climate change (when climate-related disasters uprooted whole communities). Displacement and expulsion also exacerbate issues like food insecurity and extreme hunger, which can be traced to conflict, weather extremes, and economic turbulence. Climate issues, along with conflict, persecution, hunger, and poverty, create what the High Commissioner for Refugees identifies as the new "increasingly complex emergences."[42]

These trends of displacement and expulsion are at this point somewhat less dramatic in the United States, where the fixed responses to climate-related events often reflect the dominant desire to return to an earlier sense of normality, and preserve and rebuild in place rather than reconfigure and remake. Yet those strategies of preservation and rebuild in place are also becoming problematic with respect to climate disasters (and pandemic-related displacements and expulsions)—events that have intensified the inequities that have become a structural feature of both climate- and pandemic-related situations. When the Black Lives Matter demonstrations, with their challenge to confront systemic racism and deep inequalities, erupted in summer 2020, it also became a challenge to the desire to preserve and return to that idea of normality that climate and pandemic events had already forced the United States as well as many places globally to experience.

These demonstrations and the struggle against systemic racism became the third of the all-encompassing set of events—along with the pandemic and climate change—that turned the years 2020 and 2021 into a pivotal moment challenging the dominant anticare politics of a market-centered, neoliberal global order. Beyond the Trumpian sideshow of meanness and crony capitalism, the dilemmas facing efforts among the big emitters in the United States, Europe, and China to confront the realities of a global climate crisis seemed as daunting as ever.

BLACK LIVES MATTER: REPARATIONS AND REDISTRIBUTION

The pandemic and climate change events of 2020 and 2021 made even more visible that a handful of rich people had become far richer, and people living at the edge, whose numbers had only grown, had become even more destitute. Prior to the pandemic, multiple studies underlined how changes in wealth and poverty had already become apparent since the mid-1970s, fostered by the political and economic changes during the neoliberal ascendancy. An August 2020 study by two researchers from the Rand Corporation of income trends between 1975 and 2018, for example, documented how income inequality had increased substantially during those four decades even as GDP had grown. Income then had not only failed to trickle down but the wealth gap had only widened too.[43]

It got worse during the pandemic. Between March 18, 2020 (when the first COVID-19 shutdowns began to occur) and December 7, 2020, the wealth of the 651 billionaires in the United States increased by $1 trillion to reach an astounding $4 trillion in total, as a study by the Institute for Policy Studies and Americans for Tax Fairness documented. In that period, Amazon's Jeff Bezos increased his wealth by nearly two-thirds, or $71 billion, for a total wealth of more than $184 billion, while Facebook's Mark Zuckerberg increased his wealth by 91.7 percent, from $54.7 to $104.8 billion. Several other tech-related figures such as Google cofounders Larry Page and Sergey Brin also increased their wealth by more than 50 percent—all of this in just nine months. At the same time at the global level, *Forbes* estimated that the world's 2,200 billionaires got richer by $1.9 trillion during 2020.[44]

Those wealth gaps became even more pronounced at the bottom end, especially among people of color struggling at or below the poverty line. As a result, the pandemic as well as climate change impacts, both locally in the United States and globally among a number of poor or less developed countries, threatened to create several crisis-level outcomes: a long-term increase in hunger and food insecurity; millions of residents displaced, and millions more turned into refugee and homeless populations; and health and ecological catastrophes that would mostly impact the poor. All of these scenarios were poised to continue well into the future unless political changes and a cultural shift were able to reverse those impacts.

The Black Lives Matter demonstrations in summer 2020 brought those issues of the wealth gap and its relation to systemic racism to the center of politics. They highlighted the need for an economic and cultural reckoning of the policies, practices, and legacies that had produced those disparities, and extended them to every level of society. Whether the pandemic or climate-related events, health care, education, the criminal justice system, food, employment, income, or housing, systemic racism and deep inequalities permeated the infrastructure of daily life. These inequities were historically rooted, ingrained in US institutions and culture, and required not just individual reforms but structural change too.

Take housing as one example. Two recent books—*The Color of Law* by Richard Rothstein and *Race for Profit* by Keeanga-Yamahtta Taylor— documented how history's racist legacies in homeownership have been implemented through public policies and private sector manipulations. The books differ somewhat in emphasis; Rothstein focuses on the role since the 1930s and 1940s of the Federal Housing Administration along with related government policies and actions in expanding residential segregation, while Taylor writes about the predatory practices of the real estate industry and mortgage bankers that reinforced the inequalities and segregation practices that the federal policies had established. Yet both books identify how racism and inequalities not only permeated the housing market but also had powerful implications in other areas, such as segregated and underfunded schools, increasing income inequality, and huge wealth disparities. Even when efforts were made to ameliorate that racist history through more inclusionary versus exclusionary policies, such as the 1968 Fair Housing Act, the outcomes, while more disguised, frequently deepened the problems related to racial practices. These efforts, Taylor argued, were not about "redress, restitution, or repair"—approaches that otherwise would have provided a framework more aligned with a care-centered politics.[45]

Perhaps the most visible and potent illustration of racial disparities has been the ongoing police violence and militarization of daily life directed at African Americans and communities of color. The Black Lives Matter demonstrations of 2020 were sparked by police violence, including the murders of George Floyd and Breonna Taylor. The demonstrators identified the problems as systemic to the entire criminal justice and incarceration systems, racially constructed structures that have been effectively described by writers like Michelle Alexander and Tony Platt.[46]

The arguments about a police violence gap—even African American bicycle riders have been subject to police interrogation and violence—opened up the discussion of how to do policing differently, such as by reducing funds for the continuing militarization of the police ("defund the police") and/or establishing a "system of care," as a *Los Angeles Times* editorial contended. Along those lines, Black Lives Matter demonstrators carried signs that read "Care Not Cops," while the *Los Angeles Times* argued for the need to "build a system of care that fosters health and justice and deconstruct the costly police-and-prisons infrastructure that we foolishly built instead." The Black Lives Matter demonstrations also put the spotlight on the racism and deep inequalities represented by a racial wealth gap that is manifest in every institution and dimension of daily life.[47]

The focus on the racial wealth gap during the events of 2020–2021 rekindled interest in the concept of reparations—the idea of restitution for historical and ongoing harm—in this instance, for African Americans dating back to the seventeenth century and the development of the slave trade. Reparations as a political and legal strategy has a long history in the United States, and has had multiple applications globally as well. It became one of the planks in the platform of the Black Panther Party in the 1960s, and had been raised on numerous occasions prior to the Civil War and in the aftermath of the Black Reconstruction period following it. It has been used by the *beneficiaries* of slavery too, including notoriously the government of France, which used military threats to extract huge reparations from Haiti to pay for the loss of slaves due to the overthrow of slavery in Haiti that came about with the slave rebellion in 1791, the country's formal abolition of slavery in 1803, and independence from France the following year. After the restoration of the French monarchy in 1815, France was determined to force Haiti to pay indemnities, or what amounted to a reverse form of reparations. In 1825, using the twisted logic of its loss of slaves and slave labor along with the coffee and sugar plantations that had served the French and British markets, France demanded, with gunships parked outside Haiti, a payment to the French government and French slaveholders of 150 million francs as well as a favorable trade relationship. The eventual debt that was incurred, and the interest on the debt and subsequent loans to pay the interest financed by European and US banks, amounted to as much as $21 billion by the time the reparations blackmail was paid off, devastating the Haitian economy. In 2004, then Haitian president Jean-Bertrand Aristide raised the issue that France should pay back the $21 billion to Haiti from reverse reparations. A little more than a decade later, French president François Hollande visited Haiti and stated that France had a "moral debt that exists." Yet Hollande refused to commit to any payment for reparations, instead offering development project investments. The legacy remained: a history of reparations for slaveholders, and an aftermath of debt and a type of economic bondage that had constituted its own extreme form of anticare politics.[48]

Despite the Haitian blackmail and other examples of slaveholders in the United States demanding compensation when slaves escaped in the period prior to the Civil War (e.g., through the series of Fugitive Slave Acts beginning in 1793), there were numerous other cases of reparations advocacy associated with justice for slaves and their descendants, including financial and material compensation for their lives and labor. The 1960s represented one period where reparations became an important component of civil rights and Black Power politics. Aside from the Black Panthers, former SNCC executive secretary James Forman, speaking on behalf of the National Black Economic Development Conference group, led an action at New York City's Riverside Church in May 1969 demanding that the churches and synagogues pay $500 million to support several organizations and initiatives for Black economic empowerment. Though some of the religious groups expressed sympathy for the arguments laid out in the "Black Manifesto" that Forman had written for the National Black Economic Development Conference, they rejected the idea of reparations and instead offered to expand some of their existing programs.[49]

Two decades later, in 1989, a new organization, the National Coalition of Blacks for Reparations in America, helped convince Michigan Democratic congressperson John Conyers to introduce H.R. 40, which called for a commission to be established to study and make recommendations for reparations to African Americans due to the institution of slavery, and subsequent racist policies and practices. Conyers had been inspired by congressional approval the previous year of the Civil Liberties Act of 1988, based on the recommendations of the Commission on Wartime Relocation and

Internment of Civilians, which had been authorized in 1980 and issued its report in 1983. After much maneuvering, the Commission on Wartime Relocation recommendations were adopted in the 1988 Civil Liberties Act legislation that provided for payment of $20,000 to each individual who had been interned during World War II as part of the relocation of members of the Japanese community in the United States. Another $12,000 each was provided to Aleutian Islanders who had lost traditional lands and village properties on Attu Island after they had been forcibly relocated to southeastern Alaska at the onset of World War II.[50]

Conyers obtained the number for his H.R. 40 bill based on the reparations-linked Civil War order and presidential proclamation to provide forty acres each for the freed slaves. One hundred and twenty years after the forty acres reparations order, Conyers saw the process of a commission helping facilitate the passage of reparations legislation for the Japanese and Aleutian victims of relocation providing a concrete illustration of why as well as how a new, contemporary reparations policy for African Americans could be seen as viable, initiated by a commission's deliberations capable of generating public support.[51]

For nearly thirty years, H.R. 40 failed to receive either a vote or hearing, despite Conyers's efforts to reintroduce the legislation at each congressional session until he resigned from Congress in December 2017. H.R. 40 was then introduced again by Texas Democrat Sheila Jackson Lee in January 2019 during the 116th Congress. Jackson Lee pointed to renewed interest in reparations, sparked by new advocacy and several publications, including the 2014 article "The Case for Reparations" by Ta-Nehisi Coates in the *Atlantic*. In reintroducing H.R. 40, Jackson Lee challenged opponents such as Republican senator Mitch McConnell, who although himself a descendant of slave owners, nevertheless dismissed the idea of monetary compensation by arguing that it would be for something that had happened 150 years earlier and "none of us currently living are responsible." For Jackson Lee, the issue was "whether and how this nation can come to grips with the legacy of slavery that still infects current society."[52]

As Jackson Lee suggested, the advocacy for reparations generally consisted of two sets of assertions. The first focused on the need to address as well as repair the harm and devastation associated with slavery and its legacies, including the Jim Crow era and current forms of racial inequalities. This included an acknowledgment and recognition of those legacies through direct apologies, a reconsideration of historical events and their impacts, and a willingness to make amends in some form. In his article in the *Atlantic*, Coates described this recognition as a "full acceptance of our collective biography and its consequences [which is] the price we must pay to see ourselves squarely." The National Coalition of Blacks for Reparations in America similarly defined reparations as a "process of repairing, healing and restoring a people injured because of their group identity and in violation of their fundamental human rights by governments, corporations, institutions and families."[53]

This act of recognition and repair expressed itself in numerous ways prior to and during the events of 2020–2021. It included the toppling of Confederate statues, removal of names of people on university and government buildings associated with racist actions or positions such as the promotion of eugenics, and challenges to institutions like Georgetown and Harvard University whose rich endowments were seeded by their participation in the slave trade. It involved legal actions such as the Pigford lawsuit that compensated African American farmers for discriminatory practices by the USDA. It also included formal government apologies for past actions and a commitment to provide financial compensation (and in some cases, political support) for redressing those past actions.

Among those who have sought to deflect the question of systemic racism, the demand for reparations has often been avoided or ignored even as concerns have been raised about each specific racist incident. In this environment, identifying the importance of reparations as an issue of a racial wealth gap and form of redistribution needed to also include and elevate the historical as well as contemporary cultural accounting of racism's legacies, and its continuing grip on the country's language and practices. Examples from other countries have been suggestive of possible forms that could take. These include South Africa's Truth and Reconciliation Commission and the German government's reparation agreements about Holocaust survivors, both of which provide illustrations of a form of reckoning and, in the German case, actual economic reparations.

In South Africa's case, the commission offered a searing description of apartheid's harm, especially through individual testimony, but it steered away from any discussion of how to compensate the population that suffered from it. In Germany's case, the Conference on Jewish Material Claims against Germany, known as the Claims Conference, limited itself to material claims, despite initial statements that a "moral and material indemnity" was needed, and that resolving material claims, as then West German chancellor Konrad Adenauer put it in 1951, would ease the way "to the spiritual settlement of infinite suffering." Though agreements and cash payments were made with the state of Israel for settling Holocaust survivors as well as with individual Holocaust survivors, Germany only began to achieve some partial internal form of reckoning when the country conducted its own Auschwitz war crimes trials between 1963 and 1965. Yet as pointed out by Lily Gardner Feldman, who has written about the German reparations process, such a reckoning is a continuous process. "Every new generation has to deal with this," Gardner Feldman argues, speaking of the German experience.[54]

The Black Lives Matter demonstrations helped spark renewed interest in reparations, and provided an example of the beginnings of such a generational awakening by inspiring a process of reckoning among institutions and organizations. The demonstrations also identified, through their claim of intersectionality, the need to address, reckon with, and repair other legacies and claims of harm, such as concerning Indigenous people, immigrants and refugees, sexual violence and abuse against women, and all the hidden injuries of race, class, and misogyny expressed in everyday life.

The counter to this act of recognition and repair has been denial, and in its most extreme form, the anticare approval and even contrarian celebration of that past coupled with a dismissal of the need to address those legacies. This denial politics, as articulated by McConnell, was highlighted by Trump's celebration of the past as a counter to the Black Lives Matter demonstrations. These were positions he articulated throughout his presidency and prior to it. Trump and his supporters also sought to prevent the dissemination of historical accounts that could buttress the case for reparations—accounts that could, as Coates put it, lead to "a revolution of the American consciousness, a reconciling of our self-image as the great democratizer with the facts of our history." By 2021, the anticare hostility to any racial accounting went to extreme lengths to include bans of any teaching, even in children's books available in public schools or libraries, about the country's legacies around race.[55]

Where the call for reparations has produced the greatest resistance in the United States has been the question of material compensation for the racial wealth gap. Throughout the 250 years of the advocacy of reparations, the push for such a financial accounting has produced various formula. In the 1970s, Yale University law professor Boris Bittker, influenced by the 1969 action at Riverside Church led by Forman and call for reparations in the "Black Manifesto," focused on the continuing problems of segregated education that had remained entrenched even after the 1954 Supreme Court *Brown v. Board of Education* decision. Bittker argued that school segregation was an identifiable harm that could result in monetary compensation through legal action for those who had suffered from it. His 1973 book, *The Case for Black Reparations*, became influential not as much for his assertion about segregated schools but rather as a way to open the discussion of reparations as an economic question. When Bittker's book was reissued in 2003, actions and demands for accountability directed at banks, insurance companies, and universities, among other entities, for their financial benefit from the slave trade had led reparations advocates, including Bittker, to expand their lens to address the multiple forms in which a racial wealth gap was both historically rooted and currently expressed.[56]

In one of the most comprehensive discussions of reparations and the racial wealth gap, economist William Darity and folklorist Kristen Mullen, in their 2020 book *From Here to Equality*, defined reparations as "a program of acknowledgment, redress and closure for a grievous injustice." Redress, according to Darity and Mullen, included restitution and atonement. Restitution provided the economic means to eliminate racial disparities in wealth, income, health, education, sentencing and incarceration, political participation, and an ability to participate in political and social life. While applauding grassroots actions against corporations, universities, and other institutions as building the case for reparations, Darity and Mullen contended that material compensation needed to be directed at the federal government in order to concentrate on the racial wealth gap.[57]

For Darity and Mullen, restitution needed to be linked to acknowledgment of the historical (slavery and Jim Crow) and contemporary realities of race and white supremacy. Others, however, have sought to keep the focus primarily on some form of compensation as the most important mechanism to bring about a reparations policy. A 2004 law journal article by Kyle Logue titled "Reparations as Redistribution," for example, defined the reparations debate as corrective versus redistributional strategies. Corrective measures, based on tort law, identify a specific harm caused by one party to another, like a slave master to a slave. The challenge for corrective reparations, particularly those focused on slavery and even Jim Crow policies, is the difficulty in calculating a specific historical harm such as slavery as a contemporary harm in economic terms—the McConnell defense that too much time has elapsed to warrant such corrective action. The redistributional approach, on the other hand, which is also forward-looking, seeks to deal with the current inequalities between whites and Blacks. Such an approach could involve a cash transfer (a complex, though not insurmountable issue from a legal and political perspective, Logue argues) to programs and policies designed to overcome such inequalities, such as affirmative action, tax policies, or as Bittker initially suggested, education policy.[58]

Although embedded in the discussion of race and the impact of slavery, reparations have emerged as an important strategy in global relationships too. That includes the legacies of colonialism discussed earlier. It also references the ways in which policies such as structural adjustment established by the wealthier countries, and implemented through global bodies like the International Monetary Fund or World Bank, have disadvantaged the poorer countries of the South, uprooted rural communities, and created vast urban slums. Moreover, this has led to calls for a reversal of those policies and reparations-linked demands.

Along those lines, several environmental and climate justice groups in the developing countries began to raise the issue in the 1990s of an "ecological debt." In 2002, several of these groups along with Indigenous organizations fighting fossil fuel and extractive industry efforts to develop resources on Indigenous lands met in Bali to adopt a series of principles on climate justice. These principles included reparation claims regarding the ecological debt based on the practices of transnational corporations and industrial countries. In the document they released, the "Bali Principles of Climate Justice," the groups called for corporations and nation-states to be held liable for all past as well as present impacts related to the production of greenhouse gases and the associated local pollutants. The victims of those ecological debts, they argued, should then be entitled to "receive full compensation, restoration, and reparation for loss of land, livelihood, and other damages."[59]

During the next several years after the publication of the Bali principles, the linkage of ecological debt, climate change impacts, and a call for reparations expanded to several countries already experiencing various ecological and climate impacts. Several studies bolstered those claims, including a 2008 publication in the *Proceedings of the National Academy of Sciences*. The study estimated the environmental costs of human activities from 1961 to 2000 from climate change and other environmental harms, then compared the costs borne by poor, middle-income, and rich nations to the specific activities that identified how each of those group of nations contributed to those costs. Substantial disproportionate impacts affecting the poor countries were identified, making for its own form of a climate change wealth gap that totaled $2 trillion (in 2008 dollars)—a number that exceeded the total foreign debt of the poorer countries. The next year, at the 2009 Copenhagen Conference on Climate Change, twenty of those countries raised the climate change wealth gap as requiring a type of historical debt repayment. The Bolivian ambassador to the United Nations, Pablo Solon, argued that this debt repayment constituted a form of reparations—an assertion that the Obama administration's lead negotiator at Copenhagen strongly rejected. Yet such damages have only intensified since Copenhagen, placing entire regions and even nation-states at greater risk.[60]

Reparations is essentially an argument about justice and inequalities. It is where history, to paraphrase novelist James Joyce, represents a continuing nightmare from which those suffering from those injustices and inequalities need to awaken and be freed. Redistribution through reparations provides one mechanism to address those historical and contemporary injustices and inequalities, whether individual or collective, community based or global in nature, whether brought about by systemic racism, climate change, or the pandemic. Reparations is also about a change in historical reckoning, and current and future changes in awareness and consciousness that the Black Lives Matter movements as well as earlier efforts to address systemic racism and slavery's legacies have sought to bring about. While reparations seek a historical accounting, redistribution looks forward to where and how greater equalities can be achieved. These may be difficult to achieve under the current political realities, but they become important as part of a process of change, both politically, economically, and culturally.[61]

Reparations *and* redistribution from a care-centered politics perspective is about repair *and* care along with the ability of all to live well, while recognizing how much change is needed, and where and how it can happen. The crises of 2020–2021, as Roy said about the pandemic, may well have pointed the way toward that process of change.

6 PATHWAYS FOR CHANGE: A CARE-CENTERED POLITICS AGENDA

There are periods of history in which order is dislocated, leaving behind nothing but constraints bereft of meaning. Realism no longer consists in managing what exists, but in imagining, anticipating, and initiating fundamental transformation, whose possibilities already lie in existing transformations.

—ANDRÉ GORZ, *LES CHEMINS DU PARADIS*

THE PROCESS FOR CHANGE

If care is about what we do, and how we interact with each other and the world around us, then the task of a care politics agenda, particularly in the wake of the events of 2020–2021, is to identify where the opportunities for change can be located in what we do and how we do it. Even as a care-centered politics is able to move the United States beyond a Trumpian anticare politics, the possibilities for a radical shift toward a different culture of care, a more democratic type of governance, and a change in racial, gender, and class relationships remains challenging at best. Despite the enormity of the changes required, a care politics agenda may need to initially seek changes less radical or transformative, but that nevertheless provide a direction for achieving far greater change than initially anticipated. Some of those types of changes could be found in the early actions of the Biden administration seeking to undo the anticare damage of the Trump years. At the same time, the 2020–2021 crises of a pandemic still not controlled even with the arrival of vaccines at the time of the January

20, 2021, change of the US government, a climate crisis that continues to intensify and pose severe threats around the globe, and systemic racism and deep inequalities that appear intractable—all of those made the need for transformative change more compelling than ever, despite the obstacles. The dilemma of what type of change to pursue suggests, at the extremes, differences between two distinct pathways: an incrementalism that fails to meet the challenges required versus the 1960s' imaginary and utopian slogan of transformative change: be realistic, demand the impossible.

A care-centered politics is well positioned to address that dilemma. It draws on nearly two centuries of care-related research, writing, advocating, and organizing around both immediate and structural daily life and social reproduction issues. It has accomplished small and more substantive changes while still pursuing a transformative household, community, national, and global shift. Care politics, moreover, can become associated with a wide array of constituencies, institutions, and issues, from earth care to health care, violence prevention to policing reform and criminal justice, and environmental justice to food sovereignty and climate justice. The vast majority of the people in the United States and throughout the world engage in some form of care or being cared for, from childhood to adulthood and elderhood. This fact can help stimulate a majoritarian movement while also helping change language, behavior, and the value of community and public action as opposed to anticare, profit-seeking market approaches. It elevates the desire for solidarity rather than the self-serving individualism that had become the norm in a neoliberal order.

To accomplish these kinds of changes, a care-centered politics would need to help develop and integrate several crucial building blocks.

- It would need robust *social movements* that collaborate with and bring together multiple perspectives, issues, and constituencies—an intersectional approach that can overcome racial, gender, class, and sexual identity divides, and enrich each movement's arguments and approaches. Some of that occurred from the impact of the 2020–2021 events such as when climate action groups like the Sunrise Movement embraced a racial justice and redistributional position, and some Black

Lives Matter groups focused on trans and sexism issues while also incorporating the language of global climate justice.

- It would need an approach to *electoral gains, policy advocacy, and policy goals* that recognizes how elections, policy campaigns, and victories can lead to further change that can become transformative. New studies as well as a recent film by public health historian Barbara Berney documented through interviews and archival material how the passage of Medicare in 1965 became a vehicle for the integration of hospitals throughout the South still subject to Jim Crow practices. Similarly, expanding Medicare through the passage of universal health care policies could become an instrument for addressing deep inequalities and systemic racism, and contribute to a global health for all approach. The victories of two Georgia senators in January 2021 runoff elections led to a Democratic Senate that was then able to pass the massive American Rescue Plan legislation with its transformative child benefit provisions, which prior to that Georgia election, had been considered dead on arrival.[1]

- It would need to draw on the *utopian imagination* about relationships and that another world is indeed possible by expanding the understanding of what is possible when so little change seems likely. The utopian imagination is crucial when thinking about the elimination of racism and overcoming the Black wealth gap, freeing of time from its market stranglehold, or liberation of women from the double bind of unpaid and underpaid households and jobs. The utopian imagination doesn't tell you how to get there, but it makes its language and goals central to any change trajectory.

- It would need to engage in *discourse battles and transform language,* which would be crucial for any change agenda. Language matters, as many pointed out during the events of 2020–2021, whether in relation to systemic racism, understanding climate change as a daily life issue, or contributing during a pandemic to a collective and cooperative response as well as countering the anticare and antisolidarity pandemic messages such as defiantly not wearing a mask or seeking to undermine vaccination mandates and outreach programs.

Each of these building blocks for change can reinforce each other. They can create a *process for change* that might seem gradual, but can then advance dramatically when a moment arises where the language changes, movements emerge and consolidate, utopian dreams become realistic demands, and a politics agenda comes together.

BASIC INCOME

Illustrations of where and how a care-centered politics process for change could be pursued include, but are not limited to, a universal basic income (UBI) that is unconditional, reduced work hours without reducing pay while providing opportunities for care and social connection, a Medicare for All program that is universal and prevention focused, and a Green New Deal that is participatory and community centered. These illustrations had been, prior to the crises of 2020–2021, aspirational at best, often marginalized as fanciful and unrealistic projections as opposed to obtainable policy objectives. While still considered out of reach as immediate goals, they have nevertheless changed the discussions about what is possible and not just what is likely to happen. They are examples of a process of change insofar as they point in the direction and include partial steps to what larger changes are not only possible but necessary too.

The current basic income debates are a useful starting point. South Korea provides one example of what steps have been taken and where they could lead. On September 10 and 11, 2020, the South Korean province of Gyeonggi-do and its governor, Lee Jae-myung, convened an international basic income conference, designed in part to showcase the initiatives in Gyeonggi. The province, consisting of thirty-one cities, municipalities, and rural townships surrounding Seoul, has a population of thirteen million, which constitutes about a quarter of South Korea's population.

Governor Lee, a potential candidate for South Korean president in 2022, had become a basic income champion based on his introduction of several basic income programs and policy ideas. These included a 2016 youth allowance program when Lee was mayor of Seongnam, the second-largest city in Gyeonggi Province. After his election as governor in 2018,

Lee rolled out a more ambitious youth basic income program involving an unconditional payment of 250,000 won on a quarterly basis for one year (about US$900) for all twenty-four-year-olds who had lived in the province for at least three years. The more than 150,000 young people who participated in the program were given payments in the form of local currencies designed for the money to be spent at local businesses within the region. Then in the midst of the pandemic in South Korea in 2020, Lee added supplemental funding for his province beyond the cash transfer provided by the central government to all South Korean residents. He also developed plans for a basic income for farmers and a rural township in Gyeonggi, designed in part to support small farms and women farmers, and reduce rural income disparities. In addition, he proposed a basic income program for artists.[2]

The programs in Gyeonggi as well as a two-year program in 2017–2018 in Finland along with a number of other city and regional initiatives, including in the United States, are instances of the growing—and renewed—global interest in the UBI concept. The Finland program, also highlighted at the Gyeonggi conference, involved two thousand unemployed persons receiving a monthly cash amount of 560 euros (worth about US$600). The Finnish program had received attention for its promising outcomes, including a majority expressing greater happiness in their lives, as well as criticism by those more focused on cost and the difficulties in getting participants back into the job market. Other programs referenced included a small pilot project in Stockton, California, and other similar programs also small in scale and primarily designed as pilots involving targeted groups. Michael Tubbs, Stockton's mayor, initially became a national figure for his program, though he subsequently lost reelection. He also facilitated the development of the Mayors for a Guaranteed Income network with several dozen US mayors from both small and large cities like Los Angeles, Oakland, Atlanta, and Jackson (Mississippi) who had either initiated their own pilots or expressed interest in developing a similar program. The Oakland program, established as a pilot in 2021, was notable in that it targeted the city's low-income African American population, characterizing the project as a type of reparations initiative.[3]

As with the Finnish and South Korean programs, there have been multiple arguments about the merits of the UBI as well as the definitions and intent of the concept itself. These debates date back more than two centuries, particularly with the rise of industrial capitalism and its impact on inequality. It became prominent during the 1960s and 1970s thanks to advocates like Martin Luther King Jr. and economist John Kenneth Galbraith. Shortly before his assassination, King focused on the need to address poverty in the United States as the next struggle beyond civil rights that became the centerpiece of the Poor People's Campaign, which he had helped organize. The Poor People's Campaign in turn called for a "guaranteed annual income"—a demand that was referenced in a letter to Congress and signed by Galbraith, economist James Tobin, and more than a thousand academic economists. King himself wrote about the need for a guaranteed income in the last book he published in 1968 where he contrasted the huge amounts being spent to conduct the war in Vietnam with the intractable problems of poverty and inequality amid abundance. "We must create jobs or we must create income," King contended, suggesting that full employment could be enhanced by creating new forms of work that "enhance the social good." The idea of a guaranteed basic income also became popular among welfare rights activists who wished to see an expansion of benefits *without conditions* to counter the frequently demeaning and debilitating ways in which welfare benefits were administered.[4]

In contrast to King's approach, the notion that a basic income could actually undo rather than supplement support programs and policies became popular during the 1960s and early 1970s, and again in the 1980s, among conservative, pro-market, anti–welfare state critics such as economist Milton Friedman. Friedman proposed the idea of a negative income tax that would involve cash payments to individuals based on income levels, the poorest of whom, Friedman argued, could even presumably become entrepreneurs, while also doing away with all social insurance and welfare programs. For Friedman, private charity, rather than public programs, was the preferable recourse for addressing poverty. While Friedman acknowledged in a 1980 book he cowrote with his wife that his proposal was his "utopian dream" unlikely to be adopted in the near term, he hoped it could "provide a vision of the direction in which we should be moving, a vision that can guide incremental changes."[5]

Changes involving the erosion of welfare-oriented social insurance and safety net programs, and replacing them with workfare policies and charity that Friedman and other conservative writers like Charles Murray advocated, did in fact take place during the next several decades, yet without any negative income tax or basic income support. This shift was epitomized by Bill Clinton's "end of welfare" and workfare policy enacted in 1996. Such changes reinforced and extended the problems of inequality, and were further exacerbated by a developing work economy associated with low-income, nonstable part-time work and multiple jobs with longer work hours. The stable job with benefits at a single workplace associated with the post–World War II manufacturing-based economy (the "production of things") was becoming eroded, largely replaced by a service economy with insecure low-wage jobs, including care economy jobs and unpaid work. It also witnessed the rise of online platform-based technologies and unstable contract work that rapidly expanded after 2000. By 2020–2021, a new type of gilded age had fully formed, further exacerbated by the pandemic, with wealth concentrated among individual and corporate players, such as Google, Amazon, and Facebook. The tech elites, many of whom considered themselves antiregulatory libertarians, also became advocates of a basic income policy as a strategy to deal with automation-generated unemployment. Such a position, they recognized, could at the same time serve to shield the tech giants from responsibility for their contribution to inequality and the erosion of the stable job, and the policy and regulatory initiatives designed to reduce their monopoly powers and redistribute some of their wealth.[6]

These pro-market, tech-infused versions of a basic income have been challenged by the inequality-focused critics on the Left who have become the primary advocates of an unconditional UBI and financing strategies that emphasize redistributive approaches. One socialist scholar, University of Wisconsin sociologist Eric Olin Wright, argued in 2005 that despite the barriers at the time for developing a socialist politics in the United States, a basic income approach could serve as a transition strategy to better empower workers and enhance the "social economy," including the care economy. Similarly, Li Andersson, the leader of Finland's Left Alliance Party, asserted that her country's experiment with the UBI, with its roots in left social movements, provided an opportunity to help design a different type of welfare state where people had the ability to "refuse bad jobs" and help reinvent the overall system of employment.[7]

The leading contemporary unconditional UBI global advocacy group today, the Basic Income Earth Network, has defined the UBI concept as a "periodic cash payment unconditionally delivered to all on an individual basis, without means test or work requirement." The network's cofounder, Philippe Van Parijs, along with Yannick Vanderborght, characterized basic income as a foundation from which people would have the freedom to move more easily between "paid work, education, caring, and volunteering." More than twenty years earlier, another major proponent of basic income, Gorz, argued that while the concept of an "unconditional, universal, *sufficient* income" could not be achieved immediately, it needed to be conceptualized in the present moment "in order to prepare for it," and better move toward a structural transformation and create a transition away from capitalism.[8]

The longest-standing full-scale UBI cash payment in the United States has been the Alaska Permanent Fund Dividend based on the state's oil wealth. The idea for such a fund originated in the aftermath of Alaska obtaining ownership of the Prudhoe Bay oil field, the largest in North America. This created an enormous new source of wealth for the state. To address how the wealth would be allocated, the Alaskan government created the Permanent Fund Dividend in 1976, and then legislation in 1980 to establish that the funds went to all Alaska residents. The funds began to flow to the state's residents in 1982, with amounts varying annually, depending on the amount of oil pumped and sold, and various investments the state made. During the Permanent Fund Dividend's forty-plus years, the amounts have averaged more than $1,100 annually per person, although fund amounts have at times been reduced since the late 1980s, when production was then at its peak. The Alaska model has generally been the exception to a long history of resource-rich country leaders squandering their resource through corruption, and/or by giving it away to wealthy elites and corporations that have then turned a common resource into a private asset for sale.[9]

Although the Alaska model has been an exception in relation to the size and financing mechanism of a basic income program, its dependence on oil revenue has also limited it since it involves a contested resource due to climate change and other environmental impacts. Further reductions in the Alaska fund amount are likely to occur due to the push by environmental and climate justice activists as well as sympathetic policy makers to leave all fossil fuels in the ground or ocean, and phase out all production earlier rather than later to achieve a zero carbon emissions goal.[10]

The UBI is identified by many UBI researchers and advocates primarily as a method to accomplish greater income equality through cash payments for a general population without a means test. In addition to the UBI, other approaches such as universal basic services (UBS) and universal basic vouchers (UBV) have recognized that utilizing a country's resources and other types of shared goods as a type of commons can also become an effective mechanism to establish any number of UBI, UBS, or UBV programs, including but not limited to reducing income inequality. Many of the existing initiatives are seen as transitional approaches to a full UBI, UBS, or UBV program, such as the Gyeonggi and Finland examples that have focused on targeted groups like youths or the unemployed, or programs where participants need to engage in socially useful work, whether paid or unpaid, with care work a prominent illustration.[11]

The UBS can be considered a type of income transfer in the form of establishing free consumer goods such as free internet, and free or reduced rate infrastructure services, such as health care, transportation, education, or housing. Medicare for All or a publicly run single-payer health system would be considered a UBS, as would the British National Health Service. Free or fare subsidy programs for transportation, or subsidy programs for housing, both of which have been utilized during the pandemic, could be implemented permanently on the basis that they focus on a type of commons, and constitute basic human rights for mobility and shelter. Free or subsidized care services, such as childcare, disability care, or eldercare, could also be considered a crucial commons-related UBS program, given the need and how large a population would be affected. The Biden administration's childcare support and tax credit established as part of the 2021 American Rescue Plan Act emerged early on in his Administration as an important UBS-type support initiative too.[12]

The UBV has also been implemented widely as emergency payments during the pandemic, or payments made during climate-related events such as fires, hurricanes, and flooding. Emergency pandemic-related, voucher-style payments have included the $1,200 in cash provided to individuals in March 2020 in the United States through the CARES Act, an additional $600 payment in December 2020 as part of a second economic relief bill, and a third $1,400 payment in March 2021 for qualifying individuals (with income up to $75,000) as part of the American Rescue Plan stimulus package. These payments were justified on the basis that a pandemic-impacted economy had ravaged low-income as well as some middle-income individuals and families. Other UBV-type pandemic-related strategies have included payments to employers in order pay up to 80 percent of their employees' salaries rather than have to lay them off—similar to payments instituted in Germany and France.[13]

Ongoing vouchers for targeted constituencies such as food stamps or coupons for seniors to shop at farmers' markets, low-income residents, or various housing subsidies such as Section 8 differ from the UBI due to their more traditional, welfare-type means tests. Several of these UBV programs have been in place for several decades, although food and housing justice advocates have criticized their limited nature as well as sometimes-cumbersome and demeaning bureaucratic requirements; they've also critiqued them for not being unconditional and incorporating a rights-based approach. Financing strategies for some of these programs, whether UBI, UBS, or UBV, have nevertheless identified taxes on common pool resources such as a tax on land, as proposed for some of the Gyeonggi programs, or a tax on big data to provide for free internet services and enable greater access to data-based technologies, such as computers, tablets, and cell phones.

The tax on big data and the behemoths that control the flow of data raises another crucial factor about the importance of a UBI or UBS approach due to the rise of the data-driven gig or platform economies. While the gig and platform economies have not been the only cause for the changing nature of work, including its increased precarity (creating what some have called the *precariat,* as distinct from the industrial order's proletariat), they have become a major driver for how the rapid changes to work have revealed the inadequacy of the work-based social welfare programs like unemployment insurance. During the pandemic, many of those employed as gig workers and other presumed contractors who otherwise would not have been able to receive unemployment benefits required a special provision in the initial CARES Act legislation enabling them to receive their onetime $1,200 and subsequent support payments. The pandemic also facilitated the largest single basic-income-type support payment in the form of the guaranteed income for children through the American Rescue Plan legislation, which was estimated to be able to cut child poverty in half as it became implemented.[14]

Criticisms of the existing welfare support mechanisms in the United States and other countries have also led UBI, UBS, and UBV advocates to argue for the need to develop alternative criteria for their programs to address such criticisms. These include assuring security and work prospects for the least secure; eliminating the paternalism in existing welfare programs by not imposing controls in various cases, such as workfare policies that force people into low-paying, exploitative jobs; empowering the people receiving support to have a voice in determining their future, and by doing so, allowing participants to be happier than if they didn't have any control of their life and work; structuring social entitlements as rights not charity, such as the right to food and food security, both on an individual and community basis; utilizing ecological criteria to enable access to ecological work and skills, and reduce or eliminate any unsafe and environmentally harmful conditions; and dignifying the nature of work and activity, such as in care work, both for providers and recipients—paramount for any universal care support program.[15]

Racial justice is another key criterion for UBI, UBS, and UBV initiatives. The Movement for Black Lives along with other racial equality and social justice groups, including those promoting reparations, have been among the most vocal advocates for UBI and UBS programs. These advocates make a distinction between *basic income*, which replaces core welfare and regulatory policies, and *basic income plus*, which adds to and helps restructure existing or new support programs, and could "radically redistribute security," as one group puts it, rather than diminish it. Guaranteeing everyone a sufficient income to live on, Movement for Black Lives activists argue, provides recognition that care labor done disproportionately by women is "valued as labor," while reparations can also focus on eliminating various types of discriminatory, exploitative, and disinvestment policies as well as programs negatively impacting Black communities and other communities of color.[16]

Racial justice advocates have identified the changing work economy, low wages for jobs held by African Americans and Latinx workers including care work, and lack of job stability and increased precarity as key racial justice issues that a UBI-plus approach needs to address. These conditions were exacerbated by the pandemic, and led to more calls for a new approach to work and income support.

Some influential contemporary basic income advocates, including those associated with the Basic Income Earth Network, have recognized the political barriers for the development of a full-scale unconditional basic income approach—obstacles that came into play during the late 1960s when racial justice movements constituted the leading edge of guaranteed annual income advocacy. In Van Parijs and Vanderborght's comprehensive study of basic income issues, they suggested that a partial basic income approach, including universal child benefits or subsidies to voluntary unemployment in the form of benefits for career interruption or working-time reduction, might be an effective transition strategy toward acceptance of a fully developed basic income approach. They also argued that the concept needs to be developed as a global program—an enormous challenge as well, although parallel efforts to develop a "fair deal on global warming" indicate a potential pathway for a global basic income approach. The various income support programs for children are an effective form of a partial UBI, both in relation to the immediate need as well as providing a potential pathway for acceptance of an even greater UBI that could also be elevated as a global program.[17]

The political and economic feasibility of a basic income approach in light of the changing work economy was a major topic at the September 10–11, 2020, Basic Income International Conference held in Gyeonggi. Several speakers pointed out that beyond the issue of job loss from automation and technology change, the traditional welfare and social support strategies such as unemployment insurance had not been able to address the difficulties of utilizing the existing as well as minimal support structures for the increasingly pervasive gig and platform economies of the developed countries of the North and the informal economies in the Global South. As one speaker from Finland observed at the Gyeonggi conference, the basic income approach shifts the focus from a work-centric support infrastructure to a citizen-centric (or resident-centric) approach. How to make such a transition requires not only a strategy revolving around income and inequality like basic income but also a consideration of how to make such a transition regarding work time—another area where a care-centered politics and agenda come into play.

REDUCING WORK HOURS, INCREASING CARE TIME

In 1930, as the Great Depression began its ferocious assault on the economy and unemployment eventually reached more than a quarter of the working population, English economist John Maynard Keynes penned an unusual and counterintuitive essay, at least in relation to the emerging economic situation. Written in the form of a letter to his grandchildren, Keynes sought to counter what he characterized as "a bad attack of economic pessimism" given the rapid increase in unemployment in the first months of the Depression. Keynes was a strong advocate of the idea that technology would be able to increase efficiency and productivity, and assumed the trend would continue into the next decades. Instead of just technological unemployment, a buzzword in the early months of the Depression and again today, Keynes saw opportunity, particularly in the reduction of work hours and increase in overall wealth made possible by technology gains. Keynes envisioned that over a hundred-year span, a much-shortened work time would emerge, albeit gradually, with working hours reduced to as little as fifteen hours a week. Shortened work hours would enable people to escape from always seeking more money—for Keynes, "a disgusting morbidity"—and in contrast, "live wisely and agreeably and well." In doing so, people could be encouraged to experiment with and participate in "the arts of life as well as the activities of purpose."[18]

Shortly before Keynes wrote his essay, the United States found itself far removed from the kinds of reductions in working hours Keynes had thought would eventually become possible. Although labor action had helped reduce work hours in the first two decades of the twentieth century from the sixty-hour workweek to slightly under fifty hours, those reductions stalled in the 1920s. Among manufacturing workers in the United States, more than 80 percent were still working forty-eight hours or longer per week in 1930. The United States, moreover, had become more of an outlier in relation to work time, as most other industrialized nations had by then adopted the eight-hour day. Yet conditions would soon change that dynamic, with unemployment creating a sense of urgency.[19]

Despite the hiatus around work hours in the 1920s, the demand for reduced work time was a long-standing issue for the labor movement that drew on a long history of sharp class conflict about working hours. As historians David Roediger and Philip Foner noted, the historical demands by labor for reduced hours included "America's first industrial strike, its first city wide trade union councils, its first labor party, its first general strikes, its first organization uniting skilled and unskilled workers, its first strike by females, and its first attempts at regional and national labor organizations." Furthermore, the struggle for shorter hours through the nineteenth and first decades of the twentieth centuries "unified workers across lines of age, sex, skill, race, ethnicity, and craft [and it] implied control of leisure, of intellect, even of political power." "Exercising power of when to work," Roediger and Foner argued, "could go hand in hand with exercising power over how to work."[20]

By the early 1930s, in response to the unemployment crisis and a renewed focus on work hours by labor, reduced work hours seemed once again a politically viable demand. In December 1932, Alabama senator (and later Supreme Court justice) Hugo Black introduced a bill mandating a thirty-hour workweek as the best method for dealing with the rise of unemployment. The bill passed the Senate the next year and began to work its way through the House when President Franklin Delano Roosevelt decided to oppose the bill, due to industry opposition and his own subsequent effort to pass his major employment initiative, the National Industrial Recovery Act (NIRA). Roosevelt's argument was that the NIRA, which included provisions for the right to organize unions, was a better strategy to reduce work time. When the Supreme Court ruled NIRA unconstitutional in 1935, some industries sought to increase their work hours. Unions, however, resisted those efforts, particularly the industrial unions organized into the Congress for Industrial Organizations. Some of the more militant unions began to achieve partial victories, including the adoption of the eight-hour day and forty-hour workweek. A few unions, such as those representing flat glass workers, were even able to achieve a six-hour day. Nevertheless, the primary demand of union action during much of the 1930s including among the Congress for Industrial Organizations' unions, remained focused on the right to organize and achieve union representation, with reduced work hours a secondary goal.[21]

Black and other New Deal supporters continued to seek new legislative action, especially after the Supreme Court NIRA ruling. In 1938, following another downturn in the economy, New Deal forces were able to obtain passage of the Fair Labor Standards Act, the last major piece of labor legislation of the 1930s, and in some ways the culmination of legislative efforts like the NIRA and thirty-hour workweek bill. Most provisions had to do with establishing minimum wages and workplace protections, although a phased-in forty-hour workweek was also included (forty-four hours the first year, forty-two hours the second year, and forty hours thereafter). Labor critics of the legislation raised concerns about the phase-in work hour provisions along with the lack of language regarding daily maximum hours. In addition, in order to obtain support from southern legislators to pass the bill, the Fair Labor Standards Act, similar to exclusions in the 1935 Social Security Act, exempted several categories of labor from its provisions, including agricultural and domestic workers whose workforce then was predominantly African American. Those exemptions would subsequently hinder organizing among those groups and their ability to obtain better working conditions, including pay and working hours. It also became a major issue for food justice and care work advocates about the poor working conditions of farmworkers and domestic workers.[22]

World War II interrupted the push for reduced working hours, due in part to employer attacks that the forty-hour week was unpatriotic and harmful to the war efforts. During the war, average work hours increased from slightly above forty hours a week to more than forty-three hours, while women workers, the Rosie the Riveters newly recruited into the workforce, averaged forty-eight hours per week. Yet women's household labor was not reduced, and over time the extra hours caused a number of women to quit jobs or take time off from what had become the six-day workweek. Roediger and Foner quote one study in Detroit that identified the loss of a hundred thousand worker hours per month due to women taking time off to do laundry at home. In fact, the demand for shorter hours as a primary goal, during and after the war, came to be seen in part as a women's issue, and how that issue played out involved what historian Dorothy Sue Cobble characterized as "a politics of time designed primarily with men in mind." Men, after all, were not assumed to be doing any of the laundry![23]

During the late 1940s and 1950s, some labor militants and progressive unions sought to link the issue of increased pay with reduced hours through slogans and campaigns such as thirty for forty, or a wage for thirty hours based on the pay for forty hours. Yet the predominant focus for labor remained the issues of pay scale and such pay-related benefits as overtime, vacation time, extra holidays, and, increasingly, health care coverage. Increased wages, particularly for better paid union workers, was assumed to allow greater time *after work*. Yet it was market-driven consumption rather than leisure and activity, as both Juliet Schor and Benjamin Kline Hunnicutt have written, that characterized the nature of those after work/leisure time hours. The more one consumed, the greater the need for increased pay, which also meant greater hours at work when also translated into more overtime, dual household workers, and two jobs. As then UAW President Walter Reuther put it in 1949, "our fight is not between not having enough material goods and not having enough leisure. Our fight is not having enough material goods." The shorter workweek, for Reuther, was still a long way from happening.[24]

Instead of the focus on changing and reducing work time for more leisure hours, already by the 1980s and through the next several decades, the trend became more rather than less work, jobs that were more precarious than stable, and workers with less control over their time. The neoliberal political shift that weakened unions also contributed to the limited efforts by workers to achieve reduced hours. Even when the demand was raised as part of a labor action, such as the Professional Air Traffic Controllers Organization strike in 1981 that included a demand for a thirty-two-hour week for safety reasons, the fierce response of the Reagan administration along with firing the controllers and employing strikebreakers not only led to a defeat in that strike but played a major role in the weakening of unions too.[25]

The neoliberal era didn't just diminish the role of unions, which remained the major proponent of reduced work hours; it ushered in a new era of *increased work hours*, most notably in the United States. Per capita work hours began to increase as early as the 1980s, both for those employed full time in a single job, often requiring increased overtime to meet their wage needs, and those working part-time in multiple jobs or with uneven, precarious hours. The issue of per capita rather than household paid work hours was significant since women continued to do double duty, with paid hours on the job and unpaid work in the home, and would often be the first to shift to part-time work, especially in the absence of policy support for their household and care work. Events like the 2020–2021 pandemic especially impacted women's paid work hours as the pandemic hit hardest in job sectors, mainly care related, such as retail, hospitality, health, and education where women constituted a majority, while women continued to assume primary responsibility for childcare, homeschooling, and household work when schools shut down. These sectors also had large proportions of low-income people of color, whose low wages forced many to seek more than one job, and/or face the dilemmas of potential homelessness and food insecurity without any sufficient living wages.[26]

In addition, the shift to greater work hours was influenced by consumption and technology issues, including for those people otherwise constituting middle-income labor sectors who had once been the leading edge of reduced work hour advocacy. Kathi Weeks has argued that in the neoliberal era, reinforced by the pervasive ideology of consumption, the traditional capitalist invocation of the work ethic and the Weberian asceticism associated with it had been turned on its head. People worked in order to consume, and the desire for greater consumption created the incentive to work *more*. "The work ethic," Weeks wrote in her book *The Problem with Work*, "continues to affirm the legitimacy of this connection: consumption goods are the reward for and sign of one's contributions and status as a producer. As an antinomy rather than an oxymoron, the 'worldly asceticism' of the Protestant ethic functions not despite, but because of, the pairing of terms [work and consumption]." The struggle for reduced work hours, Weeks asserted, reinforcing claims made by Gorz and others, would help free the dictates of the capitalist system's control of work *and* consumption, and instead offer to change the concept of work to one of activity. In doing so, it could create "a new work and non-work ethics and new practices of care and socialities." "By framing it in terms of this more open-ended and expansive set of goals," Weeks concludes, "by demanding shorter hours for 'what we will'—and resisting the impulse to dictate what that is or should be—we can create a more progressive coalition and sustain a more democratic discourse."[27]

At the same time, technology, despite Keynes's Depression era optimism that it could bring about increased productivity and a major reduction in work hours, has proven to be a double-edged sword. The new data-driven and platform-based technologies of the past two decades have helped reshape the workplace as much, if not more than, the machine-driven, automation-based technologies that had increased productivity and served to displace workers in manufacturing industries such as automobile production. The economic interests that developed these new technologies—companies that ranged from Google and Amazon to Uber and DoorDash—promoted the notion of job *flexibility* that was frequently only a slightly disguised form of job *precarity*. This gig economy thrived on precarity—a workforce that presumably assumed control over its own hours, but in fact often required longer hours, or second or third jobs, to even achieve minimum wages. The shifting workplace also extended downward to the rapidly growing service industries that primarily engaged women and people of color, and whose hours varied and were not stable—an inverted structure from the disappearing middle-income, stable job in manufacturing. This shift gave rise to the *flexible part-timer*: those who work fewer hours even as they experience frequent changes during the day or week about when they work. The care-related workforce has been especially subject to uneven hours, low pay, and unstable jobs.[28]

Similar to the goal of basic income, reduced hours can provide a counterpoint to the precarious workplace and need to work more. The work ethic—work hard and be able to achieve a better status—had become an instrument to reinforce the new forms of exploitation under the neoliberal forms of domination. Aside from job loss, the pandemic heightened those insecurities, extending the real dangers of exposure and illness *related to the work itself.*[29]

In the face of uncertainties and at moments of crisis, the response to the pandemic also pointed to why the idea of an income floor in the form of a cash transfer detached from a means test or job/workfare requirement—core attributes of a basic income—supplied its own logic. Similarly, the loss of jobs led to some tentative proposals to reduce working hours as a strategy to rebuild after COVID-19, such as New Zealand prime minister Jacinda Ahern's call for a four-day workweek. Her call was subsequently implemented by the global firm Unilever for its New Zealand employees, utilizing a thirty-two-for-forty framework (forty hours pay for a thirty-two-hour work week). While such changes still remain tentative and crisis driven, they nevertheless point in the direction of the more fundamental shift required, if such goals as a full basic income and deeper reduced working hours can redefine the meaning of work and income, reorient gender roles to increase men's participation in care activities, and remake the economy as a care economy in responding to pandemics, climate change, gender exploitation, racism, and inequality.[30]

THE PREVENTION PRINCIPLE: MEDICARE FOR ALL AND A
GREEN NEW DEAL

In March 2020, just as the United States and other countries experienced their first spike of COVID-19 cases, and before the fires, heat waves, and hurricanes inflicted their now-annual and increasingly destructive climate change–induced damage in several regions, the United Nations published its eighth annual *World Happiness Report*. The first *World Happiness Report* had been prepared by participants at the Earth Institute at Columbia University in collaboration with researchers at the London School of Economics and University of British Columbia, and released at a 2012 UN high-level meeting on the topic of happiness and well-being. The language of care was included in the definition and assessment of happiness and well-being, with the 2020 report noting that people are happier "when they trust each other and their shared institutions and care for the welfare of others." "Such caring attitudes," the authors noted, "are then typically extended to cover those elsewhere in the world and in future generations." The report also identified the negative impacts from "well-being inequality" related to such factors as health status, income level, discrimination, and the overall social environment that influences the availability as well as level of care and caring attitudes.[31]

The events of 2020 that followed the publication of the *World Happiness Report* juxtaposed care and anticare examples of approaches like solidarity, trust, and other individual as well as social determinants of well-being with the self-centeredness, privilege, racism, fear of the other, and meanness characteristic of an anticare individualism and politics. The pandemic in the United States witnessed numerous displays of care and caring attitudes, most notably from frontline and essential workers, including but not limited to health care workers directly at risk while providing care and support. The pandemic demonstrated the possibilities associated with those acts of social solidarity, mutual aid, and individual as well as community and institutional support for others, from the simplest, such as children and adults making masks for others, to the more complex needs associated with caretaking. Mutual aid initiatives ranged from traditional strategies such as providing meals and food aid for others, to establishing rooftop routers in areas where internet access was more limited, or providing mental health services for frontline workers or group therapy sessions in multiple languages. The massive Black Lives Matter demonstrations in summer 2020 had a care politics subtext too, such as the widely adopted "Care Not Cops" slogan mentioned earlier that originated in Portland, Oregon, in 2017, and was then picked up by numerous Black Lives Matter protesters during the 2020 protests.[32]

Similarly, climate change–related events in the United States during 2020, such as the California and Oregon wildfires as well as hurricanes and storm surges in the East, witnessed episodes where people were able to help others in danger of losing their homes and lives. Beyond illustrations of individual care, a broader care politics was visible, invoked through a type of prevention and social protection principle. Social solidarity, trust, and care were recognized as crucial immediate responses, while care politics offered some of the most direct strategies for prevention and adaptation in the longer term, including sharing and collaboration, as opposed to wasting or competing for resources.

In contrast, the pandemic and climate change events of 2020–2021 also revealed those anticare responses associated with the toxic individualism, mistrust, and defiance that had been especially stoked by Trumpian politics during the pandemic. This included the hostility expressed against mask wearers as well as threats of intimidation and violence directed at public health workers and government officials. It included the constant downplaying of the seriousness and even reality of the pandemic coupled with a type of artifact or alternative facts view of everything, ranging from the numbers of COVID-19 cases and deaths, to the assessment of risks and treatments, including vaccinations. It witnessed a jump in domestic abuse and sexual violence. It was expressed by the efforts of some companies to force their frontline and essential workers to continue working, even when COVID-19 symptoms were exhibited, or when prevention measures such as physical distancing or mask wearing were disregarded. At the same time, some of these same companies and their executives pursued liability exemptions, and sought limitations on occupational health and safety regulations.[33]

With climate change, an anticare approach was exposed when climate-related fires led to efforts by wealthy homeowners to privatize firefighting resources by purchasing those services for themselves, and not for their neighbors or the larger community. It was expressed by climate denialism as well as challenging and seeking to undermine scientific assessments of existing and future problems and potential catastrophes. It was highlighted by corporate cover-ups led by fossil fuel companies of information about climate risks that were internally available but not shared publicly, even while their actions contradicted their own findings.[34]

For both the pandemic and climate change, anticare actions represented a version of the neoliberal claim that there was no such thing as solidarity and society—only wealth, power, and the market. In contrast to such denialism and anticare actions, the prevention principle represents a long-standing, care-centered political concept embraced by health and environmental justice activists, including around such issues as reducing or eliminating toxic and hazardous wastes. Today, the language of prevention and care has been incorporated as part of the two major initiatives around health and environment: Medicare for All and the Green New Deal.

Both Medicare for All and the Green New Deal are policy templates rather than a set of policy proposals. They are aspirational and can be interpreted broadly, and serve more as a rallying cry for social movements than a legislative or regulatory action plan. This is due, in part, to the lack of sufficient support historically, especially in the United States, among legislators, government officials, and political elites for either of these approaches. Further, the sharp attacks leveled against each by health industry and fossil fuel interests had contributed to their stigmatization as too radical and costly, and thus outside the mainstream for policy action. At the same time, both Medicare for All and the Green New Deal became targets for conservative and right-wing critics, who painted them as dangerous socialist and anti-market attempts to undermine individual choice and eliminate businesses such as health insurance as well as oil, gas, and coal companies. Yet even as they were dismissed as impossible policy options, the pandemic and climate change events demonstrated why both approaches were needed to help frame future health, environmental, and climate policies.

From a prevention and care politics perspective, Medicare for All is best understood and interpreted as embodying the principle of health as a universal right. Specifically, universal health care, particularly through a publicly run single-payer system, offers the possibility of empowering care and prevention strategies, versus a corporate-driven and medicalization model for health issues. The need for a universal health approach was magnified by the pandemic. In the face of a universal and global health crisis, universal health strategies of prevention and care such as mask wearing as a form of social solidarity as well as individual reduction of potential risk and free or low-cost services that were publicly subsidized, like testing and vaccinations available to all, were essential when applied to address the spread of the disease. The pandemic further identified the enormous social inequities of the current market-centered health system in the United States, including the skewered cost of health care or immigration policies that increased the risks of immigrant populations as well as for the general public through the potential spread of the virus when care became too costly, or was not made available or even denied. Already by 2019, 67.8 million people receiving health care coverage through their work in the United States had either lost their jobs, were terminated, or needed to leave their jobs, thereby losing their existing coverage and/or being forced to find new coverage. The pandemic greatly exacerbated that situation, as many more lost their jobs and the numbers of the uninsured increased dramatically. The pandemic thus turned the challenges of access to health care, even with the coverage provided by the Affordable Care Act, into an immediate crisis not easily resolved in the short or long term by patchwork changes to the act or employer-based health insurance.[35]

Beyond the issues of health insurance and health access, the pandemic reinforced and extended health inequities at the community, national, and global levels in relation to treatment and prevention. The social determinants of health, such as housing conditions, environmental factors, diet and food availability, occupational hazards, income inequality, poverty, and homelessness, were magnified by where and how COVID-19 exposures and the pandemic had been experienced. Even the widely touted success story of the pandemic, the rapid development of vaccines, was compounded by uneven methods of distribution, patent control, wealthy people jumping the line, issues of public financing and private profiteering, and vaccine hoarding and resistance to changing World Trade Organization rules on patent protections, thereby preventing the global distribution and local manufacture of vaccines.[36]

The COVID-19 vaccine development itself built on decades of massive public investment in research and development, including research through the US National Institutes of Health. Both the German government, which initially provided $45 million for BioNTech, Pfizer's partner, and the US government, which supplied more than $2 billion to Moderna, were essential for the work of the first two vaccine developers to complete clinical trials, get approval for emergency use by the United States, United Kingdom, and other European and developed countries, and obtain preapproval advance orders. By February 2021, public funding for research and development along with advanced purchase agreements with the major vaccine developers by the United States, United Kingdom, and German governments had reached as much as $4 billion. Although pledges by some vaccine makers to make their vaccines available at low cost related to government support or relied on government programs like Medicare for vaccines at no cost, others like Pfizer decided to price their vaccines at a higher, more profitable rate. For instance, initial estimates pointed to $8 to $13 billion in sales for Pfizer from the pandemic—potentially greater than Pfizer's largest-selling drug on the market, Lipitor. Moreover, all the private pharmaceutical companies were able to capitalize enormously through huge spikes in stock prices and capital gains, while also, as happened with Moderna, unloading company shares on the same day that results from clinical trials were announced, thus reaping a huge windfall. Despite public funding for the research and development of the vaccines, governments needed to pay for their production and distribution, and absorb the costs of offering the vaccine for free, while the vaccine developers were paid up to $36 per vaccination. The public relations benefits were themselves as important as the short-term financial returns too, as one financial analyst said of Pfizer's attitude, given some of its long-standing negative public reputation.[37]

At the global level, the pharmaceutical companies made preclinical trial distribution deals with the wealthiest countries like the United States and United Kingdom to provide as much as 80 percent of the initial outlay of vaccines, creating uneven and severe shortages of the vaccine in a number of countries. At the same time, the wealthiest countries rejected a proposal from several less developed countries to waive the World Trade Organization's intellectual property rights trade-related provisions to allow the poorer countries to develop their own vaccines. Those discrepancies and differences between the wealthiest and poorest countries included the contract-related hoarding of vaccines in some countries like the United States (which considered itself a vaccine nationalist during the Trump presidency, and that view was only modestly revised initially by the Biden administration), blockage of the capacity to produce their own vaccines, and delays in achieving immunities in many of the less developed countries. These differences became part of the pandemic's global inequality outcomes, and foreshadowed a potentially dangerous public health result by extending the pandemic globally for possibly years to come.[38]

Economist Mariana Mazzucato argued throughout the pandemic that the countries that fared best prior to the availability of the vaccines, such as Vietnam or the Indian state of Kerala, were those that had invested over the years in their public sector rather than privatizing or outsourcing parts of the economy needed to address the pandemic. A publicly developed health care system is central to this approach. Public health systems and support mechanisms, including the development of vaccines, Mazzucato and others have continued to maintain, needed to be made available to all. "We are only as healthy as our neighbors—locally, nationally, and internationally," Mazzucato wrote in the *New York Times* in the first months of the pandemic.[39]

Along these lines, the World Health Organization early on in the pandemic proposed a "collective intelligence," where among other objectives, patents would be pooled. Such approaches were possible if conditions were stipulated for public financing that enabled a vaccine to be developed in the first place. Moreover, conditions like pooled patents, shared scientific and technical information, and stipulations for public financing had the capacity to help develop "a people's vaccine" rather than a "profit-centered vaccine." This was the position elaborated by the heads of state of South Africa, Senegal, Ghana, and Pakistan as well as other international leaders and academics, who argued early in the pandemic that "access to vaccines and treatments as global public goods are in the interests of all humanity." A subsequent research study modeled the consequences of wealthy nations hoarding vaccines, and indicated that nearly twice as many deaths were going to occur in less wealthy nations than if the vaccines were to be distributed equitably. In responding to the issue of vaccine access, the World Health Organization's secretary general, Tedros Adhanom Ghebreyesus, contended that a failure to move in a direction of equal global access to vaccines would effectively constitute "a catastrophic moral failure."[40]

A health for all approach, the centerpiece of a care-centered politics, makes the most sense when applied universally and globally rather than relying on a health care system that works for those who can pay for it, whether individuals or nations. From a care-centered perspective, health for all, with its inclusive, community, and global focus, also represents a global and universal extension of the Medicare for All argument about health access by incorporating a right to health, and working toward a prevention-based and community-centered health care system. The pandemic underlined that need, as would the actions needed to address climate change.

Similar to Medicare for All, the Green New Deal faced implacable opposition in the US Congress and Trump administration from the moment of its introduction, and subsequently stated opposition to the use of the name Green New Deal by the Biden administration for its climate change strategies. Nevertheless, the concept of the Green New Deal hasn't faded. It has been kept alive and sustained by social movements and progressive policy makers. These groups, particularly those led by youth participants, have been at the forefront in responding to a crisis mapped out by science and experienced globally, especially among those most vulnerable. Green New Deal movement advocates in turn have helped further speed up a decarbonization process, albeit a process that as the science has identified, still requires stronger and quicker action and far-reaching changes.

Armed with the science and a generational passion, the youth-based climate justice movements have helped induce the beginnings of a retreat by the fossil fuel interests and their financial backers. ExxonMobil, the largest of the original climate deniers, began to acknowledge by 2020 that it would need to write down some of its climate-wrecking assets due to the difficulties of bringing projects like its oil sands investments to fruition. Carbon Tracker, a financial think tank focused on changes in energy development, pointed out that between 2014 and 2019, ExxonMobil's return to its shareholders was a negative 10 percent. Those ExxonMobil shareholders, Carbon Tracker ironically noted, "would have been better off putting their cash under the mattress instead." At the same time, one of the fossil fuel industries biggest financial backers, JPMorgan Chase, announced in early 2020 that it was pulling back from certain fossil fuel financing of such projects as coal development or Arctic oil drilling. This shift was facilitated in part by the climate justice campaigners of the group Stop the Money Pipeline, led by longtime climate activist Bill McKibben. Other big banks, such as Bank of America, Goldman Sachs, Citi, Morgan Stanley, and Wells Fargo, had also declined to engage in financing Arctic oil leases, despite a last-minute push by Trump to move leasing forward just a few weeks prior to his leaving office. "Climate and Indigenous organizers have been attacking Big Energy companies and their investors, using economic pressure, boycotts, lawsuits, and disruptive direct-action tactics to impede drilling, interrupt the transportation of oil and gas, and choke off the flow of financing to, and insurance for, such projects," three sociology professors wrote in December 2020 about how the companies and their investors had begun to divest from fossil fuel extraction and infrastructure. These retreats were even further magnified by the dramatic increase in wind and particularly solar energy development, which by 2020 had already become cheaper than any of their fossil fuel competitors.[41]

An energy transition is now clearly underway, and from a Green New Deal and care-centered politics perspective, it's a welcome change in principle. It both predated and then grew quicker after the December 2018 introduction of the Green New Deal. While the Green New Deal hadn't translated into a policy change and couldn't claim responsibility for these types of changes through congressional action, it had become a marker nevertheless of the changing environment around climate change politics. As a candidate for president, Biden had attacked the Green New Deal as too costly as well as too radical in intent. As president, however, he soon faced the need to not only undo the Trump administration's anticlimate actions, such as leaving the Paris Agreement, but also rapidly scale up his own climate agenda, some of which directly resembled Green New Deal talking points. This included a care jobs agenda, an item in the Green New Deal even though it was not fully elaborated. Biden, both as a candidate and once installed as president, argued strongly for green jobs as part of his climate change approach, but without directly linking it to care-related jobs as a centerpiece for restructuring the carbon economy. While Biden advocated for strengthening care jobs such as for childcare and eldercare workers, it was traditional as well as green infrastructure development that became the centerpiece of his green jobs argument, whether in policy or funding terms. This position contrasted with the increasing recognition by climate justice, care politics advocates, and some progressive legislators that care jobs are low- or no-carbon-producing green jobs too and that a Green New Deal approach needed to focus on care sectors such as home care and schools.[42]

Both Medicare for All and the Green New Deal, while lacking a global focus as well as a stronger embrace of a care economy approach, have demonstrated that despite their presumed marginal status as policy plans, change can be achieved through other pathways. Even as their adoption as formal policy blueprints has remained elusive, Medicare for All and the Green New Deal, as visible templates, have nonetheless become crucial for the process of change. The same could be said of the two other political and policy templates described earlier in this chapter for their care-centered outcomes: the UBI and UBS, and the politics of time associated with the reduction of working hours. Similarly, as described in chapter 5, the advocacy of reparations as a form of repair along with redistribution as a strategy for moving toward greater equalities and well-being are integral to a change agenda. Furthermore, each of these—Medicare for All, the Green New Deal, the UBI, a reduction of working hours, and reparations and redistribution—require a cultural shift in how health care, climate change advocacy, income support, or reinventing work are viewed and embraced. Each score high as health and well-being indicators, as defined by the *World Happiness Report* and identified by various research studies. They have also become strong indicators of the direction that a care-centered politics needs to take.

The crises of 2020–2021 have produced pathways about just such care-centered political and cultural changes. At the same time, they have also intensified an anticare culture and politics that gathered force during the Trump years. As attempts to frame the lessons of 2020–2021 and what a future might reveal, whether in relation to climate change, the pandemic, systemic racism, or deep inequalities, a divide between a care and anticare politics is likely to become even sharper and deeper. How that divide plays out will tell us what we can expect in the presence and aftermath of each one of those crises.

7 UNIVERSAL CARE: A CONCLUSION

When the sun rose in the eastern United States on January 6, 2021, it had become clear that the multiyear efforts of thousands of organizers, working on behalf of dozens of grassroots organizations, led by young African American women, and representing a rainbow of diverse constituencies as well as ethnic and racial groups, had achieved their biggest accomplishment to date: the US Senate victories of African American preacher Raphael Warnock and Jewish filmmaker and investigative journalist Jon Ossoff. The efforts of the organizers had helped turn blue the once bright red state of Georgia.

Among the groups phoning, knocking on doors, communicating by text, and reaching out to people throughout the state was the Georgia chapter of Care in Action. The leaders and organizers of Care in Action, the political arm of the NDWA, are women of color, primarily African American domestic workers. In 2018 as part of the coalition of groups supporting Stacey Abrams for governor, and again in the 2020 presidential campaign and January 2021 Senate runoff elections, Care in Action was everywhere. It organized in rural counties where Charles Sherrod of SNCC had his life threatened in the early 1960s as he sought to register Black voters while challenging the entrenched systems of segregation and racism. It included places where Shirley Sherrod advocated for poor farmers in rural areas of the state and a groundbreaking lawsuit identified discrimination against African American farmers.

In 2018, Care in Action's domestic worker organizers texted every single Black female registered voter in Georgia. During the 2020–2021 elections for president and the Senate, organizers expanded their outreach to nearly six million messaging attempts and personal interactions in order to communicate and dialogue with Georgians. Their messages included the importance of care as a political and electoral issue—one that resonated in the midst of the pandemic. "Because of the pandemic," Care in Action executive director Jess Morales Rocketto said of their effort, "we are seeing just a seismic shift in how people are thinking about care."[1]

The Georgia organizers and care advocates celebrated on the morning of January 6, and yet that afternoon, thousands of Trump supporters cheered the president, his son, various right-wing congresspeople, and other enablers of the effort to overturn the election and keep Trump in power. The subsequent assault on the Capitol, with armed attackers smashing through windows and doors, and searching with weapons and zip ties for those they considered their congressional enemies, represented a type of apotheosis of anticare politics. With participants including former veterans and active members of police forces from around the United States, the invasion of the Capitol represented a form of combat and celebration of the warrior culture deeply embedded in the expressions of anticare politics.[2]

Anticare politics had come to signify a racial panic coupled with hostility to diversity and difference. In its most virulent form, it included climate change denial, dismissal of the pandemic and any prevention efforts to mitigate it, and more overt racist behavior and beliefs. Although associated with a type of populist politics, the anticare politics of the four years of Trump had also extended and rewarded the neoliberal forces of financialization, expulsions and dislocations, and market promotion and dominance. Anticare politics was hostile to the other—the immigrant, refugee, dark skinned, or foreigner. It engaged in gun promotion and dismissed concerns about violence. It celebrated the military and its weapons, and supported the militarization of daily life.

For even some of the neoliberals, the final phase of Trumpian anticare politics as represented by the January 6 attack on the Capitol had gone too far. Meanwhile, the neoliberal political consensus had eroded sufficiently that some form of political change seemed more possible than at any time since the 1980s. The crises of climate change, the pandemic, systemic racism, and deep inequalities were forcing the issue of whether as well as what type of social order, cultural values, and political shifts were going to emerge, and whether a care-centered or anticare politics and culture would prevail.

EXPULSIONS AND RENEWAL

In 2014, Columbia University professor Saskia Sassen published a slim volume about the material realities that were transforming places around the world. She identified those material realities as "expulsions," occurring through the continuing ascendance of financialization and its invasion of an increasing number of nonfinancial sectors. Expulsions were at the heart of the anticare worldview. They included the privatization of public resources and public spaces, or what Sassen called "life spaces." Such expulsions could be found in care settings, the environment, and multiple daily life places and situations. They were happening at the community, national, and global scales, as land, water, forests, food, and even climate were auctioned off and "securitized." Financialization and anticare politics facilitated expulsions—dead water, dead land, home expulsions, vast numbers of people in prison, displacements from communities through gentrification, immigrants and refugees fleeing from violence and climate devastations to be treated as hostile aliens, and people displaced from their village, cities, and nations, and then moving within and across borders while seeking to resettle and re-create a sense of place.[3]

There is a forbidding tone in *Expulsions*—the specter of financialization, expulsions, and anticare forces marching their way through all life spaces and everyday life. Yet Sassen's book is not all bleak. She calls for recognition and renewal of the spaces of the expelled so as to bring aboveground what has been hidden or disguised. She advocates for the making of new care-centered environments: "local economies, new histories, and new modes of membership," as she says in concluding her book.

Three years after *Expulsions* was published, Pakistani writer Mohsin Hamid, in his 2017 novel *Exit West*, described the experience of two people, Saeed and Nadia, fleeing from civil war battlefields resembling countries like Syria, Afghanistan, or Pakistan, to refugee camps on the Greek island of Mykonos, to a London suburb where immigrants are terrorized, to their eventual migration to California. Their stories are not just about the refugee and immigrant journeys but also capture the realities of displacement and expulsions to and from each of the places their migrations take them, and the search for renewal, care, and connection.[4]

Since both books were published, new or continuing crises like the pandemic, climate change, systemic racism, and deep inequalities have made expulsions even more visible and prevalent. We are left with more of those dead land and dead water bodies, and millions more refugees and immigrants moving within and across borders. We have become a planet in peril. The Trump years moved the needle ever closer to that perilous state, its anticare political agenda promoting yet more expulsions and displacements, and its anticare economic agenda that made financialization, securitization, and the new gilded age ever more ascendant.

Though describing stories of brutality and complexity, both Sassen and Hamid nevertheless envision places and environments with "plausible desirable futures." Such places and biospheres are reimagined. Expulsions still need to be contested, and communities, environments, and economies await reconstruction as well as new forms of resilience and renewal. Among multiple struggles against an anticare politics of expulsions and the creation of dead spaces, a care-centered politics along with its proposal for a more robust, universal practice of care and an agenda of resistance and renewal needs to be central to that process for challenging the anticare agendas, and regaining those life spaces and renewing life-making activities.

MIGRATIONS

In the United States, expulsions in the form of forced migrations are embedded in the country's history, recent past, and present-day struggles. The displacement of Africans into slavery; destruction of Indigenous tribal communities along with the attacks against and erosion of their livelihoods and cultures; racial exclusion and terrorism directed against the Chinese who helped make the western US expansion possible; turn-of-the-century characterization of Italians and eastern European Jews as an inferior race; and long history of Mexicans and Central Americans migrating or being brought north to work in the factories and fields—all are illustrations of the racial legacies of migrations that have defined the country's identity.

For the United States, migrations have long produced advantages for those responsible for the suffering, hostilities, and divisions experienced by migrants through exploitation, expropriation, and bondage. Slavery made possible the cotton kingdom, which was a crucial economic engine for both southern landowners and northern financiers. The displacement, eradication, and resettlement of Indigenous communities helped drive the land expansion through the South, West, and upper Midwest, and made possible a massive land base for a continental United States. The Chinese migrants from places like Guangdong Province in China laid the tracks for the railroads that crossed the Rockies and helped settle California. The Italian and eastern European Jewish immigrants at the turn of the twentieth century provided the cheap labor that facilitated the development of businesses like the garment trade along the East Coast. The cycle of migrations, expulsions, and new migrations of Mexicans and Central Americans through the twentieth and into the twenty-first century laid the basis for agribusiness and the use of food as an instrument for the penetration of foreign markets as well as a weapon in the Cold War.

This history of genocide, indenture, and exploitation is the essence of an anticare politics. Slavery, among its many other horrors, represented the original family displacement program, separating children sold to other slave owners. Human trafficking and slave-like working conditions became an economic tool, whether for garment factories in Southern California's San Gabriel Valley or the tomato fields in Immokalee, Florida. Violence has always been a possible outcome, from sexual abuse to burning homes and churches. The difficulties in achieving more permanent settlement, not least due to restrictive legislation, has created continuous fears and anxiety about further expulsions.

Yet distinctive kinds of social, cultural, and economic benefits have also been identified for receiving countries when immigrants and refugees leave their vulnerable places to arrive in wealthier countries like the United States or EU countries such as Germany. Migrants bring skills, a passion to better their lives, and a culture and ethic of care for others, including those they had to leave behind as well as their new neighbors. They bring economic value to the places where they settle and work they undertake. They enrich cultures and help establish new forms of community that also "affects the language of everyday life," writes University of Illinois sociologist Anthony Orum.[5]

Climate change has been an increasing factor for forced migrations due to climate-related disaster events such as drought, flooding, or hurricanes as well as *anticipated disasters*, including from countries most vulnerable to future climate impacts, such as below sea-level countries. Some countries, like Russia, seeking to take advantage of climate change due to warming climates in once-inhospitable regions, have encouraged rather than discouraged migrations for economic development purposes, such as making possible new agricultural or resource development. Yet migrants and refugees, even those forced to migrate due to wars, violence, climate change, and economic and political disruptions, are still also ultimately seeking to better their lives in search of well-being.[6]

Despite its uneven history of migration politics, the United States has nonetheless historically been able to absorb more immigrants and refugees than any other developed country, even accounting for its politics of hostility and racial grievance. While hostility toward migrants was magnified during the Trump years, it had been present through much of the country's past and recent history too. A time line of migration trends from the past two centuries indicate increases and declines in the immigrant share of the US population due to fluctuations between restrictive and more welcoming policies as well as the racial attitudes of the domestic population. Immigrant percentages in the United States reached a peak around the turn of the twentieth century at nearly 15 percent of the country's population, and it generally remained just below that level for the next two decades. Quota and deportation policies directed at Chinese, Japanese, and Mexican migrations, including continuing efforts to deport Mexican immigrants, saw the percentages drop significantly over the next four decades, to its lowest level of 4.7 percent by the late 1960s. Those numbers were influenced especially by the draconian deportations of Mexican immigrants living in or seeking to emigrate to the United States during the "Operation Wetback" campaigns of the 1950s, and the termination of the bracero program in 1964 that had imported temporary seasonal workers for agricultural labor in California and other areas of the country. In 1965, influenced by the language and politics of civil rights, the passage of the Immigration and Nationality Act restructured immigration quotas, thus eventually enabling far greater percentages of Asian and Latin American migrations into the United States. This partial opening of the borders increased the percentages of the foreign born in the United States and the country's overall demographic composition, with Asian, Pacific Islanders, and Latinx becoming the fastest-increasing groups by the 1980s and 1990s. By the time the Trump administration had come into power, the percentage of foreign born had grown to 13.7 percent, near the historic highs registered more than 120 years earlier.[7]

From the 1970s through the first decade of the twenty-first century, large numbers of immigrants came to settle in both rural and large urban communities that significantly diversified and transformed those places. Migrants from a particular place of origin such as Oaxaca in Mexico joined other resettled compatriots who had already taken residence in specific communities, cities, and rural towns, and provided a caring environment for immigrants to regroup and flourish. By 2020, for example, more than 150,000 Oaxacans had settled in a handful of neighborhoods in Los Angeles, creating a type of Oaxacalifornia cuisine, an expansive cultural presence symbolized by their annual Guelaguetza festival, and a renewed—and redefined—sense of place. This explosion of diversity celebrated difference and cultural breadth, and enriched the experiences of immigrant and native born alike—a hallmark of a care-centered cultural shift. In opposition to that shift, an angry, resentful, anticare backlash was unleashed, much of it in places where the new immigrants were beginning to arrive yet had previously been scarce. It was captured in the "Make America

Great Again" anticare call to arms and political ads about how "they keep on coming."[8]

In the wake of the Great Recession of 2008, and up to and through the pandemic of 2020–2021, the numbers of new immigrants began another cycle, at first leveling off and then increasing. Political factors played a role, such as the large removals of the Obama years (with the "deporter-in-chief" sobriquet ultimately tarnishing Obama's diversity legacy), to the raging hostility and mean-spirited policies of the Trump period that started with refugee bans and insults about "shithole countries," and extended to family separations and abusive actions at immigrant and refugee holding tanks. Economic factors—the Great Recession, slow recovery, and massive inequality gaps—even generated reverse migration flows, while the pandemic succeeded far more in closing borders than the deceitful and phony politics of physically constructing border walls. In late 2020 and 2021, another cycle occurred, as greater numbers of migrants, including younger ones, sought to resettle with family members and in neighborhoods now populated with those from the places in the home countries they had left. As in earlier cycles, this increase in migrations became a political opportunity for anticare forces to proclaim a crisis and seek yet another round of expulsions.[9]

The Office of the United Nations High Commissioner for Refugees has identified wars, violence, and severe disruptions such as climate-related events as the primary drivers for people fleeing places and crossing borders. These disruptions can create a massive flow of refugees as well as internal and external migrations within and beyond a country's borders. Among the more than eighty million refugees, as many as thirty-seven million people have been displaced due to the endless wars that have taken place since 9/11 and the Bush administration's evocation of the War on Terror. Climate change–related disruptions, especially drought as happened in Syria, added to those numbers of displaced people and are likely to increase exponentially unless climate triggers are addressed, although this may still only modestly blunt those disruptions in the next several decades.[10]

Increasingly, the distinction between the person fleeing wars or domestic violence, climate change refugee, or economic immigrant has narrowed, since the idea that immigrants are searching for a better life, identified largely in economic terms, has increasingly been overshadowed by the need to depart from places impacted by economic, climate, or violence-related disruptions in order to find places to resettle, and from there, renew lives and community. The historical debate between whether an immigrant is pushed or pulled has evolved into a question of whether endless wars or climate change catastrophes, which can also be related, will drive departures along with the search for minimal safety and eventual renewal. In November 2020, for example, Eta and Iota, two tropical storms that quickly turned into hurricanes that ravaged Panama, Costa Rica, Honduras, Nicaragua, El Salvador, Guatemala, and Belize in succession, displaced more than a half-million people. The intense rapid-fire buildup of the storms—Iota went from a 70 miles per hour tropical storm to a category five hurricane of 160 miles per hour in just thirty-six hours—had all the earmarks of a climate change–related disaster, according to meteorologists and other climate experts. Moreover, some of those who were displaced by the storm and witnessed their whole village destroyed joined the trek north to try to reach the United States and seek refugee status. Much of the media along with many of the policy makers who descried this new "border/immigration crisis" in the first months of the Biden administration failed to describe the displacement and migration, at least in this instance, as a climate change–related forced migration event.[11]

These refugee and immigration event outcomes have been driven as much by politics as by economics and environment. The failure in the United States, for example, to establish immigration or refugee reforms to address the marginal and uncertain status of the more than eleven million undocumented immigrants living in the United States, many having settled here for a decade or longer, reflects the hold of an anticare politics and inability to achieve policy change around immigration issues. During the Trump years, refugee issues also got caught up in his xenophobic stamp on policy, further reducing the political space for any welcoming of refugees or change in legal status, no matter the circumstances for those fleeing their country of origin. Immigration came to be associated with the militarization of the border too, with its high-tech surveillance, language of invasion, and increased use of weapons and military tactics by border patrols. The Biden administration's initial rollout of an immigration policy that included green card status for Dreamers and a shortened, though still lengthy process for achieving citizenship for the eleven million undocumented residents was a welcome change from Trumpian anti-immigrant demagoguery, but kept some of the Trump policies intact while also facing congressional barriers. At best, the Biden approach resembled more of a very modest first step than a final goal for immigration reformers and care advocates.[12]

During this long history of uneven and frequently hostile approaches in the United States (and Europe and other places) to the realities and often necessity of migrations, migrants have shown their capacity to mobilize and assert their desire to become part of their new places while remaining attached to the places where they had departed. In 2006, millions of immigrants and their supporters in the United States held rallies, took to the streets, and participated in labor actions in response to some draconian anti-immigrant proposals. As part of those events, truck drivers, as many as 90 percent of whom were immigrants, including many of them undocumented, refused to deliver or take goods from the ports of Los Angeles and Long Beach, demonstrating the enormous economic impact of just one day without immigrants. Cities not known for their large immigrant populations, such as Nashville, Tennessee, had events that drew thousands of participants, while more than 750,000 to 1 million people held rallies in New York City, Chicago and Los Angeles, the epicenters of the immigrant settlements. During 2006–2007, a brief window for limited immigration reform seemed available, but then quickly closed as yet another anti-immigrant wave took hold with the Tea Party politics of the first years of the Obama administration. When Obama subsequently established his limited opening for the Dreamer population of immigrants who had come to the United States at a young age, it was partly in response to the organizing work of the Dreamers themselves—a care-centered organizing that helped shape the initial response of the Biden administration to seek to legalize their status.[13]

With the defeat of Trump in the 2020 election, new openings for the Dreamers, refugees, and immigrant populations as a whole seemed available once again. Both a cultural shift and major political divide were becoming apparent with the pandemic, climate, and antiracism events of 2020 foreshadowing the need for political change. A subtext of the Black Lives Matter demonstrations included the notion that an integrated politics of protest and renewal also extended to immigration issues. The climate change events created an expanded awareness about the global significance of refugee issues. And the pandemic extended the advocacy of health for all—and education for all, housing for all, and universal care—to the population of immigrants that had been previously excluded or marginalized in policy and political debates about those issues. Yet the anticare language of border crisis, and the marginalization and dehumanization of the immigrant, also threatened to upend those opportunities, and underlined the broader conflict between care and anticare political debates.

Immigration and refugee status need to reside at the heart and not the margins of a care-centered politics. Care is the opposite of and challenges the xenophobia that frames an anticare politics. Care-centered politics celebrates both inclusion and understanding the importance of difference regarding people as well as experiences in a world buffeted by dislocations and expulsions. Today, the choice of a care or anticare politics and culture will shape not only how to respond to crises that lead to dislocations and expulsions but how to develop the capacity to remake caring places and environments too.

THE MILITARIZATION OF SOCIETY

One of the central features of an anticare politics is militarism along with the use of the violence that expressed itself during the events of 2020–2021. It included the murders of George Floyd, Breonna Taylor, and others at the hands of a heavily militarized as well as racialized police force. It was reflected in another increase in military spending in 2020 in the midst of major economic difficulties, particularly for the poorest and most vulnerable. It could be seen in the rise of gun-toting right-wing militias and defiant Trump supporters who were hostile to public health messaging while confronting mask wearers, including airline attendants or workers in grocery stores. It included the bombing of a Korean massage parlor and violent attacks in broad daylight of elderly Asian Americans. It was manifested in the continuing antidemocratic actions and messaging aimed at suppressing votes, contesting the validity of election results, and engaging in racial profiling. It involved the hollowing out of public agencies and care-oriented government programs, and the undermining of trust and social solidarity. It included the seizure of the Capitol under the urging of Trump, with his followers storming the building carrying Confederate flags, erecting hang nooses and guillotines, and wearing a sweatshirt emblazoned with "Camp Auschwitz".

The promise of a care politics, on the other hand, centered on pursuing decriminalization and demilitarization. It sought to expand the role of services like mental health, and programs to reduce recidivism and increase recreation, while also identifying strategies for violence reduction and healing such as gardens. The events of 2020–2021 made tangible the need for that type of care-centered politics. In some situations, an agenda for change was available, and could be expressed in small and sometimes larger steps. In other cases, a political shift seemed more distant and the recognition for change was only just reaching the surface. How such a need could be met required both an immediate focus, given the gravity of the issues related to the 2020–2021 events, including those associated with police violence and the militarization of daily life, and a longer-term commitment to far-reaching changes, including, not least, the transition away from an anticare neoliberal politics as well as a corporate- and financialization-dominated economy.

The need for demilitarization coupled with restructured budgets for the police and military as well as a reduction of prison populations became important markers related to the viability, difficulties, and possibilities for a care-centered politics. The call to defund the police that arose and was magnified by the 2020 Black Lives Matter demonstrations needed to be seen in the context of how extensively the police had become a militarized and occupying force in communities of color, especially since the late 1960s and early 1970s. The protest movements of the 1960s as well as the uprisings and riots in places like Los Angeles, Detroit, and Newark had, similar to 2020–2021, produced a "law-and-order" backlash. Law-and-order politics in turn led to increased police budgets, new police policies such as stop and frisk and the broken windows program, and new laws and government policies such as the 1968 passage of the Omnibus Crime Control and Safe Streets Act, which established the Law Enforcement Assistance Administration (LEAA) program.

LEAA, which lasted until 1982, was especially noteworthy as a national program that facilitated the heavy weaponry and overall militarization of local police forces through research, grants, and other funding, while also capturing large percentages of city and county budgets. At the same time, the large, well-endowed, and militarized police forces combined with law-and-order criminal justice policies at the federal, state, and local levels such as three strikes laws contributed to the huge incarceration numbers, particularly of African Americans. Those two issues—a militarized police force serving as a type of occupied force in communities of color and the incarceration numbers—fueled the Black Lives Matter protests, and became in their own right a scandalous illustration of the racist and anticare focus for security and community public safety in relation to what Silvia Federici called "the militarization of daily life and the shaping of a new violent concept of masculinity."[14]

A militarized police force emphasized a type of violence-prone warrior culture that overlapped with right-wing armed vigilantism and the ethic of the military. The use of technology and weaponry in turn served as an extension of the cult of the warrior. The image from the 1964 movie *Dr. Strangelove* of the air force pilot played by Slim Pickens straddling an atomic bomb and waving his cowboy hat as it headed toward its Russian destination was an earlier, yet still fitting depiction of the warrior-weaponry marriage. As the police expanded their military-like capacities, they also began to detain huge numbers of people, especially young people of color, swelling prison populations to the point that some court rulings, for health and safety reasons, started to order early release programs. The police nevertheless worked closely with district attorneys and other prosecutors to continue to feed the pipeline to the prisons of African Americans and other youths of color.

The warrior-weaponry marriage extended to the post-9/11 military operations that began with the immediate move to send troops and weapons into Afghanistan, and the "shock and awe" demonstration of military might in Iraq. From an earlier Cold War that seemed to have no end point until it transferred to other enemies, the post-9/11 endless or forever wars that began in Afghanistan and Iraq extended to Syria, Yemen, and several African countries. It also included the continual saber-rattling, economic warfare, and targeted assassinations against Iran, briefly interrupted by the Obama administration's nuclear weapons accord with Iran, and then shredded by Trump and undermined by Israeli actions, such as the covert sabotage of Iranian nuclear facilities just as talks for a renewed accord were underway. Even during the Obama years, military and police budgets continued their ascent, and the biggest innovation in weaponry and war making was a technological variant: the use of drones!

The warrior-weaponry marriage, however, did start to experience some modest, though important challenges in the aftermath of the Black Lives Matter demonstrations as well as earlier social movement and political organizing. When the Biden administration took office, it interrupted the huge increases in military and police-related spending, proposing instead a small increase in military funding while substantially boosting domestic spending on nonmilitary purposes, including for care programs and care-related agencies. While the "defund the police" slogan was widely attacked too, including by Democrats like Biden who sought to distance themselves from the defunding concept, the substantive arguments related to the slogan began to gain traction. This included the diversion of police budgets to increase funding for care services, such as mental health counseling and intervention. It was reflected in some of the community policing approaches through funding for community resources such as parks and recreational programs. The huge budgets for police and the military also began to be more contested by a wider array of social movements and progressive policy makers.

In an illustration of what a care-centered approach and organizing could accomplish, longtime social movement filmmaker, writer, and activist Norm Fruchter wrote about how community organizers in Newark,

New Jersey, in the 1960s gained the respect of and established a relationship with Hubert Williams, an African American police sergeant who patrolled the area where the organizing took root. Williams later became Newark police chief in 1973, and took an interest in an alternative high school for dropouts that Fruchter and other 1960s' community organizers had established. Williams thought that he could help them secure LEAA funds for the high school if they could demonstrate that the school, which had many students with prison records, could verify lower recidivism rates, which the school was then able to show. Thanks to Williams's effort, the school subsequently received LEAA grant funds, allowing it to continue operations, and demonstrated, as Fruchter wrote, the type of alternative services that police budgets could be used for. When Williams died in summer 2020, Fruchter honored him in a commentary published by New York University's Metropolitan Center on Equity and the Transformation of Schools. "As police brutality and the killing of Black and Brown men and women increases across the country," Fruchter remarked in August 2020, "I write this to honor a police chief who understood that an alternative high school for dropouts could reduce youth delinquency. Williams' vision of law enforcement honored the necessity to expand society's provisions for young people's academic, emotional and aesthetic capacities, rather than continuing to incarcerate them."[15]

Community organizing and social movement activism also led to the election of several new district attorneys and other law enforcement officials in cities like Philadelphia, San Francisco, and Los Angeles. Reforms began to be instituted, either through actions by the prosecutors, via the ballot box, or by legislative action. These included changes to the bail and sentencing systems; alternatives to imprisonment through education and health-based initiatives that turned out to be more successful in reducing recidivism rates like the Newark Alternative High School had accomplished; restoring the right to vote to released prisoners; and prison literacy and school-degree-based education programs as well as mindfulness and gardening programs that provide health and healing benefits. These changes have been important, though still quite modest given the overarching need for change. Some of the reform policy makers, such as the new types of district attorneys, have been challenged in their subsequent elections, and the enemies of change, from police unions to military contractors, remain poised to undo what has up to now been accomplished. Still, a care-centered-type politics, with a social justice and antiracist orientation, has demonstrated the capacity to enlarge the possibilities for a broad-based demilitarization, antiviolence, antiracist, and criminal justice approach, which in turn can redefine the purpose and strategies for the police, military, and community and global safety.

A CARING STATE AND SOCIETY

For a care-centered politics, strategies to shift resources from the military, police, prisons, or agencies like the Department of Homeland Security that enforce anticare policies such as expulsions are part of a broader effort to transform the state and its various roles. As part of a process of change approach, that includes supporting and expanding the role of institutions like libraries, schools, community health clinics, and post offices for their care-related functions. It includes the recognition that the mutual aid, expressions of solidarity, and voluntarism during the pandemic need to be scaled up into public action and more permanent redistributive policies. It gives recognition to and calls for greater commitments along with economic, political, and social support for the role of the nurses and other health care workers during the pandemic as well as other essential workers who continued to work and be exposed, partly for their own economic survival.

Publicly supported institutions such as schools, libraries, postal services, and various health institutions like clinics offer opportunities for accomplishing care-centered goals. These institutions provide multiple care functions even as efforts to privatize or otherwise undermine them have grown considerably in a market- and privatization-dominated neoliberal era—a process that had been magnified during the Trump years.

The fate of libraries and postal operations are important examples of the challenges as well as opportunities for a care-centered institutional approach. Public libraries and the postal service are among the most popular institutions in the United States. Libraries offer free services like internet and computer use, video and DVD rentals, and a wide range of books and other publications. Postal operations provide lower-cost services, from the cost of a single stamp for a first-class letter to less expensive delivery of packages and bulk items than their private counterparts like UPS. Up through the 1960s, post offices offered banking services essential for people living in rural areas and small towns without banks, and those with limited access such as immigrants or the poor. During the 1960s and 1970s, postal services also debated but never pursued the idea of providing digital services—in effect offering email addresses equivalent to the physical addresses they utilize. Both libraries and postal services have been subject to attempts at privatization, though their popularity has largely protected their public role. Their biggest challenge has been political, including restrictions imposed on them at the federal, state, and local levels, such as the 2006 legislation that postal services could not offer new services. At the same time, health care benefits for their employees now had to be paid a number of years in advance, creating a continual funding squeeze.

Yet postal operations and libraries have the capacity to become crucial and trusted community centers as well as providers of information and delivery services. They operate not as businesses but instead de facto services and infrastructure. *Los Angeles Times* columnist Michael Hiltzik argued this point in a piece about an attempt, ultimately unsuccessful after a popular vote defeated the effort, to privatize the library services in California's conservative Kern County. "When public institutions like libraries or post offices are seen as equivalent to businesses," Hiltzik wrote, "they undermine the notion that a post office, like a free public library, is a service that binds a community together. It's not a business."[16]

The brief exploration by the postal service about whether to incorporate a digital-related electronic mail service suggests how postal and library public services could be expanded while providing crucial additional resources that a care-centered politics could incorporate as part of its agenda. Internet-linked corporate entities such as Amazon along with social media and data-based platforms such as Facebook and Google function as for-profit data-mining, information, and delivery operations, not dissimilar from the role that radio and television assumed in their first decades of operation. With radio and especially television, audiences were enticed and captured to be delivered via advertising to companies targeting those audiences for their products, setting up a one-way stream for commercial transactions. Yet efforts during the 1930s and 1940s to regulate the airwaves, otherwise considered a public good and part of a social commons, and establish community and public rather than private entities was never pursued in the United States as broadcast media began to take shape. Similarly, six decades later, internet and data-based operations, benefiting from their origins made possible through publicly funded research made available through the Defense Department's Advanced Research Projects Agency and supported by the National Science Foundation, escaped any accountability or even minimal regulatory oversight that would have occurred if the internet had been established as part of a social commons. Companies like Facebook and Google also deliver audiences to their advertisers, but at a far more detailed and invasive level of penetration than broadcast media had ever imagined even in its heyday.

The changes made to postal operations points to the lost opportunity for creating such an electronic and communications commons, where "every post office in America [could have] become a neighborhood media hub equipped with a bank of computers that [would have] enabled citizens to go online for little or no expense—a service now provided by more than sixty nations around the world," wrote Winifred Gallagher in her history of the post office. The post office, she and other historians have noted, has been an invaluable democratic institution for communication and information delivery for much of its history since its founding in 1775 when Benjamin Franklin was appointed the first postmaster general. This included its ability to establish and expand rural delivery, subsidize the development of rural newspapers, and offer various financial services. Those types of initiatives were undercut in 1970, however, when Congress passed the Postal Reorganization Act, which turned the US Post Office Department into the US Postal Service (USPS), a new federal agency that was altered to be run as a business, putting a balanced budget ahead of public service.[17]

This hybrid combination of a public entity, which still maintains an important residue of public support and community service, and its obligation to act like a business was put to the test when the new postal services began to confront the new era of electronic communications. Already by the late 1970s, warnings were issued by Gaylord Freeman, chair of the Postal Regulatory Commission, that "unless the Postal Service really makes a commitment, which it has not made, to electronic message transfer, they face a really bleak future." One tentative response was the introduction in 1982 of a pilot called electronic computer-originated mail (E-COM). Through E-COM, the USPS could accept letters in electronic form, convert them to hard copy, including printing and enveloping, and deliver them, notably to those who would otherwise not have the ability to access this early version of an electronic letter. As the Office of Technology Assessment pointed out in a report on the potential for an electronic communications role for postal services, though, the role of USPS in electronic mail services was already controversial and would likely become more so if its role expanded. The Office of Technology Assessment noted that various telecommunication and computer firms viewed E-COM as an "entry of a Federal agency into competition with private industry," and as a result, raised questions about "the fairness and legality of a USPS role in EMS (electronic mail service) in general." Even though the E-COM pilot experienced an increase from two to twenty-three million transactions in the two years it operated, Congress and the Reagan administration failed to approve it as an ongoing program in 1984, and it was terminated.[18]

This absence of any community or public role became particularly troubling during the pandemic as tech-related companies raked in unprecedented earnings and their top executives commanded huge increases in wealth, even as the economy cratered, community-based institutions and local, community-oriented businesses suffered, and millions of people fell out of the safety net. For libraries and postal operations, the rise and reach of operations like Amazon and Google, and the USPS's inability to undertake such services or even compete, created additional problems that undercut their own operations, whether in relation to the delivery of goods, erosion of the book publishing industry's relationship to those services, or barriers to accessing the internet as a free public service and community information source. Though most of the critics of the internet giants and behemoths like Amazon have focused on possible antitrust action including breaking up the largest companies into smaller units, the interest in a more expansive and direct approach like a tax on their operations, or a type of public utility or social commons framework for regulatory action, is still only at a beginning stage, though it has been explored more in Europe. Enhancing the viability and capacity of libraries and postal operations through legislative or regulatory action regarding companies like Amazon, Google, and Facebook as linked public utilities could also strengthen their service as well as infrastructure, or "social commons roles," instead of the "corporate-controlled spaces" they now inhabit, as sociologist Zeynep Tufekci put it. An internet-focused social commons approach would in turn be an important institutional and public governance goal of a care-centered politics.[19]

Similar issues for health institutions—community and public roles as opposed to a market-centered and for-profit focus—were also highlighted by care advocates during the pandemic. One important care-centered strategy available has been the *promotores de salud*, or community health worker program for pandemic-related community outreach needs like contact tracing and vaccination information for communities of color and low-income and immigrant communities. Since their introduction in the United States during the 1970s and 1980s, the *promotoras*, nearly all of whom are women, have provided an essential link between health institutions and the communities those institutions seek to serve, particularly since such institutions like hospitals may be inadequate due to their corporate-industrial model and the community mistrust they may experience, or health clinics and various health programs that may lack the resources, and suffer from inadequate communication or sometimes simply fail to communicate due to a language as well as cultural disconnect. Established initially in Latin America, promotoras offer what the World Health Organization defines as "primary health care," or practical methods of care to communities that are universal as well as socially and culturally acceptable. Promotoras are considered "community caregivers" who function as "cultural brokers between their own community and the formal health care system and can play a crucial role in promoting health and wellness in their community," as one group of researchers defined them.[20]

Promotoras have been primarily utilized in Latinx communities in the United States for a wide-ranging set of health issues such as diet and obesity, diabetes, blood pressure, lead contamination, and mental health. They have been volunteers or paraprofessionals, and have worked with or been employed by community-based organizations or larger national nongovernmental organizations like Planned Parenthood or even health departments. The Affordable Care Act included language for enabling promotoras to sign up residents for its health insurance coverage in Latinx communities. Though most often associated with Spanish-speaking communities, promotoras' care-related roles have included other underserved communities where language and cultural barriers are significant. In Los Angeles during the pandemic, for example, the County Board of Supervisors established support for expanding promotores de salud programs for communities whose languages included Arabic, Armenian, Cambodian, Tagalog, Vietnamese, and Mandarin, among others, in addition to Spanish.[21]

The promotores de salud or community caregiver concept has been further elaborated by those advocating a type of health new deal or community health corps. Such an approach could be based on a public program for creating new care-related jobs modeled on the New Deal's Works Progress Administration—a type of "WPA in an age of pandemics," as one care advocate put it. Such a model could be applicable to the adaptation, resilience, and prevention initiatives in an age of climate change too. In 2020–2021, the pandemic represented the most immediate need, given the crises in testing, opposition to prevention measures like mask wearing and physical distancing, and the chaos around the vaccination rollout and hostility to vaccines by anticare forces. "COVID-19 is a crisis of social solidarity and social investment," Yale University professors Gregg Gonsalves and Amy Kapczynski wrote in the early months of the 2020–2021 pandemic in arguing for a care politics approach. Such an approach could help provide the basis for a "government as we wish it to be—caring for us, bringing us together, while also enabling us to live our different lives."[22]

The idea of redefining government's relationship to community and civil society is central to a care-centered politics approach. How to establish and structure a green energy program provides a good illustration of the differences between a community and care-centered approach, and one that favors green megaprojects such as massive solar and wind farms, or non-fossil-fuel-based energy providers such as nuclear power plants. The megaproject approach frequently constitutes a type of "technological solutionism," critic Evgeny Morozov's applicable phrase about centralized, capital-intensive technological fixes, while community-based strategies such as rooftop solar are often dismissed as too minimal and niche oriented. Yet a research study published in December 2020 concluded that a comprehensive program of installing rooftop solar panels and storing batteries in homes would be considerably less expensive than large-scale solar and wind farms (let alone nuclear plants), and had the capacity to eliminate all greenhouse gas emissions from electricity in the United States by 2050. Such a community- and home-based program could also provide community resilience along with a wider range of care-centered job opportunities, and strengthen the core care-related values of solidarity as well as individual and community empowerment working to fortify the public role.[23]

Perhaps the most significant illustration of a care-centered politics approach in reinventing community and government roles is the need for an expanded, far more comprehensive program of public health. The Trump years were the culmination of more than a decade-long erosion of public health resources and capacity, and a lack of recognition of its central role in the access and quality of care. Public health, and its message of prevention, is central to the intent and goals of a health for all program as well as a more care-centered focus for public action and government culture. It can strengthen the multidirectional flow between individuals, groups, communities, and the state, exemplifying the "caring with" paradigm. The events of 2020–2021 discussed in this book—the pandemic, climate change, systemic racism, and deep inequalities—have dramatically pointed to the need for care-centered social movements as well as a care-centered culture and politics that can empower individual and community action while facilitating a shift toward a democratically bounded "caring state."[24]

CARE POLITICS: IMAGINATION AND POWER

Among the contending and coalescing progressive and alternative social movements along with economic and cultural forces vying to shape the future, care-centered politics has a critical role to play. Care-centered politics has the capacity to provide values and ideas, and a perspective about change that not only challenges the neoliberal political consensus and its long-standing capitalist and market-centered underpinnings but the more extreme versions of the anticare politics that neoliberalism has bred too. It can be both local and global, community focused and egalitarian. It can foster solidarity and diversity. It can respect and embrace the idea of difference while challenging the anticare hostility toward the other. Moreover, it can highlight the need for redistribution and reparations for the systemic injustices of four hundred years of racism, including its contemporary expressions. It seeks to end not just the unequal status of women in the United States and globally but also affirms that women are the leading edge of change to remake social and economic relationships.

Care-centered politics is crucial in a period of environmental and health crises. It can help identify strategies for prevention and resilience, mitigation and adaptation. It is a politics that recognizes the centrality of social reproduction and the social commons, and challenges the "greed is good" toxic individualism of a capitalism that has lost any ethical bearings. It is an imaginative politics, seeking to expand what is possible rather than operating solely within the limits imposed by systems that seek to constrain or eliminate what is imaginable.

Some care advocates shy away from the notion of power or contending for power, and seek more neutral ground or limit their focus to self-empowerment rather than empowering individuals to collectively seek community empowerment. A care-centered politics, by its embrace of a shared commons, advocacy around race, class, and gender issues, and push for equality, redistribution, and a democratic governance is all about power: who has it, and how it needs to be restructured and shared.

Care-centered politics is thus about strategic and structural reformism that helps envision radical and revolutionary change. It affirms that care needs to be universal, whether health for all, care for the earth, care at work, or care for the household, shared equally by all people. It is a practical, mindful politics of daily life, and an expression of utopian potentialities and power to the imagination in identifying what is possible. It is a life-affirming, peaceful, and hopeful politics when hope sometimes seems out of reach. It is a politics of practice and an ethic of care. It is part of a larger politics, an expression of cooperation, sharing, and solidarity. Care-centered politics is about essential workers, immigrants, and refugees. It is about caring together and caring with. It is about new forms of global connection. It redefines labor as activity. It defines wealth sharing as sufficiency for all. It makes concrete the desire for change. And it affirms that hope belongs to all, including those who appear to have abandoned all hope.

Notes

CHAPTER 1

1. Joan Tronto, *Caring Democracy: Markets, Equality, and Justice* (New York: NYU Press, 2013), 33. In a 1974 book about the heritage of *La Raza* ("the people") and its resonance with care, two Mexican American writers spoke of a freedom "to be loving and participate in care for others [and] to be alive as a full human being." Elizabeth Sutherland Martínez and Enriqueta Longeaux y Vásquez, *Viva La Raza! The Struggle of the Mexican American People* (Garden City, NY: Doubleday, 1974), 6.

2. US Bureau of Labor Statistics, "Home Health and Personal Care Aides," in *Occupational Outlook Handbook*, April 9, 2021, https://www.bls.gov/ooh/healthcare/home-health-aides -and-personal-care-aides.htm.

3. Nancy Folbre, "What Is the Economy?," *Care Talk: Feminism and Political Economy* (blog), December 17, 2019, https://blogs.umass.edu/folbre/2019/12/17/what-is-the-economy -stupid; Nancy Folbre, "Measuring Care: Gender, Empowerment, and the Care Economy," *Journal of Human Development* 7, no. 2 (July 2006): 183–199; Shahra Raavi and Silke Staab, "Underpaid and Overworked: A Cross-national Perspective on Care Workers," *International Labour Review* 149, no. 4 (2010): 407–422; Oxfam International, "Time to Care: Unpaid and Underpaid Care Work and the Global Inequality Crisis," January 20, 2020, https://www.oxfam.org/en/research/time-care.

4. Ulrike Röhr, "Towards a Green and Caring Society," in *Sustainable Economy and Green Growth: Who Cares?* (Berlin: genanet, n.d.), 6, 5, https://www.genanet.de/fileadmin/user _upload/dokumente/Care_Gender_Green_Economy/Int_WS_Sustainable_Economy _Green_Growth_who_cares_EN.pdf.

5. Joan Tronto, "Care as a Basis for Radical Political Judgments," *Hypatia* 10, no. 2 (Spring 1995): 146; interview with Joan Tronto, Ethics of Care, August 4, 2019, https:// ethicsofcare.org/joan-tronto.

6. Virginia Held, *The Ethics of Care: Personal, Political, and Global* (New York: Oxford University Press, 2006), 15–16.

7. Care Collective, *The Care Manifesto: The Politics of Interdependence* (London: Verso Books, 2020), 94.

8. The phrase *les trentes glorieuses* was originally identified by French economist and demographer Jean Fourastié, and the concept of a post–World War economic expansion was elaborated (and popularized in the United States) by French economist Thomas Piketty. See Jean Fourastié, *Les trentes glorieuses: Ou, La Révolucion invisible de 1945 á 1975* (Paris: Fayard, 1979); Thomas Piketty, *Capital in the Twenty-First Century* (Cambridge, MA: Harvard University Press, 2014).

9. Cited by David Harvey, "Anti-Capitalist Politics in the Time of COVID-19," *Jacobin*, March 20, 2020, https://jacobinmag.com/2020/03/david-harvey-coronavirus-political-economy-disruptions.

10. Erik Barnouw, *The Image Empire: A History of Broadcasting in the United States from 1953* (New York: Oxford University Press, 1970).

11. David Harvey, "Neoliberalism Is a Political Project," *Jacobin*, July 23, 2016, https://www.jacobinmag.com/2016/07/david-harvey-neoliberalism-capitalism-labor-crisis-resistance.

12. André Gorz, *Capitalism, Socialism, Ecology* (London: Verso, 1994), 40–41; André Gorz, *Reclaiming Work: Beyond the Wage-Based Society* (Cambridge, UK: Polity Books, 1999). See also Christophe Fourel and Francoise Gollain, "André Gorz: Thinker of Emancipation," Books & Ideas, August 28, 2014; André Gorz, "L'écologie politique entre expertocratie et autolimitation," 1992 (English version: "Political Ecology: Expertocracy versus Self-Limitation," *New Left Review* 1, no. 202 (November–December 1993): 55–67; André Gorz, *Le Socialisme Difficile* (Paris: Editions du Seuil, 1967), 132–133; André Gorz, *Farewell to the Working Class: An Essay on Post-Industrial Socialism* (London: Pluto, 1982); André Gorz, *Les Chemins du Paradis: L'Agonie du Capital* (Paris: Éditions Galillée, 1983).

13. Johnnie Tillmon, "Welfare Is a Women's Issue," *Ms.*, no. 1, Spring 1972, https://www.bitchmedia.org/sites/default/files/documents/tillmon_welfare.pdf; Josh Levin, *The Queen: The Forgotten Life behind an American Myth* (New York: Little, Brown and Company, 2019), 89–90. At the time of the inaugural issue of *Ms.*, there were a number of domestic worker organizing efforts to claim adequate pay and also make alliance with feminists such as Gloria Steinem on the basis of fair wages for domestic work. History professor and activist Premilla Nadasen, in her discussion of one such group, the Household Technicians of America, described its campaigns as "revaluing domestic labor with a politics of rights, which became the bedrock of their feminist alliance with employers." See Premilla Nadasen, "The Care Deficit," *Dissent*, Fall 2016, https://www.dissentmagazine.org/article/care-deficit-hta-domestic-worker-organizing-history.

14. Sarah Jaffe, "Social Reproduction and the Pandemic: with Tithi Bhattacharya," *Dissent*, April 2, 2020, https://www.dissentmagazine.org/online_articles/social-reproduction-and-the-pandemic-with-tithi-bhattacharya?utm_source=Dissent+Newsletter&utm_campaign=5f7c17ea71-EMAIL_CAMPAIGN_The_First_Democratic_Debates_COPY_0&utm_medium=email&utm_term=0_a1e9be80de-5f7c17ea71-54929965; Giovanna Di Chiro,

"Living Environmentalisms: Coalition Politics, Social Reproduction, and Environmental Justice," *Environmental Politics* 17, no. 2 (April 2008): 281.

15. Silvia Federici, "Social Reproduction: Between the Wage and the Commons," interview by Marina Sitrin, *ROAR*, no. 2, https://roarmag.org/magazine/social-reproduction-between -the-wage-and-the-commons.

16. Athina Arampatzi, "Constructing Solidarity as Resistive and Creative Agency in Austerity Greece," *Comparative European Politics* 16 (2018): 50–66, https://link.springer.com/article /10.1057/s41295-016-0071-9; Vasillis Vlachokyriakos, Clara Crivellaro, Pete Wright, Evika Karamagioli, Eleni-Revekka Staiou, Dimitris Gouscos, Rowan Thorpe, et al., "HCI Solidarity Movements and the Solidarity Economy," *DisasterCHI '17: Proceedings of the 2017 CHI Conference on Human Factors in Computing Systems* (May 2017): 3126–3137.

17. Naomi Klein, *The Battle for Paradise: Puerto Rico Takes on the Disaster Capitalists* (Chicago: Haymarket Books, 2018); Alan Feuer, "Occupy Sandy: A Movement Moves to Relief," *New York Times*, November 9, 2012, https://www.nytimes.com/2012/11/11/nyregion/where -fema-fell-short-occupy-sandy-was-there.html; Rebecca Solnit, "Why Imperfect Occupy Still Had Lasting Effects," *Mother Jones*, September 16, 2013, https://www.motherjones .com/politics/2013/09/occupy-wall-street-anniversary-effects.

18. Berenice Fisher and Joan Tronto, "Toward a Feminist Theory of Caring," in *Circles of Care: Work and Identity in Women's Lives*, ed. Emily K. Abel and Margaret K. Nelson (Albany: SUNY Press, 1990), 40; Joan Tronto, "Democratic Care Politics in an Age of Limits," in *Global Variations in the Political and Social Economy of Care: Worlds Apart*, ed. Shahra Razavi and Silke Staab (New York: Routledge, 2012), 29–42.

19. Naomi Klein, "Care and Repair: Left Politics in the Age of Climate Change," *Dissent*, Winter 2020, https://www.dissentmagazine.org/article/care-and-repair-left-politics-in-the-age -of-climate-change.

20. Kate Aronoff, Daniel Aldana Cohen, and Thea Riofrancos, "We Can Waste Another Crisis, or We Can Transform the Economy," *Jacobin*, March 14, 2020, https://jacobinmag .com/2020/03/green-new-deal-coronavirus-stimulus; Seema Mehta, "Free Money? Amid the Coronavirus, a Monthly Paycheck from the Feds Doesn't Seem Crazy," *Los Angeles Times*, May 20, 2020, https://www.latimes.com/politics/story/2020-05-20/universal -basic-income-coronavirus-stimulus-aid.

21. Ai-jen Poo with Ariane Conrad, *The Age of Dignity: Preparing for the Elder Boom in a Changing America* (New York: New Press, 2016); Ai-jen Poo, "The Work That Makes All Other Work," Ted Talk, December 7, 2018, https://www.ted.com/talks/ai_jen_poo_the_work _that_makes_all_other_work_possible/transcript?language=en.

22. Klein, "Care and Repair."

23. Jennifer Gaddis, in her book *Labor of Lunch: Why We Need Real Food and Real Jobs in American Public Schools* (Berkeley: University of California Press, 2019), argues that school cafeteria employees have historically represented a crucial care sector in their interactions

with students, although that function has also been squeezed by financial and employment barriers preventing them from pursuing such roles. In my own interactions with school food service employees related to the development of farm-to-school programs across the United States, I found multiple examples where cafeteria employees, supported by school food service directors, played important roles in fostering student selections of healthy and fresh school food options. See, for example, Robert Gottlieb and Anupama Joshi, *Food Justice* (Cambridge, MA: MIT Press, 2013); Robert Gottlieb and Rodney Taylor, "Kids Like Healthy Food, so Let's Give It to Them," *Riverside Press Enterprise*, March 16, 2011, https://www.pe.com/2011/03/16/kids-like-healthy-food-so-lets-give-it-to-them.

24. Andrea Levy, "André Gorz: A Signal Legacy for the Left," *Canadian Dimension*, January–February 2008, 13. Another way of formulating the "less is better" concept from a care perspective would be "less stuff, but MORE care," as Nancy Folbre put it in her review of this manuscript.

25. Kim Stanley Robinson, *The Ministry for the Future* (New York: Hachette Books, 2020), 58; Mary Mellor, "An Eco-Feminist Proposal: Sufficiency Provisioning and Democratic Money," *New Left Review* 116–117 (March–June 2019), https://newleftreview.org/issues/II116/articles/mary-mellor-an-eco-feminist-proposal; Christine Bauhardt, "Solutions to the Crisis? Green New Deal, Degrowth, and the Solidarity Economy: Alternatives to the Capitalist Growth Economy from an Ecofeminist Perspective," *Ecological Economics* 102, no. C (June 2014): 60–68.

26. Raymond Williams, *Keywords: A Vocabulary of Culture and Society* (New York: Oxford University Press, 2015), 42.

27. Bill Gates, *How to Avoid a Climate Disaster: The Solutions We Have and the Breakthroughs We Need* (New York: Random House, 2021).

28. Raymond Williams, *Resources of Hope: Culture, Democracy, Socialism*, ed. Robin Gable (London: Verso, 1989), 118.

CHAPTER 2

1. Raymond Williams, *Keywords: A Vocabulary of Culture and Society* (New York: Oxford University Press, 2015), 266–267.

2. Nicole Cox and Silvia Federici, *Counter-Planning from the Kitchen: Wages for Housework and a Perspective on Capital and the Left* (Brooklyn: New York Wages for Housework Committee and Falling Wall Press, November 1975), https://caringlabor.files.wordpress.com/2010/10/counter-planning_from_the_kitchen.pdf. Nancy Folbre has argued that the characterization of women's "unwaged labor" has a long history, associated with the ways that household work and child-rearing have been identified as "unproductive" activity (the "unproductive housewife"), and that "family work would not be categorized as work at all." Nancy Folbre, *Greed, Lust, and Gender: A History of Economic Ideas* (New York: Oxford University Press, 1999), 251–252.

3. Mariarosa Dalla Costa, "A General Strike" (speech at an International Women's Day celebration, Mestre, Italy, 1974), https://caringlabor.wordpress.com/2010/10/20/mariarosa-dalla-costa-a-general-strike. Dalla Costa's speech is also cited in a 1994 seminar talk she gave titled "Capitalism and Reproduction," which was reproduced in 2010, See https://caringlabor.wordpress.com/2010/10/20/mariarosa-dalla-costa-capitalism-and-reproduction-2.

4. Mariarosa Dalla Costa and Selma James, *The Power of Women and the Subversion of the Community*, December 29, 1971, 1, 20, 24, http://www.e-flux.com/wp-content/uploads/2013/05/2.-Dalla-Costa-and-James-Women-and-the-Subversion-of-the-Community.pdf?b8c429.

5. Those numbers would continue to increase during the next four decades, including the participation of working mothers in the paid workforce. At the end of 2019, just prior to the pandemic, 72.3 percent of all women with children under the age of eighteen were in the paid workforce, compared to 93.4 percent of working fathers. The pandemic especially impacted these working mothers, including care workers, some of whom either lost their jobs or were forced to cut back their hours, with reduced wages as a consequence, while working fathers largely escaped that dilemma. See US Bureau of Labor Statistics, "Employment Characteristics of Families—2019," April 21, 2020, https://www.bls.gov/news.release/famee.htm; Joya Misra, "Nearly 3 in 4 US Moms Were in the Workforce before the COVID-19 Pandemic—Is That Changing?," *Conversation*, July 3, 2020, https://theconversation.com/nearly-3-in-4-us-moms-were-in-the-workforce-before-the-covid-19-pandemic-is-that-changing-141510.

6. The Lopate article was subsequently edited and published in the journal *Social Policy*. Carol Lopate, "Pay for Housework?," *Social Policy* (1974): 27–31; Carol Lopate, "Women and Pay for Housework," *Liberation* (May–June 1974): 8–11.

7. Cox and Federici, *Counter-Planning from the Kitchen*; Lopate, "Pay for Housework?," 31. Forty years later, in 2017, Federici helped gather many of the documents and materials from the New York Committee on Wages for Housework from her own collection and files, and with Arlen Austin, had them published, providing a valuable resource for understanding the wages for housework debates. Silvia Federici and Arlen Austin, *Wages for Housework: The New York Committee, 1972–1977: History, Theory, Documents* (Brooklyn: Autonomedia, 2017). See also J. C. Pan, "Love's Labor Earned," *Dissent*, Winter 2017, https://www.dissentmagazine.org/article/loves-labor-earned; Sarah Jaffe, "The Factory in the Family: The Radical Vision of Wages for Housework," *Nation*, March 14, 2018, https://www.thenation.com/article/archive/wages-for-houseworks-radical-vision.

8. Kathi Weeks said of the Dalla Costa and James manifesto, and their discussion of the home as a "social factory," that it "reminds us of the ways in which the institution of the family not only helps to absorb reductions in the price of labor and to produce lower-cost and more flexible forms of feminized labor, but also provides the ideological basis for relieving the state and capital from responsibility for much of the cost of social reproduction." Kathi Weeks, *The Problem with Work: Feminism, Marxism, Anti-Work Politics, and Post-Work Imaginaries* (Durham, NC: Duke University Press, 2011), 123.

9. Silvia Federici, *"Wages against Housework"* (Brooklyn: Power of Women Collective and Falling Wall Press, 1975), https://caringlabor.wordpress.com/2010/09/15/silvia-federici-wages-against-housework; Dalla Costa and James, *The Power of Women and the Subversion of the Community*, 47.

10. Becky Gardiner, "Selma James: A Life in Writing," *Guardian*, June 8, 2012, https://www.theguardian.com/books/2012/jun/08/life-in-writing-selma-james. See also Jenny Turner, "As Many Pairs of Shoes as She Likes," *London Review of Books*, December 15, 2011, https://www.lrb.co.uk/the-paper/v33/n24/jenny-turner/as-many-pairs-of-shoes-as-she-likes; Selma James, "Decades after Iceland's 'Day Off,' Our Women's Strike Is Stronger than Ever." *Guardian*, March 8, 2018, https://www.theguardian.com/commentisfree/2018/mar/08/iceland-global-womens-strike-protest#img-2.

11. Nancy Folbre, "Are We All Care Workers Now?," *Care Talk: Feminism and Political Economy* (blog), April 4, 2020, https://blogs.umass.edu/folbre/2020/04/04/are-we-all-care-workers-now.

12. Candace Howes, Carrie Leana, and Kristin Smith, "Paid Care Work," in *For Love and Money: Care Provision in the United States*, ed. Nancy Folbre (New York: Russell Sage Foundation, 2012), 66.

13. Rachel E. Dwyer, "The Care Economy? Gender, Economic Restructuring, and Job Polarization in the US Labor Market," *American Sociological Review* 78, no. 3 (June 2013): 394–396; Jennifer Cheeseman Day and Cheridan Christnacht, "Your Health Care Is in Women's Hands," US Census Bureau, August 19, 2019, https://www.census.gov/library/stories/2019/08/your-health-care-in-womens-hands.html.

14. These trends have also produced a low-wage and imported care worker cycle, or global care chain, generating the need for yet more low-wage immigrant workers. The available supply of this paid care work sector allows more women with the means to pay for their home care needs to then enter or reenter the workforce, or increase their hours at work, which then, as part of the cycle, leads to increased demands for yet more of that same low-wage labor pool, including immigrant and foreign-born care workers. Howes, Leana, and Smith, "Paid Care Work," 70, 74–75; Robyn Rodriguez, "Service Workers or Servile Workers? Migrant Reproductive Labor and Contemporary Global Racialized Capitalism," Law and Political Economy, December 4, 2019, https://lpeblog.org/author/robynrodriguez; Eleanor Laise, "Private Equity Takeover of Nursing Homes Has Reduced Quality of Care at Critical Moment, Research Suggests," *MarketWatch*, March 14, 2020, https://www.marketwatch.com/story/coronavirus-pandemic-puts-private-equity-ownership-of-nursing-homes-under-microscope-2020-03-14; Atul Gupta, Sabrina T. Howell, Constantine Yannelis, and Abhinav Gupta, "Does Private Equity Investment in Healthcare Benefit Patients? Evidence from Nursing Homes," Working Paper 28474, National Bureau of Economic Research, February 2021, https://www.nber.org/system/files/working_papers/w28474/w28474.pdf. See also Shahra Razavi and Silke Staub, "Underpaid and Overworked: A Cross-National Perspective on Care Workers," *International Labour Review* 149, no. 4 (December 2010):

407–408; Barbara Ehrenreich and Arlie Hochschild, eds., *Global Woman: Nannies, Maids, and Sex Workers in the New Economy* (New York: Henry Holt and Co., 2002).

15. "Time-Use Statistics," UN Department of Economic and Social Affairs, https://unstats.un.org/unsd/gender/timeuse; AARP and National Alliance for Caregiving, *Caregiving in the United States 2020* (Washington, DC: AARP, .May 2020), https://www.aarp.org/ppi/info-2020/caregiving-in-the-united-states.html; Diane Elson, "Recognize, Reduce, and Redistribute Unpaid Care Work: How to Close the Gender Gap," *New Labor Forum* 26, no. 2 (2017): 57. Despite the increased attention for men to share in unpaid household and care activities, the 2019 "American Time Use Survey" still reported women spending twice the amount of time as men in nearly all household and care activities, with the exception of lawn mowing. See "American Time Use Survey—2019 Results,' Bureau of Labor Statistics, June 25, 2020, table 1, https://www.bls.gov/news.release/pdf/atus.pdf.

16. Paula Englund, Michelle Budig, and Nancy Folbre, "The Wages of Virtue: The Relative Pay of Care Work," *Social Problems* 49, no. 4 (November 2002): 455–473; Mignon Duffy, *Making Care Count: A Century of Gender, Race, and Paid Care Work* (New Brunswick, NJ: Rutgers University Press, 2012), 113–127. Following Duffy, Rachel Dwyer has categorized nonnurturant jobs as manual "reproductive labor" essential for maintaining bodies and homes, as distinct from (or an expansion of) maintaining and reproducing the workforce in capitalism. Rachel Dwyer, "The Care Economy? Gender, Economic Restructuring, and Job Polarization in the US Labor Market," *American Sociological Review* 78, no. 3 (June 2013): 395. Eileen Boris and Rhacel Salazar Parreñas also expand the notion of nurturant and nonnurturant jobs to include what they define as "intimate labor," which includes "bodily and household upkeep, personal and family maintenance, and sexual contact or liaison." Eileen Boris and Rhacel Salazar Parreñas, *Intimate Labors: Culture, Technologies, and the Politics of Care* (Stanford, CA: Stanford University Press, 2010), 2.

17. Nancy Folbre, "Demanding Quality of Care: Worker/Consumer Coalitions and 'High Road' Strategies in the Care Sector," *Politics and Society* 34, no. 1 (March 2006): 15–16; Emma Dowling, *The Care Crisis* (London: Verso, 2021), 3. Eileen Boris and Jennifer Klein argue that the "home health care" workforce, "once considered economically marginal, has moved to the center of the economy" in relation to job growth. This includes the low-wage sector of home health aides. Eileen Boris and Jennifer Klein, *Caring for America: Home Health Workers in the Shadow of the Welfare State* (New York: Oxford University Press, 2012), 3.

18. Jonathan Vespa, "The Graying of America: More Older Adults than Kids by 2035," US Census Bureau, March 13, 2018 (revised October 8, 2019), https://www.census.gov/library/stories/2018/03/graying-america.html; US Bureau of Labor Statistics, "Home Health Aides and Personal Care Aides: Job Outlook," in *Occupational Outlook Handbook*, September 2019, https://www.bls.gov/ooh/healthcare/home-health-aides-and-personal-care-aides.htm#tab-6.

19. "Robots May Be the Right Prescription at Nursing Homes," Q&A with Karen Eggleston and Yong Suk Lee, Freeman Spogli Institute for International Studies, Stanford University,

June 11, 2020, https://fsi.stanford.edu/news/robots-may-be-right-prescription-struggling-nursing-homes. See also Nancy Folbre, "Nursebots to the Rescue? Immigration, Automation, and Care," *Globalizations* 3, no. 3 (2006): 349–360; "Your Next Home Health Aide: A Robot?," Complia Health, August 22, 2018, http://www.compliahealth.com/blog/home-health-aide-robot; Corinne Purtill, "Stop Me If You've Heard This One: A Robot and a Team of Irish Scientists Walk into a Senior Living Home," *Time*, October 4, 2019, https://time.com/longform/senior-care-robot.

20. *It's Time to Care: A Detailed Profile of America's Direct Care Workforce*, PHI, January 21, 2020, 4, https://phinational.org/resource/its-time-to-care-a-detailed-profile-of-americas-direct-care-workforce/. On the patient-dumping issue, see, for example, Jack Dolan and Brittny Mejia, "City Attorney Accuses LA Nursing Home of Dumping Patients to Profit from Coronavirus," *Los Angeles Times*, July 9, 2020, https://www.latimes.com/california/story/2020-07-09/coronavirus-nursing-home-sued-patient-dumping.

21. *Notes from the Storm: Black Domestic Immigrant Workers in the Time of COVID-19*, Institute for Policy Studies and National Domestic Workers Alliance We Dream in Black Program, June 2020, https://www.domesticworkers.org/reports-and-publications/notes-from-the-storm-black-immigrant-domestic-workers-in-the-time-of-covid-19; Herr Research Center, Erikson Institute, "Family Child Care Providers: Unsung Heroes in the COVID-19 Crisis," Research-to-Policy Brief, September 2020, https://www.erikson.edu/wp-content/uploads/2020/09/Family-Child-Care-Providers_Unsung-Heroes-in-the-COVID-19-Crisis.pdf.

22. Louise Aronson, *Elderhood: Redefining Aging, Transforming Medicine, Reimagining Life* (New York: Bloomsbury Publishing, 2019), 205, 380–381.

23. Silvia Federici, *Revolution at Point Zero: Housework, Reproduction, and Feminist Struggle* (Oakland, CA: PM Press, 2012).

24. Ai-jeen Poo with Ariane Conrad, *The Age of Dignity: Preparing for the Elder Boom in a Changing America* (New York: New Press, 2015); "Why Care?," Caring across Generations, https://caringacross.org/why-care.

25. "Domestic Workers' Bill of Rights," New York State Department of Labor, https://dol.ny.gov/domestic-workers-bill-rights; Bryce Covert, "The New Federal Domestic Workers Bill of Rights Would Remedy Decades of Injustice," *Nation*, November 29, 2018, https://www.thenation.com/article/archive/federal-domestic-workers-bill-of-rights-harris-jayapal-labor; "Build Back Better: Joe Biden's Jobs and Economic Recovery Plan for Working Families," Biden Harris, https://joebiden.com/build-back-better.

26. Hunter Britt, "Virginia Is 10th State to Pass Domestic Worker Protections," Capital News Service, Associated Press, March 2, 2021, https://apnews.com/article/race-and-ethnicity-richmond-virginia-laws-0f89753ee471d5cf1e92c62b1efc399b.

27. Benjamin W. Veghte, Alexandra A. Bradley, Marc Cohen, and Heidi Hartmann, eds., *Designing Universal Family Care: State-Based Social Insurance Programs for Early Child Care Education, Paid Family and Medical Leave, and Long-Term Services and Support*

(Washington, DC: National Academy of Social Insurance, 2019), https://universalfamilycare
.org/wp-content/uploads/2019/06/Designing-Universal-Family-Care_Digital-Version
_FINAL.pdf.

28. David Dayen, "An Interview with Ai-jen Poo," *American Prospect*, October 21, 2020,
https://prospect.org/familycare/an-interview-with-ai-jen-poo.

29. Ai-jen Poo, "The Work That Makes All Other Work Possible," TEDWomen, November
2018, https://www.ted.com/talks/ai_jen_poo_the_work_that_makes_all_other_work_possible
?language=en; Ai-jen Poo, "This Is Our (Caring) Revolution," On Being with Krista Tip-
pett, April 2, 2020, https://onbeing.org/programs/ai-jen-poo-this-is-our-caring-revolution;
"Community Health Care Associates," Community-Wealth.org, https://community-wealth
.org/content/cooperative-home-care-associates.

30. *U.S. Home Care Workers: Key Facts* (Bronx: PHI, 2018), https://phinational.org/wp
-content/uploads/2018/08/U.S.-Home-Care-Workers-2018-PHI.pdf; *Hidden Work, Hidden Pain: Injury Experiences of Domestic Workers in California*, Research Brief (Los Angeles:
UCLA Labor Occupational Safety and Health Program, July 2020), https://losh.ucla.edu
/wp-content/uploads/sites/37/2020/06/Hidden-Work-Hidden-Pain.-Domestic-Workers
-Report.-UCLA-LOSH-June-2020.pdf.

31. Poo, "This Is Our (Caring) Revolution."

32. Rosalynn Carter, "Ask 2020 Candidates for Their Agenda on Caregiving," *Des Moines Register*, August 10, 2019, https://www.rosalynncarter.org/register-op-ed.

33. Poo with Conrad, *The Age of Dignity*, 14.

34. Joan Tronto, "Democratic Care Politics in an Age of Limits," in *Global Variations in the
Political and Social Economy of Care*, ed. Shahra Razavi and Silke Staab (New York: Routledge, 2012), 29–42.

35. Nancy Folbre and Thomas Weisskopf, "Did Father Know Best? Families, Markets, and the
Supply of Caring Labor," in *Economics, Values, and Organization*, ed. Avner Ben-Ner and
Louis Putterman (Cambridge: Cambridge University Press, 1999), 173.

36. Marc P. Federici, "Designate Grocery Workers as First Responders," *Washington Post*, May
14, 2020, https://www.washingtonpost.com/opinions/local-opinions/designate-grocery
-workers-as-first-responders/2020/05/14/94db668a-952c-11ea-91d7-cf4423d47683
_story.html.

37. Jake Bittle, "The Postal Service Is Breaking Down," *Nation*, March 27, 2020, https://www
.thenation.com/article/society/post-office-coronavirus.

38. Susan Orlean, *The Library Book* (New York: Simon and Schuster, 2018), 267. See also
Eric Klinenberg, *Palaces for the People: How Social Infrastructure Can Help Fight Inequal-
ity, Polarization, and the Decline of Civic Life* (New York: Crown, 2018). The Little Free
Library movement was first launched in 2009 amid the Great Recession, and in just a
decade expanded to a hundred thousand libraries in more than one hundred countries.
While the pandemic presented challenges due to fears about contamination, the concept of

free or nonmarket "sharing" still resonated, and took on multiple forms during 2020 and 2021. "The History of Little Free Library," Little Free Library, https://littlefreelibrary.org /ourhistory; Adriana Ramírez, "Are Little Free Libraries Helping Locals Survive COVID? LA Weighs In," *Los Angeles Times*, August 20, 2020, https://www.latimes.com /entertainment-arts/books/story/2020-08-20/little-free-libraries-in-the-time-of-covid.

39. Dorany Pineda, "As COVID-19 Cases Surge, L.A. Librarians Join the Ranks of Contact Tracers," *Los Angeles Times*, July 31, 2020, https://www.latimes.com/california/story/2020 -07-31/la-librarians-becoming-contact-tracers; Nita Lelyveld, "How Do You Go to the LA Public Library When COVID-19 Has Closed Its Buildings? It's Easy, Fun, and Surprisingly Comforting," *Los Angeles Times*, September 26, 2020, https://www.latimes.com/california /story/2020-09-26/how-la-public-library-adjusted-covid-19-pandemic.

40. Liz Daehnke, "Stories of Rural Resilience: Libraries Live On with Community Support," Center for Rural Affairs, July 2, 2020, https://cfra.org/news/200702/stories-rural-resiliency -libraries-live-community-support?emci=a01791f7-32c1-ea11-9b05-00155d03bda0&emdi =7afea214-34c1-ea11-9b05-00155d03bda0&ceid=2575808.

41. "Meat and Poultry Processors: Interim Guidance from CDC and the Occupational Safety and Health Administration (OSHA)," Center for Disease Control, updated February 6, 2021, https://www.cdc.gov/coronavirus/2019-ncov/community/organizations/meat-poultry -processing-workers-employers.html; Michael Corkery and David Yaffe-Bellany, "As Meat Plants Stayed Open to Feed Americans, Exports to China Surged," *New York Times*, June 16, 2020 (updated July 4, 2021), https://www.nytimes.com/2020/06/16/business/meat -industry-china-pork.html; Leah Douglas, "Covid-19 Cases Appear to Be Slowing at Meatpacking Plants. But Companies Are Not Releasing Test Results," *Fern's Ag Insider*, July 27, 2020, https://thefern.org/ag_insider/covid-19-cases-appear-to-be-slowing-at-meat-plants -but-companies-arent-releasing-test-results; Alexandra Kelley, "Union Says 93 Meatpack- ing Employees Have Died from Coronavirus," *Hill*, June 25, 2020, https://thehill.com /changing-america/well-being/medical-advances/504562-union-says-93-meatpacking -employees-have-died.

42. Arlie Russell Hochschild, *The Outsourced Self: Intimate Life in Market Times* (New York: Metropolitan Books, 2012).

43. The preschool teacher comment was made by Marcy Whitebook, director of the Center for the Study of Child Care Employment at the University of California at Berkeley, and is cited in Jeneen Interlandi, "Why Are Our Most Important Teachers Paid the Least," *New York Times Magazine*, January 9, 2018, https://www.nytimes.com/2018/01/09/magazine /why-are-our-most-important-teachers-paid-the-least.html.

44. André Gorz, *Reclaiming Work: Beyond the Wage-Based Society* (Cambridge, UK: Polity Books, 1999), 39, 52–53.

45. Gorz, *Reclaiming Work*, 98, 54.

46. Weeks, *The Problem with Work*, 124 (emphasis added), 13.

47. Weeks, *The Problem with Work*, 30.

48. Janet Gornick, Candace Howe, and Laura Braslow, "The Care Policy Landscape," in *For Love and Money: Care Provision in the United States*, ed. Nancy Folbre (New York: Russell Sage Foundation, 2012), 112–139.

49. Nancy Fraser, "Contradictions of Capital and Care," *New Left Review*, July–August 2016, https://newleftreview.org/issues/II100/articles/nancy-fraser-contradictions-of-capital-and-care; Nancy Fraser, "Capitalism's Crisis of Care," interview by Sarah Leonard, *Dissent*, Fall 2016, https://www.dissentmagazine.org/article/nancy-fraser-interview-capitalism-crisis-of-care.

50. Tronto, "Democratic Politics in an Age of Limits." 31.

CHAPTER 3

1. Leonard Arrington, Feramorz Fox, and Dean May, *Building the City of God: Community and Cooperation among the Mormons* (Salt Lake City: Deseret Book Company, 1976); Robert Gottlieb and Peter Wiley, *America's Saints: The Rise of Mormon Power* (New York: G. P. Putnam's Sons, 1982).

2. Gifford Pinchot, *Breaking New Ground* (New York: Harcourt, Brace, 1947), 190.

3. In the wake of the George Floyd's murder by chokehold and the Black Lives Matter demonstrations, Sierra Club leader Michael Brune issued a statement on July 22, 2020, about Muir's racism and its foreshadowing of environmental connections to eugenics. Michael Brune, "Pulling Down Our Monuments," Sierra Club, July 22, 2020, https://www.sierraclub.org/michael-brune/2020/07/john-muir-early-history-sierra-club. See also Stephen Fox, *John Muir and His Legacy: The American Conservation Movement* (Boston: Little, Brown, 1981), 117–118; Robert Gottlieb, *Forcing the Spring: The Transformation of the American Environmental Movement* (Washington, DC: Island Press, 2015).

4. Robert Marshall, *Arctic Village* (New York: Harrison Smith and Robert Haas, 1933), 198; George Marshall, "Bob Marshall and the Alaska Arctic Wilderness," *Living Wilderness*, (Autumn 1970): 29–32; Gottlieb, *Forcing the Spring*, 48–49.

5. Robert Marshall, *The People's Forests* (New York: Harrison Smith and Robert Haas, 1933), 123; James M. Glover and Regina B. Glover, "Robert Marshall: Portrait of a Liberal Forester," *Journal of Forest History* 30, no. 3 (July 1986): 112–119.

6. See my discussion of Marshall, Muir, Pinchot, Hamilton, Addams, and Kelley in *Forcing the Spring*, 47–63. Hamilton, for example, championed a type of "shoe leather epidemiology" in identifying health hazards for workers and community members that focused on where people lived as well as worked as central to an urban and workplace environmentalism.

7. Liana Aghajanian, "Ron Finley: South Central LA's Guerilla Gardener," *LA Weekly*, May 14, 2014, https://www.laweekly.com/ron-finley-south-central-l-a-s-guerilla-gardener.

8. "Our History," Green Guerillas, http://www.greenguerillas.org/history.

9. Ron Finley, "A Guerrilla Gardener in South Central LA," TED2013, https://www.ted.com /talks/ron_finley_a_guerrilla_gardener_in_south_central_la?language=en.

10. Jeanette Marantos, "His 'Eco-lutionary Call to Action," *Los Angeles Times*, July 11, 2020, https://www.latimes.com/lifestyle/story/2020-07-10/gardening-with-gangsta-gardener -and-masterclass-teacher-ron-finley; Finley, "A Guerrilla Gardener in South Central LA"; LA Green Grounds, https://www.lagreengrounds.org/about.

11. The term *mainstream environmental groups* was introduced during the 1970s and 1980s as a way to identify the largest, most effective organizations operating as professional and expertise-oriented groups at the national level that were able to influence, and in some cases, become integrated into, an emerging legal, legislative, and regulatory environmental infrastructure at the national and state levels. See my discussion of the mainstream groups and their environmental justice counterparts in my *Forcing the Spring*, 83–114. For a look at the rise of the environmental justice groups in this same period, see, for example, Luke Cole and Sheila Foster, *From the Ground Up: Environmental Racism and the Rise of the Environmental Justice Movement* (New York: NYU Press, 2001); Robert Bullard, *Dumping in Dixie: Race, Class, and Environmental Quality* (Boulder, CO: Westview Press; 2000); Bunyan Bryant and Paul Mohai, eds., *Race and the Incidence of Environmental Hazards: A Time for Discourse* (Boulder, CO: Westview Press, 1992).

12. "The Principles of Environmental Justice (EJ)," October 27, 1991, https://www.nrdc.org /sites/default/files/ej-principles.pdf; Dana Alston, "Our Vision of the Future" (talk at the First National People of Color Environmental Leadership Summit, Washington, DC, October 26, 1991).

13. John Lewis, *Walking in the Wind: A Memoir of the Movement* (New York: Simon and Schuster, 1998), 182.

14. "Shirley Miller Sherrod Oral History Interview Conducted by Joseph Mosnier in Albany, Georgia," September 15, 2011, https://www.loc.gov/item/afc2010039_crhp0050.

15. Charles Sherrod, interview in the documentary *Arc of Justice: The Rise, Fall, and Rebirth of a Beloved Community* (Newburgh, NY: New Day Films, 2016).

16. "Charles Melvin Sherrod Oral History Interview Conducted by Joseph Mosnier in Albany, Georgia," June 4, 2011, https://www.loc.gov/item/2015669121.

17. Shirley Sherrod, *The Courage to Hope: How I Stood Up to the Politics of Fear* (New York: Atria Books, 2012).

18. Carlton Fletcher, "Resora Community Will Make Public, Private Debuts, Saturday," *Albany Herald*, June 6, 2014, http://www.albanyherald.com/news/resora-community-will -make-public-private-debuts-saturday-/article_af6f476d-947b-5e54-b308-b75ab0e692cc .html. Unfortunately, despite the vindication for the Sherrods, the implementation of the Pigford settlement for the Black farmers then still operating proved to be inadequate. Many of those farmers, faced with huge debts, didn't have the legal recourse to save their lands. Ultimately, the Pigford settlement, according to Lloyd Wright, director of the USDA's

Office of Civil Rights during the Clinton and Obama administrations, turned out to be "a big promise that didn't deliver much." New expectations about support for Black farmers were raised again in 2021 with the passage of the American Rescue Plan Act, the Biden administration's stimulus relief legislation, with about half of the $10 billion designated for agriculture earmarked for disadvantaged farmers, including Black farmers. Although seen by some advocates as a game-changing provision, the long history of discrimination and broken promises reinforced the need for continuing pressure for structural change at the USDA, and a far more extensive effort at reparations for Black farmers. Laura Reiley, "Relief Bill Is Most Significant Legislation for Black Farmers since Civil Rights Act, Experts Say," *Washington Post*, March 8, 2021, https://www.washingtonpost.com/business/2021/03/08 /reparations-black-farmers-stimulus.

19. Shirley Sherrod continued to play an important role in community land initiatives as well as other care and cooperation-based initiatives in Georgia. She also experienced one of the bleakest moments of the Obama presidency when Tom Vilsack, the then secretary of agriculture, fired her without warning from her then position as the Georgia director of rural development at the USDA. Vilsack acted on misinformation provided by right-wing extremist Andrew Breitbart from a doctored tape by a talk that Shirley had given. When Vilsack—and Obama—realized the tape had been doctored to say the opposite of what Sherrod had said, they offered her back her job, but she refused, and instead sued Breitbart and then settled with his estate after he had died. The Breitbart and Vilsack episode is described in Shirley Sherrod's *The Courage to Hope* memoir and would later become a flash point in the opposition to Vilsack's second appointment as USDA secretary by the Biden administration. Helena Bottemiller Evich, Ximena Bustillo, and Liz Crampton, "Black Farmers, Civil Rights Advocates Seething over Vilsack's Pick," *Politico*, December 9, 2020, https://www.politico.com/news/2020/12/09/black-farmers-tom-vilsack-agriculture-usda -biden-cabinet-444077.

20. Terry Lewis, "Stacey Abrams Attempts to Solidify Her Voter Base," *Albany Herald*, August 25, 2018.

21. "COVID-19 Stimulus: Bailout for Corporate Agribusiness or a Lifeline for Our Food System," Food Tank, April 2020, https://foodtank.com/news/2020/04/covid-19-stimulus -bailout-for-corporate-agribusiness-or-a-lifeline-for-our-food-system; "Trump's Farmer Bailout," Environment Working Group, https://www.ewg.org/key-issues/farming/bailout.

22. Natasha Bowens, "CSA Is Rooted in Black History," *Mother Earth News*, February 13, 2015, https://www.motherearthnews.com/organic-gardening/csas-rooted-in-black-history -zbcz1502?fbclid=IwAR33z2BOv1RYJ4NhcJKfWotnN05iApwNSHGztCKnS97k CPARbdptVJyCVi4; Lyn Fraser, review of *How to Make $100,000 Farming 25 Acres*, by Booker T. Whatley, *Southern Changes* 10, no. 3 (1988): 22–23, http://southernchanges .digitalscholarship.emory.edu/sc10-3_1204/sc10-3_004.

23. Hannah Ricker and Mara-Kardas Nelson, "Community Supported Agriculture Is Surging amid the Pandemic," *Civil Eats*, April 9, 2020, https://civileats.com/2020/04/09/community -supported-agriculture-is-surging-amid-the-pandemic; Kim Severson, "The Farm-to-Table

Connection Comes Undone," *New York Times*, April 9, 2020, https://www.nytimes.com
/2020/04/09/dining/farm-to-table-coronavirus.html.

24. Chip Giller, "Why Local Food Matters—Especially during a Pandemic," *Grist*, May 23, 2020, https://grist.org/fix/why-local-food-matters-especially-during-a-pandemic. Soul Fire in the City in the Albany/Troy, New York, area as well as La Cosecha Colectiva of the East Yard Communities for Environmental Justice in the East Los Angeles and West Long Beach areas of Sothern California provide illustrations of groups with innovative strategies helping establish food and garden initiatives in low-income communities. See "Soul Fire in the City," Soul Fire Farm, https://www.soulfirefarm.org/food-sovereignty-education/soul-fire -in-city; "La Cosecha Colectiva," East Yard Communities for Environmental Justice, http:// eycej.org/la-cosecha-colectiva.

25. Judith Redmond and Thomas Nelson, CSA pioneers and alternative food and farm system advocates, elaborated a food ethic concept in a document that circulated in 2001 among food activists. They defined a food ethic as a series of practices, including a "land steward-ship in the way that people garden," a "marketing relationship that allows the consumer to know the farmer," and a culture in which "eating and preparation of meals become a mean-ingful part of our lives." All of these practices were relevant during the pandemic. Judith Redmond and Thomas Nelson, "Defining a Food Ethic: Common Values for the Sustain-able Food and Farm Movement," Guinda, CA, January 28, 2001 (in author's possession). See also Anne Barnard, "Why Outdoor Farmers Markets Matter More Than Ever," *New York Times*, April 1, 2020, https://www.nytimes.com/2020/04/01/nyregion/coronavirus -greenmarkets-nyc.html.

26. Rachel Wharton, "'If All the Stores Close, We Need Food,' Community Gardens Adapt to the Pandemic," *New York Times*, April 10, 2020, https://www.nytimes.com/2020/04/10 /dining/community-garden-coronavirus.html.

27. Laura J. Lawson, *City Bountiful: A Century of Community Gardening in America* (Berkeley: University of California Press, 2005); Joachim Wolschke-Bulmahn, "From the War-Garden to the Victory Garden: Political Aspects of Garden Culture in the United States during World War I," *Landscape Journal* 11, no. 1 (1992): 51–57.

28. The potato patch farms of the 1890s in Detroit were developed on vacant lands due to the economic recession at that time, similar to what developed after the 2008–2009 Great Recession more than a hundred years later. See Frederic W. Speirs, Samuel McCune Lind-say, and Franklin B. Kirkbride, "Vacant-Lot Cultivation," *Charities Review* 8, no. 3 (1898): 74–107.

29. Grace Lee Boggs, "Living for Change: Love and Revolution," *Michigan Citizen*, July 19–25, 2009; Grace Lee Boggs with Scott Kurishage, *The Next American Revolution: Sustainable Activism for the 21st Century* (Berkeley: University of California Press, 2012), xxii; Grace Lee Boggs, "Detroit's 'Quiet Revolution': How We Came to See Vacant Lots Not as Blight but as Opportunities to Grow Our Own Food," *Nation*, September 2, 2009, https://www .thenation.com/article/archive/detroits-quiet-revolution.

30. The author played a direct role in the Santa Monica farm-to-school story as a parent of a child in the school that established the pilot as well as the director of the Urban & Environmental Policy Institute that established the farm-to-school program in Santa Monica and then helped expand it nationally into all fifty states through the National Farm to School Network. That role is described in Robert Gottlieb and Anupama Joshi, *Food Justice* (Cambridge, MA: MIT Press, 2013), 171–174. My coauthor, Joshi, was an Urban & Environmental Policy Institute staff member and became the first director of the National Farm to School Network.

31. Taylor's comment about the transformation of his role was first made to me and also became a key point in the numerous talks he gave. This included his talk as a keynote speaker at the National Farm to School Network conference in 2018 and subsequently after receiving the California Endowment's Health Happens Heroes award in 2011. On the evaluation of the SMMUSD program, see Michelle Mascarenhas and Robert Gottlieb, "The Farmers' Market Salad Bar: Assessing the First Three Years of the Santa Monica–Malibu Unified School District Program," Community Food Security Project, Urban & Environmental Policy Institute, Los Angeles, October 2000.

32. The Urban & Environmental Policy Institute, for example, undertook a study of school gardens in the Los Angeles Unified School District shortly after the California superintendent of schools issued a statement proclaiming that a garden in every school ought to be an objective of all the state's schools. Although the study identified that as many as 50 percent of the schools in the district (the second largest in the country) had gardens, it also indicated how many earlier gardens had to be abandoned due to a lack of resources and effective supervision, and some of those overseeing existing gardens felt uncertainty about the future of them. Andrea Azuma, Tegan Horan, and Robert Gottlieb, *A Place to Learn and a Place to Grow: School Gardens in the Los Angeles Unified School District; a Survey, Case Studies, and Policy Recommendations* (Los Angeles: Center for Food and Justice, Urban & Environmental Policy Institute, July 2001).

33. Janelle Guthrie, "Corrections Hope Gardens to Help Fight Hunger in Response to COVID-19 Pandemic," Washington Department of Corrections, May 29, 2020, https://www.doc.wa.gov/news/2020/05292020.htm; Kelsey Timler, Helen Brown, and Colleen Varcoe, "Growing Connection beyond Prison Walls: How a Prison Garden Fosters Rehabilitation and Healing for Incarcerated Men," *Journal of Offender Rehabilitation* 58, no. 5 (2019): 444–463.

34. Petra Mayer, "Pandemic Gardens Satisfy a Hunger for More Than Just Good Tomatoes," NPR, May 9, 2020, https://www.npr.org/2020/05/09/852441460/pandemic-gardens-satisfy-a-hunger-for-more-than-just-good-tomatoes.

35. Andrew Keshner, "Why Gardening during a Pandemic Is So Comforting," *MarketWatch*, May 3, 2020, https://www.marketwatch.com/story/this-earth-day-especially-remember-plants-are-non-judgmental-what-its-like-to-start-gardening-during-a-pandemic-2020-04-22.

36. Robert Gottlieb and Simon Ng, *Global Cities: Urban Environments in Los Angeles, Hong Kong, and China* (Cambridge, MA: MIT Press, 2014), 25–59.

37. "Position Paper of La Vía Campesina: Environmental and Climate Justice Now!," La Vía Campesina, 2014, https://viacampesina.org/en/environmental-and-climate-justice-now -position-paper-of-la-via-campesina; "The Six Pillars of Food Sovereignty," in *Food Sovereignty NOW! A Guide to Food Sovereignty* (Brussels: European Coordination via Campesina, 2018), 14–15, https://viacampesina.org/en/wp-content/uploads/sites/2/2018/02 /Food-Sovereignty-A-guide-Low-Res-Vresion.pdf.

38. Joan Martínez Alier, "Environmental Justice and Economic Degrowth: An Alliance between Two Movements," *Capitalism, Nature, Socialism* 23, no. 1 (2012): 56, 60.

39. Julian Agyeman, David Schlosberg, Luke Craven, and Caitlin Mathews, "Trends and Directions in Environmental Justice: From Inequity to Everyday Life, Community, and Just Sustainabilities," *Annual Review of Environmental Resources* 41 (2016): 330. Progressive congressperson Alexandria Ocasio-Cortez has frequently associated her evolution as a social and climate justice champion to her time as a participant at Standing Rock. See, for example, "How Standing Rock Resistance Inspired the Green New Deal," Democracy NOW!, March 22, 2019, https://www.youtube.com/watch?v=De9Ah_nyluo.

40. Kevin Morgan, "Local and Green, Global and Fair: The Ethical Foodscape and the Politics of Care," *Environment and Planning A* (2010): 1860–1861, 1863.

41. Damian Carrington, "'Hypocrites and Greenwash': Greta Thunberg Blasts Leaders over Climate Crisis," *Guardian*, November 9, 2020, https://www.theguardian.com/environ ment/2020/nov/09/hypocrites-and-greenwash-greta-thunberg-climate-crisis. See also Robert Gottlieb, "Care Is Key to Nations' Response in Crises," *China Daily*, March 19, 2020, https://global.chinadaily.com.cn/a/202003/19/WS5e72c86aa31012821728046a.html.

CHAPTER 4

1. "Build Back Better: Joe Biden's Jobs and Economic Recovery Plan for Working Families," https://joebiden.com/build-back-better/#, Biden Harris, ; Taryn Morrissey, "Addressing the Need for Affordable, High-Quality Childhood Care and Education for All in the United States," Washington Center for Equitable Growth, February 18, 2020, https:// equitablegrowth.org/addressing-the-need-for-affordable-high-quality-early-childhood -care-and-education-for-all-in-the-united-states; Katy Lederer, "A Gen-X Adviser to Biden Argues Equality Is Good for Growth," *New York Times*, August 28, 2020, https://www .nytimes.com/2020/08/28/business/heather-boushey-biden-economic-inequality.html; Bryce Covert, "Biden's Quietly Radical Care Plan," *New York Times*, August 2, 2020, https://www.nytimes.com/2020/08/02/opinion/biden-child-care.html.

2. Mignon Duffy and Kim Price-Glynn, "A 'Care' Agenda Is Essential Policy," WBUR, April 8, 2021, https://www.wbur.org/cognoscenti/2021/04/08/biden-infrastructure-care-policy -structure-mignon-duffy-kim-price-glynn-care; "Carework Network Statement to the

Biden-Harris Administration," Carework Network, March 5, 2021, http://careworknet workresponds.com/2021/03/05/carework-network-statement-to-the-biden-harris -administration.

3. Folbre's comments are summarized in *Economics, Care and Education: Cornerstones of Sustainable and Just Economies*, Make Mothers Matter, July 16, 2020, https://makemothers matter.org/wp-content/uploads/2020/07/2020-HLPF-SE-Care-Economics-Report.pdf, 3. See also Nancy Folbre," *Valuing Children: Rethinking the Economics of the Family* (Cambridge, MA: Harvard University Press, 2010), where she argues that efforts to align care with the market can be problematic. "Not all inputs and outputs come with price tags attached," Folbre writes. "Somewhere along the way, babies are conceived, nurtured, educated, and launched into adulthood in a process that requires considerable time and effort as well as money," 2.

4. Silvia Federici, "Social Reproduction: Between the Wage and the Commons," interview by Marina Sitrin, *Roar Magazine* 2, https://roarmag.org/magazine/social-reproduction -between-the-wage-and-the-commons; Graciela Monteagudo, "Women Reclaim the Commons: A Conversation with Silvia Federici," *NACLA Report on the Americas* 51, no. 3 (2019): 256–261; Massimo de Angelis, "Social Reproduction and the Transformation at the Edge of Chaos," *South Atlantic Quarterly* 118, no. 4 (October 1, 2019) 747–766; "A Conversation with Massimo de Angelis and Stavros Stavrides," *An Architekture*, June– August 2010, http://worker01.e-flux.com/pdf/article_8888150.pdf.

5. "Regional Cap and Trade Programs," World Resources Institute, February 16, 2011, https://www.wri.org/resources/maps/regional-cap-and-trade-programs; *State and Trends of Carbon Pricing, 2020* (Washington, DC: World Bank Group, May 2020), https:// openknowledge.worldbank.org/bitstream/handle/10986/33809/9781464815867.pdf ?sequence=4; Nathanael Johnson, "Cap and Trade-Offs," *Grist*, October 19, 2020, https:// grist.org/climate/the-biggest-fight-over-cap-and-trade-isnt-about-what-you-think-it-is.

6. In relation to housing, for example, health researchers Joshua Barocas and Esther Choo emphasize that the pandemic underlined how "housing for all is a critical part of our public health response and of sustaining the viability of our health systems," including by reducing the rate of hospitalizations, among other outcomes. Joshua A. Barocas and Esther K. Choo, "Housing Is an Essential Part of Health Care: 'Treat 'Em and House 'Em," JAMA Network, March 2, 2021, https://jamanetwork.com/journals/jamanetworkopen/fullarticle/2776925.

7. Kate Raworth, *Doughnut Economics: Seven Ways to Think Like a 21st Century Economist* (White River Junction, VT: Chelsea Green, 2017), 23.

8. Rutger Hoekstra, *Replacing GDP by 2030: Towards a Common Language for the Wellbeing and Sustainable Communities* (Cambridge: Cambridge University Press, 2019), xx.

9. Wellbeing Economy Alliance, https://wellbeingeconomy.org/wego; "Nicole Sturgeon: Wellbeing as Important as Economic Growth," BBC, January 22, 2020, https://www.bbc .com/news/uk-scotland-scotland-politics-51200821; Nicola Sturgeon, "Why Governments

Should Prioritize Well-being," TedSummit 2019, July 29, 2019, https://www.ted.com /talks/nicola_sturgeon_why_governments_should_prioritize_well_being?language=en.

10. Thomas Barrett, "Wales to Trial 'Experimental' Foundation Economy Approach," *Rethinking Poverty*, November 20, 2020, https://www.rethinkingpoverty.org.uk/rethinking-poverty /wales-to-trial-experimental-foundation-economy-approach.

11. Justin Bentham, Andrew Bowman, Marta de la Cuesta, Ewald Engelen, Ismail Ertürk, Peter Folkman, Julie Froud, et al., "Manifesto for the Foundational Economy," CRESC Working Paper No. 131, November 2013, https://foundationaleconomycom.files.wordpress.com /2017/01/wp131.pdf.

12. Foundational Economy Collective, "2020 Manifesto for the Foundational Economy," https://foundationaleconomycom.files.wordpress.com/2020/04/2020-manifesto-for -the-foundational-economy.pdf.

13. Andrew Bowman, Ismail Ertürk, Julie Froud, Sukhdev Johal, John Law, Adam Leaver, Michael Moran, and Karel Williams, *The End of the Experiment? From Competition to the Foundational Economy*, (Manchester: Manchester University Press, 2014); Foundational Economy Collective, *Foundational Economy: The Infrastructure of Everyday Life* (Manchester: Manchester University Press, 2018).

14. J. K. Gibson-Graham [Julie Graham and Kathie Gibson], *A Post-Capitalist Politics* (Minneapolis: University of Minnesota Press, 2006), xxiv.

15. Ethan Miller, "Solidarity Economy: Key Concepts and Issues," in *Solidarity Economy: Building Alternatives for People and Planet*, ed. Emily Kawano, Tom Masterson, and Jonathan Teller-Ellsberg (Amherst, MA: Center for Popular Economics, 2010), http://www .communityeconomics.org/sites/default/files/paper_attachment/Miller_Solidarity_Economy _Key_Issues_2010.pdf; Nathan Schneider, *Everything for Everyone: The Radical Tradition That Is Shaping the Next Economy* (New York: Nation Books, 2018), 83; "Building Regional Solidarity Economies," New Economy Coalition, https://neweconomy.net/solidarity -economy/#what-is-the-solidarity-economy; Lara Maestripieri, "Creating Alternative Economic Spaces: The Socially Innovative Practices of Solidarity Purchasing Groups," in *Creating Economic Space for Social Innovation*, ed. Alex Nicholls and Rafael Ziegler (New York: Oxford University Press, 2019), 225–244; Gibson-Graham, *A Post-Capitalist Politics*, 7–8.

16. Isaac Stanley, *Love's Labours Found: Industrial Strategy for Social Care and the Everyday Economy* (London: Nesta, February 2020), 8.

17. Edward R. Barbier, *A Global Green New Deal: Rethinking the Economic Recovery* (Cambridge: Cambridge University Press, 2010).

18. *Global Green New Deal: An Update for the G20 Pittsburgh Summit* (Nairobi: UN Environment Programme, September 2009).

19. Christine Wong, "The Fiscal Stimulus Programme and Public Governance Issues in China," *OECD Journal on Budgeting* 11, no. 3 (2011), https://www.oecd.org/gov/budgeting /Public%20Governance%20Issues%20in%20China.pdf.

20. Christine Bauhardt, "Solutions to the Crises? The Green New Deal, Degrowth, and the Solidarity Economy," *Ecological Economics* 102 (2014): 61.

21. World Commission on Environment and Development, *Our Common Future* (Oxford: Oxford University Press, 1987).

22. Becky Yerak, "Exide Bankruptcy Leaves Toxic Site as California's Problem," *Wall Street Journal*, October 16, 2020, https://www.wsj.com/articles/exide-bankruptcy-leaves-toxic -site-as-californias-problem-11602888947; Tony Barboza, "Story So Far: How a Battery Recycler Contaminated L.A.-Area Homes for Decades," *Los Angeles Times*, December 21, 2015, https://www.latimes.com/local/lanow/la-me-exide-cleanup-story-so-far-20151121 -story.html.

23. "Special Report: Global Warming of 1.5 °C," Intergovernmental Panel on Climate Change, October 2018, https://www.ipcc.ch/sr15; Robinson Meyer, "The Democratic Party Wants to Make Climate Policy Exciting," *Atlantic*, December 5, 2018, https://www.theatlantic.com /science/archive/2018/12/ocasio-cortez-green-new-deal-winning-climate-strategy/576514.

24. H.R. 109, 116th Cong., 1st Sess., https://www.congress.gov/116/bills/hres109/BILLS- 116hres109ih.pdf; "Green New Deal FAQ," Congresswoman Alexandria Ocasio-Cortez, February 5, 2019, https://web.archive.org/web/20190207191119/https:/ocasio-cortez .house.gov/media/blog-posts/green-new-deal-faq.

25. John Cassidy, "The Good News about a Green New Deal," *New Yorker*, March 4, 2019, https://www.newyorker.com/news/our-columnists/the-good-news-about-a-green-new -deal; Dan Drollette Jr., "We Need a Better Green New Deal: An Economist's Take," *Bulletin of the Atomic Scientists*, March 25, 2019, https://thebulletin.org/2019/03/we -need-a-better-green-new-deal-an-economists-take.

26. Parris Bergquist, Matto Mildenberger, and Leah Stokes, "Combining Climate, Economic, and Social Policy Builds Political Support for Climate Action in the US," *Environmental Research Letters* 15, no. 5 (May 12, 2020), https://iopscience.iop.org/article/10.1088 /1748-9326/ab81c1; Robinson Meyer, "So Has the Green New Deal Won Yet?," *Atlantic*, November 15, 2019, https://www.theatlantic.com/science/archive/2019/11/did-green -new-deal-win-look-after-one-year/602032.

27. Naomi Klein, *On Fire: The (Burning) Case for a Green New Deal* (New York: Simon and Schuster, 2019), 178; Naomi Klein, *This Changes Everything: Capitalism vs the Climate* (New York: Simon and Schuster, 2015).

28. Ipec llkkaracan, "The Purple Economy as a Gender-Egalitarian Strategy for Employment Generation," in *Economics and Austerity in Europe: Gendered Impacts and Sustainable Alternatives*, ed. Hannah Bargawi, Giovanni Cozzi, and Susan Himmelwait (London: Routledge, 2016), 27–39; Christa Wichterich, "Contesting Green Growth, Connecting Care, Commons, and Enough," in *Practising Feminist Political Ecologies: Moving beyond the "Green Economy,"* ed. Wendy Harcourt and Ingrid L. Nelson (London: Zed Books, 2015), 79; Eileen Boris, "Making Care Work Green," LPE, December 3, 2019, https://lpeblog .org/2019/12/03/making-care-work-green/#more-3036.

29. Mary Mellor, "An Eco-Feminist Proposal: Sufficiency Provisioning and Democratic Money," *New Left Review* 116–117 (March–June 2019): 192, https://newleftreview.org /issues/II116/articles/mary-mellor-an-eco-feminist-proposal.

30. Ashley Dawson, "A Greener New Deal?," *New Politics* 17, no. 2 (Winter 2019), https:// newpol.org/issue_post/a-greener-new-deal.

31. Naomi Klein, "Care and Repair: Left Politics in the Age of Climate Change," *Dissent*, Winter 2020, https://www.dissentmagazine.org/article/care-and-repair-left-politics-in-the-age -of-climate-change; Juliet B. Schor, *The Overspent American: Why We Spend What We Don't Need* (New York: Harper Perennial, 1999); Juliet B. Schor, "Sustainable Consumption and Worktime Reduction," *Journal of Industrial Ecology* 9, no. 1–2 (2005): 38–50; Dean Snyder and Matt Guardino, "The Green New Deal and a New Politics of Consumption," *Jacobin*, March 21, 2020, https://www.jacobinmag.com/2020/03/green-new-deal-politics -consumption.

32. Raymond Williams, *Keywords: A Vocabulary of Culture and Society* (New York: Oxford University Press, 2015), 78–79; David Graeber, "The Very Idea of Consumption: Desire, Phantasms, and the Aesthetics of Destruction, from the Medieval Times to the Present," in *Possibilities: Essays on Hierarchy, Rebellion, and Desire* (Oakland, CA: AK Press, 2007), 76–77.

33. For the transcript of the Nixon-Khrushchev kitchen debate, see https://www.cia.gov/read ingroom/docs/1959-07-24.pdf.

34. Herbert Marcuse, *One-Dimensional Man: Studies in the Ideology of Advanced Industrial Capitalism* (Boston: Beacon Press, 1964).

35. David Gilbert, Bob Gottlieb, and Susan Sutheim, *Consumption: Domestic Imperialism: A New Left Introduction to the Political Economy of American Capitalism* (New York: Movement for a Democratic Society, 1968).

36. "Real Personal Consumption Expenditures Per Capita," FRED, updated June 24, 2021, https://fred.stlouisfed.org/series/A794RX0Q048SBEA.

37. Robert Bocock, *Consumption* (London: Routledge, 1993), 2.

38. Juliet B. Schor, "Can the North Stop Consumption Growth? Escaping the Cycle of Work and Spend," in *The North, the South, and the Environment: Ecological Constraints and the Global Economy*, ed. Venkataraman Bhaskar and Andrew Glyn (London: Earthscan, 1995), http://archive.unu.edu/unupress/unupbooks/80901e/80901E0b.htm; Naomi Jagoda, "Lawmakers: Leave Advertising Tax Break Alone," *Hill*, May 17, 2017, https://thehill.com /policy/finance/333743-lawmakers-leave-advertising-tax-break-alone.

39. Gary Cross, *An All-Consuming Century: Why Commercialism Won in Modern America* (New York: Columbia University Press, 2000), 200; Robert E. Lane, *The Loss of Happiness in Market Democracies* (New Haven, CT: Yale University Press, 2000), 233. The term *consumer choice* has also been given different meanings by the disability rights movement, which has challenged cultural perceptions of disability as well as medical and state control

over the lives of people with disabilities. Instead, this social movement affirms "autonomy and choice in life decisions" as a type of interpretation of the concept of consumer choice. Deborah Little, "Efficacy, Utility, and Disability Rights Movement Recruitment," *Disability Rights Quarterly* 30, no. 1 (2010), https://dsq-sds.org/article/view/1013/1226.

40. Michael J. Enright, Edith E. Scott, and Ka-mun Chang, *Regional Powerhouse: Greater Pearl River Delta and the Rise of China* (Singapore: John Wiley and Sons, 2005); Robert Gottlieb and Simon Ng, *Global Cities: Urban Environments in Los Angeles, Hong Kong, and China* (Cambridge, MA: MIT Press, 2014), 26; Emily Elhacham, Liad Ben-Uri, Jonathan Grozovski, Yinon M. Bar-On, and Ron Milo, "Global Human-Made Mass Exceeds All Living Biomass," *Nature*, December 9, 2020, https://www.nature.com/articles/s41586-020-3010-5.

41. "Consumer Sentiment and Behavior Continue to Reflect the Uncertainty of the COVID-19 Crisis," McKinsey & Company, October 26, 2020, https://www.mckinsey.com/business-functions/marketing-and-sales/our-insights/a-global-view-of-how-consumer-behavior-is-changing-amid-covid-19#.

42. Alibaba organized the first Singles' Day to create a consumer buy-in for young singles to contrast with the consumer-oriented purchases for couples around Valentine's Day. The 2020 Singles' Day event, by far the largest in its brief history, led to purchases of more than $75 billion for Alibaba and another $41 billion for JD.com. It involved the shipment of more than three billion parcels—an outcome with its own massive environmental footprint. For China consumers, according to an article in the *Harvard Business Review*, Singles' Day had come to represent "a unifying cultural event of unabashed retail therapy." China's central government, however, through its state-run central consumer organization, the China Consumer Association, became increasingly concerned about Alibaba's preeminent position as a private corporation in shaping China's domestic consumer economy, including through its online microlending services Huabei and Jiebel ("just spend" and "just borrow" in Mandarin). The Consumer Federation instead called for a more "rational consumption." Sherisse Pham, "Singles Day: Alibaba Sales Blitz Rakes in $75 Billion as Chinese Shake Off Covid-19," CNN, November 11, 2020, https://www.cnn.com/2020/11/10/tech/singles-day-2020-alibaba-intl-hnk/index.html; Quy Huy, "For Alibaba, Singles Day Is about More Than Huge Sales," *Harvard Business Review*, December 11, 2019, https://hbr.org/2019/12/for-alibaba-singles-day-is-about-more-than-huge-sales; Alice Su, "Young Chinese Balking at His Call to Borrow and Spend," *Los Angeles Times*, March 10, 2021. See also Li Yiping, "'Dual Circulation' New Choice for Economy," *China Daily*, July 27, 2020, https://www.chinadaily.com.cn/a/202007/27/WS5f1e0c65a31083481725c184.html.

43. Jack Manno, "Commoditization: Consumption Efficiency and an Economy of Care and Connection," in *Confronting Consumption*, ed. Thomas Princen, Michael Maniatas, and Ken Conca (Cambridge, MA: MIT Press, 2002).

44. Mellor, "An Eco-Feminist Proposal"; Mary Mellor, "Contribution to GTI Roundtable 'On Degrowth': An Exchange on the Viewpoint," *The Degrowth Alternative*, February 2015, https://greattransition.org/commentary/mary-mellor-the-degrowth-alternative-giorgos-kallis.

45. Christa Wichterich, "Contesting Green Growth," 92.

46. Leonard Cohen, "Everybody Knows," April 13, 2011, https://www.youtube.com/watch?v=Lin-a2lTelg.

47. Federico Demaria, Giorgos Kallis, and Karen Bakker, "Geographies of Degrowth: Nowtopias, Resurgencies, and the Decolonization of Imaginaries and Spaces," *Environment and Planning E: Nature and Space* 2, no. 3 (2019): 433.

48. André Gorz, *Ecology as Politics* (Boston: South End Press, 1980); Nicholas Georgecu-Roegen, *The Entropy Law and the Economic Process* (Cambridge, MA: Harvard University Press, 1971); Valérie Fournier, "Escaping from the Economy: The Politics of Degrowth," *International Journal of Science and Social Policy* 28, no. 11–12 (2008): 531; Giorgos Kallis, *In Defense of Degrowth: Opinions and Minifestos*, ed. Aaron Vansintjan (Open Commons, March 2017), 27.

49. Herman Daly, *Toward a Steady-State Economy* (New York: W. H. Freeman, 1973); Herman Daly, *Beyond Growth: The Economics of Sustainable Development* (Boston: Beacon Press, 1996), 32–33.

50. Giorgos Kallis, Christian Kerschner, and Joan Martínez Alier, "The Economics of Degrowth: Introduction," *Ecological Economics* 84 (2012): 1–9.

51. Beatriz Rodríguez-Labajos, Ivonne Yánez, Patrick Bond, Lucie Greyl, Serah Munguti, Godwin Uyi Ojo, and Winfridus Overbeek, "Not So Natural an Alliance: Degrowth and Environmental Justice Movements in the Global South," *Ecological Economics* 157 (2019): 177–178; Fournier, "Escaping from the Economy," 532. In one modest modification of the language of degrowth, the globally oriented environmental justice group Ecologistas en Acción launched a campaign in 2009 that reoriented the slogan "less is better" to become "less to live better" (*Menos para vivir major*). "2009: The Year of the Decrease with Fairness (Equitable Decrease)," Ecologistas en Acción, December 30, 2008, https://www.ecologistasenaccion.org/13158/2009-the-year-of-the-decrease-with-fairness-equitable-decrease.

52. The term *intersectionality* was elaborated by University of California at Los Angeles law professor Kimberlé Crenshaw in her 1991 article, "Mapping the Margins: Intersectionality, Identity Politics, and Violence against Women of Color," *Stanford Law Review* 43, no. 6 (1991): 1241–1299. Crenshaw illustrated how her own identity as a Black woman should reference a connected rather than separate set of identities. An awkward word (akin to the awkward term *degrowth*), the concept of intersectionality nevertheless has resonated among social movements, including significantly Black Lives Matter, and helped identify a new political framework that has highlighted not subtracted from the connections between various identities and movements that began to make common cause, such as the Black Lives Matter demonstrations during 2020. Corinna Dengler and Birte Strunk, "The Monetized Economy versus Care and the Environment: Degrowth Perspectives on Reconciling an Antagonism," *Feminist Economics* 24, no. 3 (2018): 160–183. On the importance of defining limited or no growth as a political project with respect to climate change, see Juliet B. Schor and Andrew Jorgensen, "Is It Too Late for Growth?," *Review of Radical Political Economics* 5, no. 2 (2019): 320–329.

CHAPTER 5

1. Branko Milanovic, "Trump as the Ultimate Triumph of Neo-Liberalism," *Global Policy Journal*, May 14, 2020, https://www.globalpolicyjournal.com/blog/14/05/2020/trump-ultimate-triumph-neoliberalism; Daniel Bessner and Matthew Sparke, "Don't Let His Trade Policy Fool You: Trump Is a Neoliberal," *Washington Post*, March, 22, 2017, https://www.washingtonpost.com/posteverything/wp/2017/03/22/dont-let-his-trade-policy-fool-you-trump-is-a-neoliberal.

2. Julia Horowitz, "Steve Mnuchin's Wife Strikes a Pose with a Sheet of Money," CNN Money, November 15, 2017, https://money.cnn.com/2017/11/15/news/louise-linton-steven-mnuchin-dollar-bills-treasury/index.html.

3. Linda Greenhouse, "Four Years of the Trump Administration in Court: One Word Stuck in My Head," *New York Times*, November 19, 2020, https://www.nytimes.com/2020/11/19/opinion/trump-policy-mean.html?action=click&module=Opinion&pgtype=Homepage.

4. Louis Menand, "The Making of the New Left," *New Yorker*, March 22, 2021, https://www.newyorker.com/magazine/2021/03/22/the-making-of-the-new-left.

5. "'We Clap Because We Care': New Yorkers Applaud Frontline Coronavirus Workers—Video," *Guardian*, March 28, 2020, https://www.theguardian.com/world/video/2020/mar/28/we-clap-because-we-care-new-yorkers-applaud-frontline-coronavirus-workers-video; Sam Byers, "We're All Keen to Show We Care, but We've Shaped a Society That Doesn't Care at All," *Guardian*, May 17, 2020, https://www.theguardian.com/commentisfree/2020/may/17/show-care-lockdown-clap-transgressors-rontline-workers-pandemic.

6. Jean Chaisson, "Nurses Devalued and Abandoned," *Health Affairs* 21, no. 2 (March–April 2002), https://www.healthaffairs.org/doi/full/10.1377/hlthaff.21.2.304.

7. "PPHF," Centers for Disease Control and Prevention, https://www.cdc.gov/funding/pphf/index.html#:~:text=The%20Prevention%20and%20Public%20Health,our%20nation's%20public%20health%20system.

8. "What We Are Learning from COVID-19 about Being Prepared for a Public Health Emergency: Lessons We Already Knew," Trust for America's Health, Issue Brief, May 27, 2020, https://www.tfah.org/wp-content/uploads/2020/05/TFAH2020CovidResponseBriefFnl.pdf; "Accomplishing CDC's Mission with Investments from the Prevention and Public Health Fund, FY 2010-FY 2016," Centers for Disease Control and Prevention, https://www.cdc.gov/funding/documents/CDC-PPHF-Funding-Impact.pdf.

9. Distinguishing between a Medicare for All perspective and the types of reforms elaborated in the American Rescue Plan, Medicare for All advocates have argued that interim reforms ought to incorporate three core goals: expanded health care access in order to move toward a universal health access goal, the utilization of public means to achieve interim goals such as a public option, and a reduction of the power and influence of health care corporations along with the industrial health model as a pathway toward an alternative public and community health system model. See, for example, Natalie Shure, "Opponents of Medicare

for All Are Deathly Afraid," *Nation*, March 1, 2021, https://www.thenation.com/article/culture/opponents-of-medicare-for-all-are-deathly-afraid.

10. Christopher C. Krebs, "Advisory Memorandum on Ensuring Essential Critical Infrastructure Workers Ability to Work during the COVID-19 Response," US Department of Homeland Security, Cybersecurity and Infrastructure Security Agency, August 18, 2020, https://www.cisa.gov/sites/default/files/publications/Version_4.0_CISA_Guidance_on_Essential_Critical_Infrastructure_Workers_FINAL%20AUG%2018v3.pdf.

11. "COVID-19: Essential Workers in the States," National Conference of State Legislatures, May 21, 2020, https://www.ncsl.org/research/labor-and-employment/covid-19-essential-workers-in-the-states.aspx#Map.

12. Daniel A. Medina, "As Amazon, Walmart, and Others Profit amid Coronavirus Crisis, Their Essential Workers Plan Unprecedented Strike," *Intercept*, April 28, 2020, https://theintercept.com/2020/04/28/coronavirus-may-1-strike-sickout-amazon-target-whole-foods; Makenzie Huber, "Essential Worker Just Means You're on the Death Track," *USA Today*, May 12, 2020, https://www.usatoday.com/in-depth/news/2020/05/04/meat-packing-essential-worker-hogs-south-dakota-smithfield-food-chain-covid-19-coronavirus-inside/3064329001; Anna Hensel, "'Hero Is an Overused Word': Despite Public Hand-Waves, Essential Retail Workers Still Face a Daily Minefield," *Modern Retail*, July 24, 2020, https://www.modernretail.co/retailers/hero-is-an-overused-word-despite-public-hand-waves-essential-retail-workers-still-face-a-daily-minefield.

13. Suhauna Hussain and Dakota Smith, "Ralphs and Food 4 Less Locations to Close in Los Angeles over Hazard Pay Rules," *Los Angeles Times*, March 10, 2021, https://www.latimes.com/business/story/2021-03-10/ralphs-food-4-less-locations-close-los-angeles-hazard-pay.

14. Tithi Bhattacharya, "Social Reproduction Theory and Why We Need It to Make Sense of the Corona Virus Crisis," April 2, 2020, http://www.tithibhattacharya.net/new-blog.

15. Elise Gould and Valerie Wilson, "Black Workers Face Two of the Most Lethal Preexisting Conditions for Coronavirus: Racism and Economic Inequality," Economic Policy Institute, June 1, 2020, https://files.epi.org/pdf/193246.pdf.

16. Thomas M. Selden, Terceira A. Bedahl, and Zhengyi Fang, "The Risk of Severe COVID-19 within Households of School Employees and School-Age Children," *Health Affairs* 39, no. 11 (September 17, 2020), https://www.healthaffairs.org/www.healthaffairs.org/doi/10.1377/hlthaff.2020.01536.

17. "Morbidity and Mortality Weekly Report (MMWR)," Centers for Disease Control and Prevention, August 24, 2020, https://www.cdc.gov/mmwr/volumes/69/wr/mm6933e1.htm; Thomas M. Selden and Terceira A. Berdahl, "COVID-19 and Racial/Ethnic Disparities in Health Risk, Employment, and Household Composition," *Health Affairs*, July 24, 2020, https://www.healthaffairs.org/doi/full/10.1377/hlthaff.2020.00897.

18. Michael D. Shear, Katie Benner, and Michael S. Schmidt, "'We Need to Take Away Children,' No Matter How Young, Justice Dept. Officials Said," *New York Times*, October 6,

2020, https://www.nytimes.com/2020/10/06/us/politics/family-separation-border-immigration-jeff-sessions-rod-rosenstein.html.

19. José Olivares and John Washington, "'A Silent Pandemic': Nurse at ICE Facility Blows the Whistle on Coronavirus Dangers," *Intercept*, September 14, 2020, https://theintercept.com/2020/09/14/ice-detention-center-nurse-whistleblower; Kari Paul, "ICE Detainees Faced Medical Neglect and Hysterectomies, Whistleblower Alleges," *Guardian*, September 14, 2020, https://www.theguardian.com/us-news/2020/sep/14/ice-detainees-hysterectomies-medical-neglect-irwin-georgia; Nomaan Merchant, "More Migrant Women Say They Did Not Consent to Surgeries at ICE Center," *Guardian*, September 18, 2020, https://www.theguardian.com/us-news/2020/sep/18/migrant-women-us-detention-center-georgia; Nomaan Merchant, "US Deports Migrant Women Who Alleged Abuse by Georgia Doctor," AP, November 11, 2020, https://apnews.com/article/us-deports-migrant-women-georgia-doctor-b6a5fc1e2d4a822eb3767f9a858ea670.

20. One concern of immigrant rights advocates was the new Biden administration's focus on high-tech strategies for border security that extended the role of what border researcher Todd Miller called the border-industrial complex. It did so by further magnifying the role of companies like Northrop Grumman with its "VADER 'man-hunting' radar system" used in Afghanistan, and General Atomics with its Predator B drones—companies that donated more funds to Biden than Trump in the 2020 election, recognizing Biden's embrace of high-tech border security during the campaign. Todd Miller, "The Greater the Disaster, the Greater the Profits: The Border-Industrial Complex in the Post-Trump Era," TomDispatch, March 23, 2021, https://tomdispatch.com/the-greater-the-disaster-the-greater-the-profits/#more.

21. "Goal 2: End Hunger, Achieve Food Security, and Improved Nutrition and Promote Sustainable Agriculture," United Nations Statistics Division, https://unstats.un.org/sdgs/report/2016/goal-02/#:~:text=SDG%20Goals-Goal%202%3A%20End%20hunger%2C%20achieve%20food%20security%20and%20improved%20nutrition,to%20lead%20a%20healthy%20life; *The State of Food Security and Nutrition in the World: Transforming Food Systems for Affordable Healthy Diets* (Rome: Food and Agriculture Organization of the United Nations, 2020), http://www.fao.org/3/ca9692en/CA9692EN.pdf; *The Sustainable Development Goals Report, 2020* (New York: United Nations, 2020), 26, https://unstats.un.org/sdgs/report/2020/The-Sustainable-Development-Goals-Report-2020.pdf.

22. Helen Lambert, Jaideep Gupte, Helen Fletcher, Laura Hammond, Nicola Lowe, Mark Pelling, Neelam Raina, et al., "COVID-19 as a Global Challenge: Towards an Inclusive and Sustainable Future," *Lancet Planetary Health*, August 2020, https://www.thelancet.com/journals/lanplh/article/PIIS2542-5196(20)30168-6/fulltext; US Census Bureau, "Week 1 Household Pulse Survey: April 23–May 5," United States Census Bureau, May 20, 2020, https://www.census.gov/data/tables/2020/demo/hhp/hhp1.html; US Census Bureau "Household Pulse Survey, "Week 21 Household Pulse Survey: December 9–21," United States Census Bureau, January 6, 2021, table 2a, https://www.census.gov/data/tables/2020/demo/hhp/hhp21.html; "Tracking the COVID-19 Recession's Effect on Food, Housing, and Employment Hardships," Center for Budget and Policy Priorities,

September 18, 2020, https://www.cbpp.org/research/poverty-and-inequality/tracking-the
-covid-19-recessions-effects-on-food-housing-and; Stacy Dean, Lauren Hall, Brynne
Keith-Jennings, and Dottie Rosenbaum, "SNAP Benefit Boost Would Get Needed Food
Aid to the Poorest Participants, Who Have Been Left Out," Center for Budget and Policy Priorities, September 17, 2020, https://www.cbpp.org/research/food-assistance/snap
-benefit-boost-would-get-needed-food-aid-to-the-poorest-participants.

23. "Food Security and COVID-19," brief, World Bank, April 13, 2021, https://www
.worldbank.org/en/topic/agriculture/brief/food-security-and-covid-19.

24. Presentation by Derek Polka, policy and research manager, Los Angeles Regional Food
Bank, to the Los Angeles Food Policy Council, September 17, 2020; Caitlin Welsh,
"E84: COVID Highlights Need to Change Food Security Strategy, Duke Sanford World
Food Policy Center (podcast), August 18, 2020, https://wfpc.sanford.duke.edu/podcasts
/covid-highlights-need-change-food-security-strategy.

25. *Impact of COVID-10 on School Nutrition Programs: Part 2* (Arlington, VA: School Nutrition
Association, May 2020), https://schoolnutrition.org/uploadedFiles/11COVID-19/3
_Webinar_Series_and_Other_Resources/COVID-19-Impact-on-School-Nutrition
-Programs-Part2.pdf.

26. Jessica Fu, "School Lunch as We Know It Is Over. Here's How School Nutrition Directors
Are Reinventing It for an Uncertain Year," *Chalkbeat*, June 23, 2020, https://www
.chalkbeat.org/2020/6/23/21300529/school-lunch-as-we-know-it-is-over-coronavirus
-school-nutrition-directors.

27. Rong-Gong Lin II, "Fauci Says Coronavirus Could Remain a Threat through 2021," *Los
Angeles Times*, October 10, 2020.

28. "The America We Need," *New York Times* series, https://www.nytimes.com/series/the
-america-we-need.

29. Anh Do, "How Is Little Saigon Curbing Coronavirus? By Respecting Elders, Authorities,
and Masks," *Los Angeles Times*, September 22, 2020, https://www.latimes.com/california
/story/2020-09-22/little-saigon-secret-covid-19-prevention-respect.

30. Phys.org News, "Hottest Day Ever in Shanghai as Heat Wave Bakes China," July 21, 2017,
https://phys.org/news/2017-07-hottest-day-shanghai-china.html.

31. Leyland Cecco, "'Lytton is Gone': Wildfire Tears through Village after Record-Breaking
Heat." *The Guardian*, July 1, 2021.

32. Matt Compton, "President Obama Describes an All-of-the-Above Strategy for Energy,"
White House, February 23, 2012, https://obamawhitehouse.archives.gov/blog/2012/02/23
/president-obama-describes-all-above-strategy-energy.

33. "Princeton Prof: 'Shut Up' over Climate Change," CNBC, July 14, 2014, https://www
.cnbc.com/video/2014/07/14/princeton-prof-shut-up-over-climate-change.html; Coral Dav-
enport and Mark Landler, "Trump Administration Hardens Its Attack on Climate Science,"

New York Times, May 27, 2019, https://www.nytimes.com/2019/05/27/us/politics/trump-climate-science.html?action=click&module=Top%20Stories&pgtype=Homepage.

34. Parrish Bergquist, Matto Mildenberger, and Leah C. Stokes, "Combining Climate, Economic, and Social Policy Builds Political Support for Climate Action in the US," SSRN, November 8, 2019, https://papers.ssrn.com/sol3/papers.cfm?abstract_id=3477525.

35. Anna Lappé, *Diet for a Hot Planet* (New York: Bloomsbury, 2011).

36. For a discussion of China's high-speed rail network, see Robert Gottlieb and Simon Ng, *Global Cities: Urban Environments in Los Angeles, Hong Kong, and China* (Cambridge, MA: MIT Press, 2014), 193–195. On California's effort, see Ralph Vartabedian, "How California's Faltering High-speed Rail Project Was 'Captured' by Costly Consultants," *Los Angeles Times*, April 26, 2019, https://www.latimes.com/local/california/la-me-california-high-speed-rail-consultants-20190426-story.html.

37. Thadeus Greenson, "Why the Supes Denied Terra-Gen's Wind Project, despite a Series of 11th Hour Concessions by the Company," *North Coast Journal*, December 17, 2019, https://www.northcoastjournal.com/NewsBlog/archives/2019/12/17/why-the-supes-denied-terra-gens-wind-project-despite-a-series-of-11th-hour-concessions-from-the-company.

38. Richard Sennett, *Building and Dwelling: Ethics for the City* (New York: Farrar, Straus and Giroux, 2018); Sonia Shah, *The Next Great Migration: The Beauty and Terror of Life on the Move* (New York: Bloomsbury Publishing, 2020).

39. Mark Pelling, *Adaptation to Climate Change: From Resilience to Transformation* (New York: Routledge, 2011), 3.

40. Jason Hickel, "Quantifying National Responsibility for Climate Breakdown: An Equality-Based Attribution Approach for Carbon Dioxide Emissions in Excess of the Planetary Boundary," *Lancet Planetary Health*, September 1, 2020, https://www.thelancet.com/journals/lanplh/article/PIIS2542-5196(20)30196-0/fulltext, E-399.

41. Daniel Macmillen Voskoboynik, "Bridging Colonialism and Climate Change," *Utne Reader*, June 2019, https://www.utne.com/environment/neocolonialism-and-environment-ze0z1906zhoe. See also the framing paper solicited by the Heinrich Böll Stiftung (foundation) on the links between racial and climate justice that situated colonialization as central to the changes that ultimately fueled the climate crisis, including the global overexploitation of natural resources and land use changes. Olumide Abimbola, Joshua Kwesi Aikins, Tselane Makhesi-Wilkinson, and Erin Roberts, *Racism and Climate (In)Justice: How Racism and Colonialism Shape the Climate Crisis and Climate Action* (Washington, DC: Heinrich Böll Stiftung, March 2021, https://us.boell.org/sites/default/files/2021-03/FINAL%20-%20Racism%20and%20Climate%20(In)Justice%20Framing%20Paper.pdf.

42. *Global Trends: Forced Displacement in 2019* (Copenhagen: United Nations High Commissioner for Refugees, 2020), https://www.unhcr.org/be/wp-content/uploads/sites/46/2020/07/Global-Trends-Report-2019.pdf.

43. Carter C. Price and Kathryn A. Edwards, *Trends in Income from 1975 to 2018* (Santa Monica, CA: Rand Corporation, August 14, 2020), https://www.rand.org/content/dam/rand/pubs/working_papers/WRA500/WRA516-1/RAND_WRA516-1.pdf.

44. Chuck Collins, "Updates: Billionaire Wealth, US Job Losses, and Pandemic Profiteers," Inequality.org, December 9, 2020, https://inequality.org/great-divide/updates-billionaire-pandemic; Chase Peterson-Withorn, "The World's Billionaires Got $1.9 Trillion Richer in 2020," *Forbes*, December 16, 2020, https://www.forbes.com/sites/chasewithorn/2020/12/16/the-worlds-billionaires-have-gotten-19-trillion-richer-in-2020/?sh=283e39a27386.

45. Richard Rothstein, *The Color of Law: A Forgotten History of How Our Government Segregated America* (New York: Liveright Publishing, 2017); Keeanga-Yamahtta Taylor, *Race for Profit: How Banks and the Real Estate Industry Undermined Black Homeownership* (Chapel Hill: University of North Carolina Press, 2019), 18..

46. Michelle Alexander, *The New Jim Crow: Mass Incarceration in the Age of Color Blindness* (New York: New Press, 2010); Tony Platt, *Beyond These Walls: Rethinking Crime and Punishment in the United States* (New York: St. Martin's Press, 2018).

47. Nicole Santa Cruz and Alene Tchekmedyian, "Deputies Killed Dijon Kizzee after a Bike Stop: We Found 15 Similar Law Enforcement Shootings, Many Fatal," *Los Angeles Times*, October 16, 2020, https://www.latimes.com/california/story/2020-10-16/examining-dijon-kizzee-bike-stop-police-shootings; "System of Care: When America Chose Prisons over Public Health," editorial, *Los Angeles Times*, June 10, 2020.

48. Westenley Alcenat, "The Case for Haitian Reparations," *Jacobin*, January 14, 2017, https://www.jacobinmag.com/2017/01/haiti-reparations-france-slavery-colonialism-debt; Peter Granitz, "Hollande Promises to Pay 'Moral Debt' to Former Colony Haiti," Reuters, May 12, 2015, https://uk.reuters.com/article/uk-haiti-hollande-idUKKBN0NX2KR20150512.

49. "Jim Forman Delivers Black Manifesto at Riverside Church," SNCC Digital Gateway, May 1969, https://snccdigital.org/events/jim-forman-delivers-black-manifesto-at-riverside-church; "Black Manifesto," in *The Church Awakens: African Americans and the Struggle for Justice*, April 26, 1969, https://episcopalarchives.org/church-awakens/items/show/202.

50. Civil Liberties Act, H.R. 442, 100th Cong., (1987–1988), https://www.congress.gov/bill/100th-congress/house-bill/442.

51. The forty acres order and presidential proclamation has been discussed by Black Reconstruction historians such as Eric Foner (*Reconstruction: America's Unfinished Revolution, 1863–1877*) and cultural critics such as Henry Louis Gates Jr., who called the order a systematic attempt at reparations that involved "a methodical redistribution" of land and wealth to the freed slaves. Following Abraham Lincoln's death, Andrew Johnson, who replaced Lincoln as President, revoked the order and returned the land to the former plantation owners. Henry Louis Gates Jr., "The Truth behind 'Forty Acres and a Mule,'"

Root, January 7, 2013, https://www.pbs.org/wnet/african-americans-many-rivers-to-cross /history/the-truth-behind-40-acres-and-a-mule. See also the discussion about reparations initiatives in Nkechi Taifa, "Reparations—Has the Time Finally Come?," American Civil Liberties Union, May 26, 2020, https://www.aclu.org/news/racial-justice /reparations-has-the-time-finally-come.

52. Ta-Nehisi Coates, "The Case for Reparations," *Atlantic*, June 2014, https://www.theatlantic .com/magazine/archive/2014/06/the-case-for-reparations/361631; Ta-Nehisi Coates, *We Were Eight Years in Power: An American Tragedy* (New York: One World Publishing, 2017), 151–208; Corky Siemaszko, "Senator Mitch McConnell's Great-Great Grandfathers Owned 14 Slaves, Bringing Reparations Issue Closer to Home," NBC News, July 8, 2019, https://www.nbcnews.com/politics/congress/mitch-mcconnell-ancestors-slave-owners -alabama-1800s-census-n1027511; "Congresswoman Sheila Jackson Lee Introduces Legislation for a Commission to Consider Reparations Proposals for African Americans," United States Congresswoman Sheila Jackson Lee, January 9, 2019, https://jacksonlee.house.gov /media-center/press-releases/congresswoman-sheila-jackson-lee-introduces-legislation -for-a-commission.

53. Coates, "The Case for Reparations"; "What Is Reparations," National Coalition of Blacks for Reparations in America, https://www.ncobraonline.org/reparations.

54. Annabelle Timsit, "The Blueprint the US Can Follow to Finally Pay Reparations," *Quartz*, October 13, 2020, https://sports.yahoo.com/blueprint-us-finally-pay-reparations-11000 6016.html; David Marchese, "What Can America Learn from South Africa about National Healing," *New York Times Magazine*, December 11, 2020, https://www.nytimes.com /interactive/2020/12/14/magazine/pumla-gobodo-madikizela-interview.html; "History," Conference on Jewish Material Claims against Germany, http://www.claimscon.org/about /history; Greg Rienzi, "Other Nations Could Learn from Germany's Efforts to Reconcile after WWII," *Johns Hopkins Magazine*, 2015, https://hub.jhu.edu/magazine/2015/summer /germany-japan-reconciliation. The action of the German government was not without controversy, both from German citizens who were initially opposed to the policy and some of the Holocaust survivors who felt it wasn't a sufficient form of redress and repair. The reparations program has continued to be implemented, however, including additional funds made available during the COVID-19 pandemic for the remaining survivors. Elana Lyn Gross, "Germany Will Pay $662 Million to Holocaust Survivors Struggling Because of the Pandemic," *Forbes*, October 14, 2020, https://www.forbes.com/sites/elanagross/2020 /10/14/germany-will-pay-662-million-to-holocaust-survivors-struggling-because-of-the -pandemic/#b13902c1e6.

55. Alison Flood, "Sharp Rise in Parents Seeking to Ban Anti-Racist Books in Schools," *The Guardian*, April 6, 2021, https://www.theguardian.com/books/2021/apr/06/sharp-rise -in-parents-seeking-to-ban-anti-racist-books-in-us-schools; Coates, *We Were Eight Years in Power*, 202.

56. Boris Bittker, *The Case for Black Reparations* (Boston: Beacon Press, 2003).

57. William Darity and A. Kristen Mullen, *From Here to Equality: Reparations for Black Americans in the Twenty-First Century* (Chapel Hill: University of North Carolina Press, 2020), 263.

58. Kyle D. Logue, "Reparations as Redistribution," *Boston University Law Review* 84, no. 5 (2004): 1319–1374.

59. "Bali Principles of Climate Justice," August 29, 2002, https://www.ejnet.org/ej/bali.pdf.

60. U. Thara Srinivasan, Susan P. Carey, Eric Hallstein, Paul A. T. Higgins, Amber C. Kerr, Laura E. Koteen, Adam B. Smith, et al., "The Debt of Nations and the Distribution of Ecological Impacts from Human Activities," *Proceedings of the National Academy of Sciences* 105, no. 5 (February 5, 2008): 1768–1773, https://www.pnas.org/content/pnas/105/5/1768 .full.pdf; Joan Martínez Alier, "Environmental Justice and Economic Degrowth: An Alliance between two Movements," *Capitalism, Nature, Socialism* 23, no. 1, (2012): 51–73.

61. The legislative push through H.R. 40 for a reparations commission was advanced for the first time in 2021, when it was voted on favorably by the House Judiciary Committee. It also generated concerns among some Republicans that instead of a historical reckoning, reparations actually represented a "redistribution of wealth, or socialism," as Utah Republican congressperson Burgess Owens complained. Nicholas Fandos, "House Panel Advances Bill to Study Reparations in Historic Vote," *New York Times*, https://www.nytimes .com/2021/04/14/us/politics/reparations-slavery-house.html?action=click&module=Top %20Stories&pgtype=Homepage.

CHAPTER 6

1. *Power to Heal*, produced by Barbara Berney (BLB Film Productions, 2015), https://www .blbfilmproductions.com; Mike Konczal, *Freedom from the Market: America's Fight to Liberate Itself from the Grip of the Invisible Hand* (New York: New Press, 2021), 96–136; David Lauter, "Lifting Kids out of Poverty Could Be Biden's Legacy, but Costs Raise Doubts," *Los Angeles Times*, April 13, 2021, https://www.latimes.com/politics/story/2021-04-13/lifting -kids-out-of-poverty-biden-legacy-long-term-price-tag. In her discussion of how to move toward what she called the green state, University of Melbourne professor Robyn Eckersley has argued that the challenge in seeking to accomplish such a transition would be to find the ways to "gain political traction while also being transformative and not merely ameliorative"—a challenge central to the process of change that requires what Eckersley labels "a disciplined imagination." Robyn Eckersley, *The Green State: Rethinking Democracy and Sovereignty* (Cambridge, MA: MIT Press, 2004), 4.

2. Ock Hyun-ju, "Gyeonggi Province Sets Example for Universal Basic Income," *Korean Herald*, August 10, 2020, http://www.koreaherald.com/view.php?ud=20200811000938; Jeong-Ho Lee and Sam Kim, "Free Cash for All Boosts South Korea Star to Top of Polls," *Bloomberg*, October 4, 2020, https://www.bloomberg.com/news/articles/2020-10-05/free -cash-for-all-boosts-rising-south-korea-star-to-top-of-polls; Lee Hyo-jin, "Gyeonggi Province to Test Basic Income Scheme for Farmers," *Korea Times*, September 23, 2020, https://

www.koreatimes.co.kr/www/nation/2020/11/356_296548.html; The Gyeonggi Korean "2020 Korea Basic Income Fair International Conference, Sessions 3, 4, 5 (English)," September 11, 2020, https://www.youtube.com/watch?v=EPEQtHBLT2E.

3.   Reuters, "Finland's Basic Income Trial Boosts Happiness, but Not Employment," *New York Times*, February 9, 2019, https://www.nytimes.com/2019/02/09/world/europe/finland-basic-income.html; Amy Castro Baker and Stacia Martin-West, "Mayors for a Guaranteed Income, Learning Agenda," Center for Guaranteed Income Research, University of Pennsylvania School of Social Policy and Practice, 2020, https://static1.squarespace.com/static/5ee2a523bbc68e71ffac27c9/t/5f9046ab03730c5288b6185f/1603290796288/Center+For+Guaranteed+Income+Research+Learning+Agenda.pdf; Erika D. Smith, "It's a GuaranteedI Income Program, but Think of It as a Test Case for Reparations," *Los Angeles Times*, March 27, 2021, https://www.latimes.com/california/story/2021-03-27/oakland-guaranteed-income-reparations-slavery-black-california.

4.   Martin Luther King Jr., *Where Do We Go from Here: Chaos or Community?* (Boston: Beacon Press, 1968), 172. The leading welfare rights organization during the late 1960, the National Welfare Rights Organization, had already highlighted a guaranteed income goal at its founding convention in 1967. Brian Steensland, *The Failed Welfare Revolution: America's Struggle over Guaranteed Income Policy* (Princeton, NJ: Princeton University Press, 2008), 58. The economists' letter to Congress is detailed in a May 28, 1968, *New York Times* article, "Economists Urge Assured Income," which argued that a "system of national guarantees and supplements" was "feasible and compatible with our economic system." See also Premilla Nadasen, *Welfare Warriors: The Welfare Rights Movement in the United States* (Abingdon, UK: Routledge, 2005).

5.   Friedman's comment and his discussion of the negative income tax was addressed in several of his books, including his more personal coauthored book (with his wife, Rose Friedman), *Free to Choose: A Personal Statement* (San Diego, CA: Harcourt Brace Jovanovich, 1980), 120, 121–124.

6.   Lauren Smiley, "Silicon Valley's Basic Income Bromance," *Wired*, December 15, 2015, https://www.wired.com/2015/12/silicon-valleys-basic-income-bromance/#.nfqba4sem.

7.   Eric Olin Wright, "Basic Income as a Socialist Project," *Rutgers Journal of Law and Public Policy* 2, no. 1 (Fall 2005): 202; Ronan Burtenshaw, "Where Next for Finland's Welfare System: An Interview with Li Andersson," *Jacobin*, December 21, 2017, https://www.jacobinmag.com/2017/12/li-andersson-left-alliance-true-finns. For a different perspective from the Left on the Finish program, see Jimmy O'Donnell, "Why Basic Income Failed in Finland," *Jacobin*, December 1, 2019, https://www.jacobinmag.com/2019/12/basic-income-finland-experiment-kela.

8.   For the Basic Income Earth Network's definition, see https://basicincome.org. Philippe Van Parijs and Yannick Vanderborght, *Basic Income: A Radical Proposal for a Free Society and a Sane Economy* (Cambridge, MA: Harvard University Press, 2017), 26; André Gorz, *Reclaiming Work: Beyond the Wage-Based Society* (Cambridge, UK: Polity Books, 1999), 91 (emphasis added).

9. Karl Wilderquist and Michael W. Howard, eds., *Alaska's Permanent Fund Dividend: Examining Its Suitability as a Model* (New York: Palgrave Macmillan, 2012), xvi. Though not utilized for a basic income approach, the discovery of oil in the North Sea in the late 1960s enabled Norway to eventually establish the largest sovereign wealth fund in the world, its Government Fund Pension Global, which has been used to make global investments that contribute to the wealth of the Norwegian economy. Since the fund's inception, it has proven to be a more stable funding mechanism than the Alaskan program.

10. See, for example, Bill McKibben, "Why We Need to Keep 80% of the Fossil Fuels in the Ground," *YES!*, Spring 2016, https://www.yesmagazine.org/issue/life-after-oil/2016/02/15 /why-we-need-to-keep-80-percent-of-fossil-fuels-in-the-ground; "Keep It in the Ground (Pipelines and Drilling)," Greenpeace, https://www.greenpeace.org/usa/issues/keep-it-in -the-ground.

11. Sophia Seung-Yoon Lee, Ji-eun Lee, and Kyo-seung Kim, "Evaluating Basic Income, Basic Service, and Basic Voucher for Social and Ecological Sustainability," *Sustainability* 12, no. 20 (October 10, 2020), https://www.mdpi.com/2071-1050/12/20/8348.

12. Katharina Bohnenberger, "Money, Vouchers, Public Infrastructures? A Framework for Sustainable Welfare Benefits," *Sustainability* 12, no. 2 (January 14, 2020), https://www .mdpi.com/2071-1050/12/2/596.

13. Philip Olterman, "Germany to Extend Coronavirus Furlough to 24 Months," *Guardian*, August 18, 2020, https://www.theguardian.com/world/2020/aug/18/germany-to-extend -coronavirus-furlough-to-24-months; Lee, Lee, and Kim, "Evaluating Basic Income, Basic Service, and Basic Voucher for Social and Ecological Sustainability."

14. Jason DeParle, "In the Stimulus Bill, a Policy Revolution in Aid for Children," *New York Times*, March 7, 2021, https://www.nytimes.com/2021/03/07/us/politics/child-tax -credit-stimulus.html; Thomas M. McInerney and Andrew M. Massara, "CARES Act Impact on Independent Contractors and Gig Workers," *National Law Journal*, April 6, 2020, https://www.natlawreview.com/article/cares-act-and-its-impact-independent-contractors -and-gig-workers.

15. Guy Standing, *Basic Income: And How We Can Make It Happen* (London: Pelican Books, 2017). See also "LSE III | Professor Guy Standing | Basic Income: And How We Can Make It Happen," May 11, 2017, https://www.youtube.com/watch?v=dZwljkrlutc.

16. Undercommons, "No Racial Justice without Basic Income," *Boston Review*, May 3, 2017, http://bostonreview.net/class-inequality-race/undercommons-no-racial-justice-without -basic-income; "Reparations," Movement for Black Lives, https://m4bl.org/policy-platforms /reparations.

17. Van Parijs and Vanderborght, *Basic Income*, 167, 244.

18. John Maynard Keynes, "Economic Possibilities for Our Grandchildren," 1930, reprinted in John Maynard Keynes, *Essays in Persuasion* (New York: W. W. Norton and Co., 1963), 358–373. Keynes wrote that a fifteen-hour workweek in a hundred years was not only

possible but also a likely outcome of technology-induced greater productivity and the elimination of work hours. The focus on technology and increased productivity has become a widely used talking point among various and sometimes widely different basic income proponents, such as leading UBI advocates like Guy Standing, and pro-market and anti–welfare state advocates like Charles Murray. Andrew Yang, who helped make visible a basic income concept during his 2020 presidential run, in his book *The War on Normal People: The Truth about America's Disappearing Jobs and Why Universal Basic Income Is Our Future* (New York: Hachette Books, 2018), and in positions he articulated during his unsuccessful run for New York City mayor, sought to steer a path between conservative interpretations of basic income that eliminated some or all safety net programs, and liberal, radical, and progressive interpretations that expanded income as well as social supports for the poor (and middle class) above and beyond a baseline of basic income support. See, for example, Bryce Covert, "Andrew Yang Isn't Doing UBI Right," *New York Times*, March 16, 2021, https://www.nytimes.com/2021/03/16/opinion/andrew-yang-ubi-nyc-mayor .html?action=click&module=Opinion&pgtype=Homepage; Michael Gartland, "Mayoral Candidate Andrew Yang's Plan to Give Cash to NYC's Poor Remains Vague, Opponents Call It a Gimmick," *New York Daily News*, March 13, 2021, https://www.nydailynews .com/news/politics/new-york-elections-government/ny-nyc-mayoral-race-andrew-yang -ubi-20210314-676heopn5nhhrmi6fdu5vkjohy-story.html.

19. Irving Bernstein, *The Lean Years: A History of the American Worker, 1920–1933* (Chicago: Haymarket Books, 2010).

20. David R. Roediger and Philip S. Foner, *Our Own Time: A History of American Labor and the Working Day* (London: Verso, 1989), viii.

21. Benjamin Kline Hunnicutt, *Work without End: Abandoning Shorter Hours for the Right to Work* (Philadelphia: Temple University Press, 1988).

22. Larry DeWitt, "The Decision to Exclude Agricultural and Domestic Workers from the 1935 Social Security Act," *Social Security Bulletin* 70, no. 4 (2010), https://www.ssa.gov/ policy/docs/ssb/v70n4/v70n4p49.html; Roediger and Foner, *Our Own Time*, 256.

23. Dorothy Sue Cobble, *The Other Women's Movement: Workplace Justice and Social Rights in Modern America* (Princeton, NJ: Princeton University Press, 2004), 104; Roediger and Foner, *Our Own Time*, 261.

24. The Reuther quote is from Christoph Hermann, *Capitalism and the Political Economy of Work Time*, Abingdon and New York: Routledge, 2015, p. 196; See also, Benjamin Kline Hunnicutt, *Free Time: The Forgotten American Dream*, Philadelphia: Temple University Press, 2013; Juliet B. Schor, *The Overspent American: Why We Want What We Don't Need*, New York: Harper Perennial, 1999; In 1949, General Motors had pushed Congress to pass a forty-five-hour workweek and apply that to its workforce. The United Auto Workers union, however, fought back, with UAW president Walter Reuther arguing that "reductions in the unit cost of production must be made possible by improved technology and production processes . . . and not by placing an unfair workload on workers." The next year, UAW

and GM "guaranteed a cooperative agreement on introduction of labor-saving technology which meant that wages were linked to productivity increases." Cited by Jamie McCollum in his book *Worked Over: How Round-the-clock work is killing the American Dream* (New York: Basic Books, 2020), 110.

25. Reagan's action was clearly designed to undercut not just the Professional Air Traffic Controllers Organization but also unions in general—a message reinforced by the Reagan administration's unwillingness to negotiate a contract even prior to the strike, despite just months after the air traffic organization had endorsed Reagan for election. Allen Pusey, "August 5, 1981: Reagan Fires Air Controllers," *ABA Journal*, August 1, 2015, https://www .abajournal.com/magazine/article/august_5_1981_reagan_fires_air_traffic_controllers.

26. A Census Bureau story on mothers, job loss, and care responsibilities during the pandemic indicated that working mothers were either willingly leaving jobs or were being forced out in extraordinary numbers. According to the report, "Mothers' V-shaped employment patterns are becoming prolonged and more severe in this global crisis." Misty L. Heggeness, Jason Fields, Yazmin A. García Trejo, and Anthony Schulzetenberg, "Tracking Job Losses for Mothers of School-Age Children during a Health Crisis," United States Census Bureau, March 3, 2021, https://www.census.gov/library/stories/2021/03/moms-work-and-the -pandemic.html.

27. Kathi Weeks, *The Problem with Work: Feminism, Marxism, Anti-Work Politics, and Postwork Imaginaries* (Durham, NC: Duke University Press, 2011), 49; Kathi Weeks, "'Hours for What We Will': Work, Family, and the Movement for Shorter Hours," *Feminist Studies* 35, no. 1 (Spring 2009): 124.

28. Hermann, *Capitalism and the Political Economy of Work Time*, 194.

29. The mantra of work hard to achieve greater status became especially prevalent in China's rapidly expanding state capitalist economy, including its tech sector. "Overwork," highlighted in one 2016 Chinese publication as responsible for as many as 600,000 annual deaths, became by 2019 the Chinese tech sector slogan of "996" (9 to 9 work day, six days a week). The term 996 was first made popular by an anonymous tech worker's post that went viral, arguing that the pressure to work 996 would send tech developer workers to the intensive care unit and that "developers' lives matter," riffing on the Black Lives Matter slogan. Although the term 996 became linked to tech worker discontent, the criticism was challenged by China's tech industry leaders like Alibaba's Jack Ma, who argued that "young people should be aware that happiness comes from hard work" and that the long hours could be considered crucial to achieve national superiority in the tech field. Yingzhi Yang, "'Developers' Lives Matter': Chinese Software Engineers Use Github against the Country's 996 Work Schedule," *South China Morning Post,* March 29, 2019, https://www.scmp.com /tech/start-ups/article/3003691/developers-lives-matter-chinese-software-engineers -use-github; "'Developers' Lives Matter': Chinese Tech Firms' Overwork Culture Touches Off Debate," *China Plus,* April 15, 2019, http://chinaplus.cri.cn/news/china/9/20190415 /275849.html.

30. Eleanor Ainge Roy, "Jacinda Ahern Flags Four-Day Working Week as Way to Rebuild New Zealand after Covid-19," *Guardian*, May 19, 2020, https://www.theguardian.com/world /2020/may/20/jacinda-ardern-flags-four-day-working-week-as-way-to-rebuild-new -zealand-after-covid-19; Reuters staff, "Unilever to Try Out Four-Day Working Week in New Zealand," Reuters, November 30, 2020, https://www.reuters.com/article/unilever -newzealand/unilever-to-try-out-four-day-working-week-in-new-zealand-idUSL1N2IG2DF

31. John F. Helliwell, Richard Layard, Jeffrey D. Sachs, and Jan-Emmanuel De Neve, *World Happiness Report* (New York: Sustainable Development Solutions Network, March 2020), https://happiness-report.s3.amazonaws.com/2020/WHR20.pdf.

32. Nearly a thousand mutual aid groups formed during 2020, with many of the participants and volunteers articulating a type of care ethic as part of their motivation. "It's about building the world we want to see," one mutual aid volunteer told the *New York Times*. Kimko de Freytas-Tamura, "Mutual Aid Groups Frantically Patch Holes in the Safety Net," *New York Times*, March 7, 2021, https://www.nytimes.com/2021/03/03/nyregion/covid-19-mutual -aid-nyc.html; Rebecca Solnit, "'The Way We Get through This Is Together': The Rise of Mutual Aid under Coronavirus," *Guardian*, May 14, 2020, https://www.theguardian.com /world/2020/may/14/mutual-aid-coronavirus-pandemic-rebecca-solnit; editors, "'Care, Not Cops': Our Society Has Become Too Reliant on Police," *Commonweal Magazine*, June 2, 2020, https://www.commonwealmagazine.org/%E2%80%98care-not-cops%E2%80%99.

33. See, for example, Patrick McGreevy and Suhauna Hussain, "California Demands That Amazon Comply with COVID-19 Investigation," *Los Angeles Times*, December 14, 2020, https://www.latimes.com/california/story/2020-12-14/california-lawsuit-amazon-work place-conditions-covid-19.

34. Katie Jennings, Dino Grandoni, and Susanne Rust, "How Exxon Went from Leader to Skeptic on Climate Change Research," *Los Angeles Times*, October 23, 2015, https:// graphics.latimes.com/exxon-research; Geoffrey Supran and Naomi Oreskes, "What Exxon Mobil Didn't Say about Climate Change," *New York Times*, August 22, 2017, https://www .nytimes.com/2017/08/22/opinion/exxon-climate-change-.html; Evan Varian, "While California Fires Rage, the Rich Hire Private Firefighters," *New York Times*, October 26, 2019, https://www.nytimes.com/2019/10/26/style/private-firefighters-california.html.

35. Peter S. Arno and Philip Caper, "Medicare for All: The Social Transformation of US Health Care," *Health Affairs*, March 25, 2020, https://www.healthaffairs.org/do/10.1377 /hblog20200319.920962/full.

36. Olivier J. Outers, Ken Shadlen, Maximilian Salcher-Konrad, Andrew J. Pollard, Heidi J. Larson, Yot Teerawattananon, and Mark Jit, "Challenges in Ensuring Global Access to COVID-19 Vaccines: Production, Affordability, Allocation, and Deployment," *Lancet*, March 13, 2021, https://www.thelancet.com/journals/lancet/article/PIIS0140-6736 (21)00306-8/fulltext; Lori Wallach, *Waiver of the WTO's Intellectual Property Rights Rule (TRIPS): An Indispensable Tool to Fight the COVID-19 Pandemic*, Global Trade Watch, March, 2021, https://mkus3lurbh3lbztg254fzode-wpengine.netdna-ssl.com/wp-content /uploads/TRIPS-waiver_Facts-vs-Common-Myths.pdf.

37. Arlene Weintraub, "Pfizer CEO Says It's 'Radical' to Suggest Pharma Should Forego Profits on COVID-19 Vaccine," *Fierce Pharma*, July 30, 2020, https://www.fiercepharma.com/pharma/pfizer-ceo-says-it-s-radical-to-suggest-pharma-should-forgo-profits-covid-19-vaccine-report; Michael Gibney, "Pfizer May Be 1st to File for COVID-19 Vaccine, But Profits Likely Short-lived," *S&P Market Intelligence*, November 18, 2020, https://www.spglobal.com/marketintelligence/en/news-insights/latest-news-headlines/pfizer-may-be-1st-to-file-for-covid-19-vaccine-but-profits-likely-short-lived-61287896; Stephen Buranyi, "Big Pharma Is Fooling Us," *New York Times*, December 17, 2020, https://www.nytimes.com/2020/12/17/opinion/covid-vaccine-big-pharma.html?action=click&module=Opinion&pgtype=Homepage.

38. The unequal global distribution of vaccines predated the COVID-19 pandemic. In numerous earlier instances, according to a *Lancet* task force, it "would often take years if not decades for new vaccines to achieve the same level of uptake in LMICs [low- and middle-income countries] as in high-income countries." This created an even greater fear that this would again be the case with COVID-19, given its virulence and capacity to spread—a fear borne out in fact by the events of 2020–2021. *Lancet* Commission on COVID-19 Vaccines and Therapeutics Task Force members, "Operation Warp Speed: Implications for Global Vaccine Security," *Lancet*, March 26, 2021, https://www.thelancet.com/journals/langlo/article/PIIS2214-109X(21)00140-6/fulltext. See also Megan Twohey, Keith Collins, and Katie Thomas, "With First Dibs on Vaccines, Rich Countries Have Cleared the Shelves," *New York Times*, December 15, 2020, https://www.nytimes.com/2020/12/15/us/coronavirus-vaccine-doses-reserved.html?action=click&module=Spotlight&pgtype=Homepage; Ernest Aryeetey, Eivind Engebretsen, Åse Gornitzka, Peter Maassen, and Svein Stølen, "A Step Backwards in the Fight against Global Vaccine Inequities," *Lancet*, December 9, 2020, https://www.thelancet.com/journals/lancet/article/PIIS0140-6736(20)32596-4/fulltext.

39. Tran Le Thuy, "Vietnam Fighting Covid without Pitting Economic Growth against Public Health," *Guardian*, October 20, 2020, https://www.theguardian.com/commentisfree/2020/oct/20/vietnam-covid-economic-growth-public-health-coronavirus; Mariana Mazzucato, Henry Lishi Li, and Els Torreele, "Designing Vaccines for People, Not Profits," *Social Europe*, December 2, 2020, https://www.socialeurope.eu/designing-vaccines-for-people-not-profits; "The Next Big Idea: Climate Change and the Economy with Mariana Mazzucato and Tom Steyer," *Washington Post*, December 8, 2020, https://www.washingtonpost.com/washington-post-live/2020/12/08/next-big-idea-climate-change-economy; Mariana Mazzucato, "Capitalism Is Broken: The Fix Begins with a Free Covid-19 Vaccine," *New York Times*, October 8, 2020, https://www.nytimes.com/2020/10/08/opinion/international-world/capitalism-covid-19-vaccine.html; Bob Simison, "Economics Agitator," International Monetary Fund, Fall 2020, https://www.imf.org/external/pubs/ft/fandd/2020/09/economics-agitator-mariana-mazzucato.htm.

40. "The People's Vaccine. Available to All. In All Countries. Free of Charge," UNAIDS, May 14, 2020, https://www.unaids.org/en/resources/presscentre/featurestories/2020/may/20200514_covid19-vaccine-open-letter; Matteo Chinazzi, Jessica T. Davis, Natalie E.

Dean, Kunpeng Mu, Ana Pastore y Piontti, Xinyue Xiong, M. Elizabeth Halloran, et al., "Estimating the Effect of Cooperative versus Uncooperative Strategies of COVID-19 Vaccine Allocation: A Modeling Study," November 4, 2020, https://www.mobs-lab.org/uploads/6/7/8/7/6787877/global_vax.pdf; Owen Dwyer, "COVID-19: Countries Are Learning What Others Paid for Vaccines," *BMJ* 372, no. 281 (January 29, 2021), https://www.bmj.com/content/372/bmj.n281.

41. Kevin Young, Michael Schwartz, and Richard Lachmann, "A Tipping Point for the Defeat of Fossil Fuels? How to Stop Big Energy in Its Tracks (Quite Literally)," TomDispatch, December 10, 2020, http://www.tomdispatch.com/post/176784/tomgram%3A_lachmann%2C_schwartz%2C_and_young%2C_is_a_green_new_deal_planet_possible/#more; "How the Almighty Have Fallen—How Chasing Growth Destroyed Value in ExxonMobil," Carbon Tracker, October 28, 2020, https://carbontracker.org/reports/how-the-mighty-are-fallen; "Our Targets," Stop the Money Pipeline, https://stopthemoneypipeline.com; Patti Wetli, "JP Morgan Chase Pulls Back on Lending to Oil, Gas, and Coal Companies—Too Little, Too Late?," WTTW News, February 29, 2020, https://news.wttw.com/2020/02/29/jp-morgan-chase-pulls-back-lending-oil-gas-and-coal-companies-too-little-too-late.

42. Mindy Isser, "A Low-Carbon Economy Will Be Built by Nannies, Caregivers, and House Cleaners," *In These Times*, October 22, 2019, https://inthesetimes.com/article/green-new-deal-climate-labor-domestic-workers-nannies-house-cleaners; Jacqueline Alemany, "New York Lawmaker Rolls Out Green New Deal for Public Schools," *Washington Post*, July 15, 2021, https://www.washingtonpost.com/politics/2021/07/15/climate-change-reconciliation-bill.

CHAPTER 7

1. Sue Halpern, "Can Boosting Child Care and Elder Care Help Democrats Win Control of the Senate?," *New Yorker*, January 3, 2021, https://www.newyorker.com/news/campaign-chronicles/can-boosting-child-and-elder-care-help-democrats-win-control-of-the-senate; Susan Chira, "In Frenzied Georgia Canvassing, No Door Goes Unlocked," *New York Times*, November 5, 2018, https://www.nytimes.com/2018/11/05/us/politics/georgia-governors-canvassing-voters.html; "Women of Color in Georgia Showed Up in Record Numbers to Make Their Voices Heard in 2020," *11Alive*, January 8, 2021, https://www.11alive.com/article/news/local/women-of-color-in-georgia-showed-up-in-record-numbers-to-make-their-voices-heard-for-2020-election/85-e171e02a-150e-4859-b791-e06b20f11621.

2. The analogy to fascism, though imperfect in some respects, was nevertheless telling, and reminiscent of the infamous cry of the Spanish fascists during the Spanish Civil War. At an August 15, 1936, rally in Seville, José Millán-Astray, founder of the Foreign Legion, in his confrontation with Miguel de Unamuno, rector of the university in Salamanca, declared "Down with intelligence, long live death!" He and others repeated that and similar

declarations on other occasions during the Spanish Civil War. Hugh Thomas, *The Spanish Civil War* (London: Eyre and Spottiswoode, 1961).

3. Saskia Sassen, *Expulsions: Brutality and Complexity in the Global Economy* (Cambridge, MA: Belknap Press, 2014). Christa Wichterich provides a feminist frame to the concept of expulsions by linking it to the concept of "othering." "Othering land, nature, and women constructs a hierarchical set of cultural values and mechanisms of externalization, exclusion, and expulsion," Wichterich writes. Christa Wichterich, "Contesting Green Growth, , Connecting Care, Commons, and Enough," in *Practising Feminist Political Ecologies: Moving beyond the "Green Economy,"* ed. Wendy Harcourt and Ingrid L. Nelson (London: Zed Books, 2015), 79.

4. Mohsin Hamid, *Exit West: A Novel* (New York: Riverhead Books, 2017).

5. Anthony M. Orum, "Circles of Influence and Chains of Command: the Social Processes Whereby Ethnic Communities Influence Host Societies," *Social Forces*, December 2005, 922.

6. Amy Maxmen, "Migrants and Refugees Are Good for Economies," *Nature*, June 20, 2018, https://www.nature.com/articles/d41586-018-05507-0; Abrahm Lustgarten, "How Russia Wins the Climate Crisis," *New York Times Magazine*, December 16, 2020, https://www.nytimes.com/interactive/2020/12/16/magazine/russia-climate-migration-crisis.html?launch_id=9206665.

7. Abby Budiman, "Key Findings about U.S. Immigrants," Pew Research Center, August 20, 2020, https://www.pewresearch.org/fact-tank/2020/08/20/key-findings-about-u-s-immigrants.

8. Tejal Rao, "A Delicious Link to Oaxaca in South Los Angeles," *New York Times*, March 4, 2019, https://www.nytimes.com/2019/03/04/dining/oaxaca-food-los-angeles.html; Robert Gottlieb, *Reinventing Los Angeles: Nature and Community in the Global City* (Cambridge, MA: MIT Press, 2007), 323–324.

9. On Obama's immigration policy, which emphasized the removal of those with a criminal record, and its comparison to the Clinton and George W. Bush approaches (and the numbers of removals and deportations), see Muzzaphar Chisti, Sarah Pierce, and Jessica Bolter, "The Obama Record on Deportations: Deporter in Chief or Not?" Migration Policy Institute, January 26, 2017, https://www.migrationpolicy.org/article/obama-record-deportations-deporter-chief-or-not. A more critical view is presented by Jean Guerrero, "3 Million People Were Deported under Obama. What Will Biden Do about It?," *New York Times*, January 23, 2021, https://www.nytimes.com/2021/01/23/opinion/sunday/immigration-reform-biden.html.

10. "Costs of War," Watson Institute International and Public Affairs, Brown University, September 2020, https://watson.brown.edu/costsofwar/costs/human; Rebecca Gordon, "Can We Finally Stop Marching to Disaster," *Nation*, December 30, 2020, https://www.thenation.com/article/world/stop-endless-war-2021.

11. Sarah Marsh and Sofia Menchu, "Storms That Slammed Central America in 2020 Just a Preview, Climate Change Experts Say," Reuters, December 3, 2020, https://www.reuters.com/article/us-climate-change-hurricanes/storms-that-slammed-central-america-in-2020-just-a-preview-climate-change-experts-say-idUSKBN28D2V6.

12. Caroline Weill, *Beyond Borders: Understanding, Fighting and Overcoming the Walls That Surround Us* (Coredem, March 2019), https://www.coredem.info/IMG/pdf/beyond borders.pdf.

13. Michael Jones-Correa, Sophia J. Wallace, and Chris Zepeda-Millán, "The Large-Scale Protests over Immigrants' Rights in 2006 Shifted How Latinos View the U.S. Political System and Their Own Abilities to Influence Government Outcomes," LSE USCentre, October 14, 2013, https://blogs.lse.ac.uk/usappblog/2013/10/14/latino-immigration-protests-government-attitudes; Gottlieb, *Reinventing Los Angeles*, 253–290.

14. Silvia Federici, "Social Reproduction: Between the Wage and the Commons," interview by Marina Sitrin, *ROAR*, no. 2, https://roarmag.org/magazine/social-reproduction-between-the-wage-and-the-commons.

15. Norm Fruchter, "An Alternative High School and a Police Chief," Metropolitan Center for Research on Equity and the Transformation of Schools, New York University, August 9, 2020, https://steinhardt.nyu.edu/metrocenter/alternative-high-school-and-police-chief.

16. Michael Hiltzik, "A Handy Sign That a Local Government Is Shirking Its Public Duty: Privatizing the Library," *Los Angeles Times*, February 1, 2016, https://www.latimes.com/business/hiltzik/la-fi-mh-privatizing-the-library-20160201-column.html.

17. Winifred Gallagher, *How the Post Office Created America: A History* (New York: Penguin Press, 2016), 266; Wayne E. Fuller, *The American Mail: Enlarger of the Common Life* (Chicago: University of Chicago Press, 1972).

18. Office of Technology Assessment, *Implications of Electronic Mail and Message Systems for the U.S. Postal Service* (Washington, DC: US Government Printing Office, August 1982), https://ota.fas.org/reports/8214.pdf; University of California San Diego Data Services Librarian Anita Schiller already warned in a 1981 article that electronic information services could challenge and even displace libraries instead of expanding their reach due to "the erosion of the public character of the library's role [and] the increasing proprietary interest in information as a profitable resource as opposed to the diminishing concern for the social interest in information as a shared resource." Anita Schiller, "Shifting Boundaries in Information," *Library Journal*, April 1, 1981, 706–707.

19. Zeynep Tufekci, "GoogleBuzz: The Corporatization of Social Commons," http://technosociology.org/?p=102; Rachel Premack, "USPS Is Subsidizing Jeff Bezos' Quest to Turn Amazon into a Delivery Machine That Competes with UPS and FedEx—but USPS Can't Break Up with Bezos," *Business Insider*, May 6, 2020, https://www.businessinsider.com/amazon-usps-rural-packages-deliveries-2020-5.

20. *Primary Health Care: Report of the International Conference on Primary Health Care, Alma-Ata, USSR, 6–12 September 1978* (Geneva: World Health Organization, 1978), https://apps.who.int/iris/handle/10665/39228; Emma K. WestRasmus, Fernando Pineda-Reyes, Montelle Tamez, and John M. West fall, "Promotores de Salud and Community Health Workers: An Annotated Bibliography," *Family and Community Health* 35, no. 2 (April–June 2012): 172–182.

21. "LA County to Expand Promotores Program to Reach More Diverse Communities," Los Angeles County Supervisor Hilda L. Solis, May 26, 2020, https://hildalsolis.org/la-county-to-expand-promotores-program-to-reach-more-diverse-communities.

22. Gregg Gonsalves and Amy Kapczynski, "The New Politics of Care," *Boston Review*, April 27, 2020, http://bostonreview.net/politics/gregg-gonsalves-amy-kapczynski-new-politics-care.

23. Sammy Roth, "How Rooftop Solar Could Save $473 Billion," *Los Angeles Times*, January 7, 2021, https://www.latimes.com/environment/newsletter/2021-01-07/how-rooftop-solar-could-save-americans-473-billion-dollars-boiling-point. From an environmental justice perspective, opposition to megawind or solar projects also includes issues of "defense of indigenous territories, local livelihoods and community development Projects." Sofia Avila, "Environmental Justice and the Expanding Geography of Wind Power Conflicts," *Sustainability Science* 13, no. 3 (March 2018): 599–616.

24. The notion of a caring state, or caring government and public sector, was elaborated by public administration professors Ralph Hummel and Camilla Stivers, who described the importance of a care-focused government culture of "attentiveness" to people's lived experiences that would enable connections with "things and people in our world and to be aware of those connections." In doing so, it would also facilitate a type of "democratic knowledge in representative government." Those concepts were further filled out by DeLysa Burnier in her discussion of a "care-centered public administration." Ralph Hummel and Camilla Stivers, "Government Isn't Us: The Possibility of Democratic Knowledge in Representative Government," In *Government Is Us: Public Administration in an Anti-Government Era*, ed. Cheryl Simrell King and Camilla Stivers (Newbury Park, CA: Sage, 1998), 38; DeLysa Burnier, "Other Voices/Other Rooms: Towards a Care-Centered Public Administration," *Administrative Theory and Praxis* 25, no. 4 (December 2003): 529–544. .

Index